NICHE TOURISM IN QUESTION -

INTERDISCIPLINARY PERSPECTIVES ON PROBLEMS AND POSSIBILITIES

Edited by

Donald V. L. Macleod

2003
UNIVERSITY OF GLASGOW
CRICHTON PUBLICATIONS

University of Glasgow
Crichton Publications

General Editor
Mark G. Ward

Rutherford/McCowan Building
Crichton University Campus
Dumfries, DG1 4ZL
Scotland

First published 2003

ISBN 0 85261 771 2

CONTENTS

PREFACE

On Saturday 22nd June 2002 a conference was held in Browne House, University of Glasgow, Crichton Campus, Dumfries. The theme was 'Niche Tourism in Question: Interdisciplinary Perspectives on Problems and Possibilities', and the host was the Crichton Tourism Research Centre. Given that the centre had been established less than one year earlier, and that this was to be the first major academic conference held in Browne House, everything went surprisingly well. Academic experts from universities around the UK brought their vast experience and knowledge to the event and tackled the conference theme with vigour and originality. The majority of chapters in this volume are based on the various presentations and testify to the breadth and depth of interests present on the conference day.

One of the intentions of the conference was to draw together academics from different disciplines in order to gain a rich and varied perspective on issues related to tourism as well as engender an exchange of ideas, information and methodology. This proved successful and contributors to this volume reflect backgrounds in History, Geography, Sociology, Anthropology, Marketing, Management, Literature, Tourism Studies, Film Studies and Conservation. Added to this variety is the fact that different types of organisations, apart from numerous universities, are represented among the chapters

Furthermore, industry professionals from Dumfries and Galloway's Council, Tourist Board and Scottish Enterprise provided a panel drawing attention to the local dimension of tourism and practical issues and the conference itself was opened by Norma Hart, Chief Executive of the Dumfries and Galloway Tourist Board. The presence of specialists who are involved with tourism is also apparent among the chapters with contributions from representatives of the Dumfries and Galloway Council, Scottish Natural Heritage and the Tourism and Environment Forum.

Thanks go to the following: Dumfries and Galloway Tourist Board for sponsoring the opening event at the conference; Scottish Enterprise Dumfries and Galloway for funding the Research Fellowship enabling the editing of this book; presenters at the conference who did not contribute to this book, Luiz Moutinho, Keith Hollinshead, Rex Pyke, Colin Bell, Vicki Miller, and Chris Wybrew; to Mark Ward for helping with the creation of this book, and to Rex Taylor for his support of the project throughout its development.

Don Macleod
Dumfries, September 2003

PART I

OVERVIEW

Chapter 1

Introduction:
Perspectives on Niche Tourism

Donald Macleod

Niche tourism is a relatively new term that describes activities that are themselves substantially older. Like many terms in the world of tourism and of academia, it is subject to various definitions and interpretations – a problem that is tackled in this book. For the purpose of this collection, which is fundamentally a critical examination and questioning of the subject matter, niche tourism has been limited to its cultural and environmental manifestations. As can be seen, these alone are hugely embracing and the diversity of topics and variety of places referred to admits of this. This book offers a serious, challenging, instructive and entertaining enquiry into a current phenomenon in tourism: the increasing specialisation of interest and offering that is leading to specific markets and highly differentiated products.[1]

Tourism is often described as the world's biggest industry,[2] and within this industry niches are continually being created and are expanding – a good example being ecotourism in its manifold guises. Consequently the timing of this book is appropriate, and the need for a critical approach from a variety of academic disciplines is recognised. This enables the reader to fully appreciate the different areas of life that niche tourism impacts upon, and its multiple aspects: historical, geographical, anthropological, sociological, as well as economic. That tourism has a profound effect on the arts, music, literature, films, and is stimulated by cultural fashions is made clear in this collection; as is the vital relationship it has with the natural environment in terms of impact and influences that can veer from the destruction to the preservation of nature. There are many areas of life

---

[1] It is worth pointing out that there are areas of 'special interest tourism' that overlap with niche tourism, including museums and nature-based tourism, and the reader may wish to pursue work that deals with this topic, for example: Alpine (1986), Hall (1989), Hall and Weiler (1992), Read (1980). The volume *Niche Tourism: Contemporary Issue, Trends and Cases,* edited by Marina Novelli, is due to be published in 2004 by Butterworth-Heinemann.

[2] 'By the mid-1990s, the World Travel and Tourism Council (WTTC) estimated that tourism was the world's largest industry' (Cooper *et al* 1998: 2). See also Sharpley and Telfer (2002), and Burns and Holden (1995) for a critical approach towards assertions about the size of the industry.

that are influenced by tourism, and similarly, tourist activities reflect many aspects of contemporary society. Niche tourism might be regarded as a response to an increasing consumer-driven market place, as well as reflecting a growing awareness of opportunities, greater propensity to experience the unusual, and the desire to undertake benign or socially and environmentally beneficial vacations.

The various chapters take different approaches to the subject with some dealing with abstract ideas, matters of definition, practical concerns of management, the reality of sustainable tourism in different regions, the representation of place through literature, the different types of media used to represent places and peoples, and different understandings of the concept 'culture' among the subject matter.[3] Consequently there is a continuum of approaches from the abstract theoretical to the empirical and concrete. And this is the fascination of tourism as a topic of study: its sheer diversity, an inexhaustible subject of enquiry for a spectrum of disciplines. The book is divided into three parts, first an overview of the subject matter, then a focus on tourism and culture, and finally tourism and the natural environment: this introduction guides the reader along the central issues dealt with by the contributors.

In his Keynote chapter, Derek Hall sets the context for the collection and raises a number of questions for discussion, having examined various definitions of niche tourism. He has four objectives: to revisit the definition of niche; to pose questions concerning the recognition of niche tourism; to draw out inconsistencies and paradoxes, and to draw on ideas from the above, reflecting on the role of niche tourism in South West Scotland. He concludes that there may be multiple conceptual niche tourisms, as well as multiple operational niches, and sees it as a major driving force in tourism's global growth – with concomitant problems: it could all be part of a fashionable marketing ploy and divert us away from the progress of mass tourism.

Culture and tourism forms a major part of the collection's interest. The subject of culture is approached in a variety of ways including the broad embrace of the anthropological perspective in contrast to its definition and utilisation by the tourism industry; culture as a means of group identity; as well as the use of the arts, including literature, music, film and history, in the promotion of place and products.

---

[3] The majority of the chapters are composed of full-length papers, although three are extended abstracts: Chapter 4 (Murray Pittock), Chapter 8 (Belle Doyle) and Chapter 13 (Sandy Dear).

Different ways of 'capturing' culture are also examined – through music, live and recorded: through literature, read, imagined, revisited; through multi-media technology – the CD ROM in which local people, song, history and place can be accessed in many languages; through the ubiquitous medium of the moving image – an increasingly potent form of attracting interest, and through festivals and events.

Murray Pittock advocates culture as a way of profiling a country through its cultural identity, a form of branding. He sees culture as a key component in defining human identity that can enrich the lives of citizenry through its use in tourism. There is a need to reconsider the Scottish cultural image, its development and its potential, and examples are given of missed opportunities – architectural tourism being one. The culture of Scotland can be used to boost tourism and it needs to be explored further through such avenues as genealogical tourism. Furthermore, cultural tourism should be aligned with the achievements of the arts in Scotland.

This argument can, of course, be applied widely to other places and situations, and further, the concept of culture enlarged to take us out of our ethnocentric limitations. Examples of the various contexts of defining the term ' culture' are given by Donald Macleod: he seeks to show how destinations are constructed through presentation, description, interpretation and promotional activities. The presentation of Dumfries and Galloway (D&G) as a tourist destination is deconstructed, as well as the process of delineating niches such as cultural tourism. The anthropological approach to understanding 'culture' is employed – the better to understand its inherent determination in the context of time and space – and emphasising the tourism professionals' adoption of culture in terms of the 'high arts'. Changing contexts and fashions have influenced many regions, and the Romantic Movement is shown to have had an impact on D&G as well as its neighbour destination, the Lake District. Tourist brochures provide examples of the construction of a regional destination by individuals with a specific agenda and reinvention of place becomes apparent. It is suggested that only the human imagination limits the scope for commodification: although specific branding can bring risks as well as rewards.

In terms of reinventing, constructing or imagining place, the writers of fiction, in all its forms, must rank among the masters. The Lake District comes to mind with its association with poets, and equally, the poet Robert Burns has influenced many people's image of Scotland. In his examination of literary places and tourism, David

Herbert sees the influence of writers in terms of their biography and factual material on literary places, as well as their imagined worlds – the fictional environment – what he regards as social constructions, the results of processes of signification. But, he wonders, how do such places fit into the landscape of tourism; how do they relate to matters of authenticity and preservation? Other areas for exploration include the tourist experience, the presentation of literary places and their interpretation. Examples of literary places, including those in Wales, are given, showing the variety of types and their attraction; and the literary tourist is also examined. Herbert sees the root of literary places in culture, rather than in the economy, and argues that the issue of authenticity pervades the whole process at literary sites in relation to the site itself and the visitor experience.

Just as writers can become iconic symbols of a region, so can less animate things represent a place, create a sense of identity. However, Mike Paterson argues that icons may become limiting and prescriptive forces: for example, bagpiping is stereotyped and abounds in promotional material for Scotland that is often misleading. Bagpiping is nevertheless a strongly differentiating and value added marketing tool. He outlines the major developments in contemporary piping in Scotland, such as technical improvements, greater awareness of traditional music, the growth of youth participation and the growing popularity of Celtic music. Furthermore, interest in the bagpipes is growing internationally. Icons have meaning only because people have invested them with their culturally determined values and attitudes; but, we are warned, these values may become outmoded and irrelevant, leading to the possible 'death' of the icon. Paterson advocates the establishment of brandings that are based on the actual experience of activities to which successful icons point – an example being Robert Burns and associated literary characters in Scotland.

Robert Burns remains an iconic figure for South West Scotland (his silhouette is even sported on some taxis) and he has helped to shape the imagined landscape of Dumfries and Galloway, to have directed his reader's gaze towards its scenic aspects, as have other writers including Sir Walter Scott, who also helped bring the Victorian public's attention to the ballads of the region. Lesley Stevenson notes these influences and seeks to discover to what extent it is appropriate for music to be considered a niche form of tourism. Her thesis addresses the historical context of tourism, involving figures from the past and outlining the historic role that music has played in shaping visitor's perception: traditional music is to be regarded as a vital source of cultural capital. Current activities, such as the Gaelforce initiative, serve to spotlight the region's musical and artistic activities, and we mustn't forget that the region is host to Scotland's largest country music festival. Stevenson argues that the influence of music on tourism has not been adequately gauged, and concludes that music was once predominantly an indicator of place, whereas of late it has become a means of attracting visitors. Marketing should continue to promote the region's specific place identity as an additional and important part of any musical product.

Music is still undoubtedly an important component in the cultural identity of a region and a nation, as is the literature produced; however, increasingly the moving image, through television, cinema, video, the Internet and other means, is growing in importance. It is now recognised that film-based tourism is a major factor in visitor numbers for many regions and locations associated with specific productions. Belle Doyle points out that money generated by the filmmaking process alone can be vast – about £2million has been spent during the production of '2000 Acres of Sky' on the SW coast of D&G. Furthermore, the tourism generated by films can be enormous. The film BraveHeart has encouraged a rise of 52% in the numbers of visitors to the Wallace Monument in Stirling. Customer questionnaires suggest that films influenced some 14% of visitors to visit Scotland. However, opportunities to promote a site are often missed, but occasionally unexpected hits arise. There is, on the downside, always the possibility that films can create a bad image for a place in the minds of some of the local population, as was the case with The Wicker Man in D&G, believed to be attracting the 'wrong sort'. Nevertheless, as is apparent, D&G has discovered its own niche in that it can easily be turned into 'an island location' through the magic of the lens.

Film, music, text, history, literary places: all of these can be captured by new technology, the CD ROM and digital media; this might enable the 'armchair traveller' to visit a region without leaving the comfort of home: this opportunity, brought about by 'virtual tourism', is addressed by Valentina Bold in her exploration of Scotland by CD ROM. She considers the potential and the disadvantages of using digital media, which can be used to introduce and represent a region to an audience, even potential tourists. Digital tours allow people, be they indigenous or outsiders, to experience a place in a self-directed and thoughtful way. Valentina Bold gives an example from a CD ROM she helped to develop on North East Scotland, detailing its production, aims, outcomes and the intellectual issued involved. This case study provides an excellent introduction to the construction, uses and problems of creating such a versatile record of a region's culture and composition. It is suggested that the CD ROM provides a model format for promoting tourism and educating people about a destination.

Many of the chapters in this collection make reference to Scotland: its cultural richness as well as geographic diversity is made apparent; in this manner it becomes an ideal model for other parts of the world, and the same goes for the intellectual points of theory and subject matter with which the authors deal. Niche tourism knows few (if any) boundaries, and incidents that seem ostensibly to be severe catastrophes, can often be capitalised upon by the tourism industry and imaginative (or mercenary) individuals. Nevertheless, it is generally accepted that those in the tourist industry must make efforts to preserve the assets from which they prosper, especially the natural environment, and a developing awareness about 'culture' is also entering discussions on sustainability. The chapters by John Lennon and Jonathan Skinner deal with the subject of disasters, drawing our attention to the vulnerability of the tourism destination, the extraordinary diversity of attractions and the resilience that some demonstrate.

The year 2001 brought with it some exceptional disasters for the world: two in particular have strong resonance for the UK in relation to tourists: the Foot and Mouth Disease (FMD) outbreak, and the September 11th attack on the USA. The FMD outbreak led to the restriction of access to the country-side through severely limiting visitor access, and the September 11th disaster substantially reduced visitors numbers from the USA in the period following. John Lennon examines responses to market downturns calling for adequate planning and marketing to cope with 'shocks' to the operating environment. He gives a case study of responses to the FMD outbreak on visitor attractions in Scotland and the efforts made to assist and develop support to the tourism industry. There were already problems for the tourist industry in early 2001 relating to the rising cost of sterling and fuel prices; subsequent disasters dealt a strong blow to a weakened industry. VisitScotland estimates a loss of £225 million in gross revenue terms. However, lessons should be learned for the future, and the link between agriculture and tourism has been clarified, and the importance of implementing disaster plans to ensure rapid responses that are cost-effective and user friendly has been established.

A different and spectacular natural disaster visited the Caribbean Island of Montserrat: a volcanic explosion killed many local people and destroyed the homes of thousands more. Yet, there are some who can profit from this experience, offering volcano tours among other services. Jonathan Skinner describes how Monteserrat once marketed itself as 'the way the Caribbean used to be' and was referred to as 'The Emerald Island of the Caribbean'. It was constructed as an up-market 'colonial' residential tourist location – which unfortunately left the local populace perceiving themselves as the 'Black Irish of the Caribbean'. However, following the initial volcanic episode in 1995 and the consequent deaths, relocation of inhabitants and evacuation of tourists, there has been an orientation by the tourist industry to the 'niche' tourism product of 'disaster tourism', a weak variant of 'dark tourism'. Jonathan Skinner argues that this new promotion of 'volcanic tourism' indicates the extent to which tourism has seeped into the consciousness of some in the island community. A nostalgia for nature has grown, rather than for colonialisation, whilst the history of suffering is glossed over. But, on the positive side, the disaster has (more recently) spurred a spirit of survival rather than the initial response of avoidance and denial. This is a superb and graphic example of how tourist locations may be prone to disaster, due to their qualities and natural settings, but can be rapidly re-branded and even recover. Ironically, volcanic tourism is offering Montserrat and her islands a temporary economic stability.

That the natural environment is an extremely important part of a tourism destination's composition has become very apparent in the examples given above. This fact has long been recognised within the industry and by many observers and critics of tourism and its impacts. Increasingly the natural environment is becoming the principal attraction for visitors to a tourism destination and as such it is commanding importance as the focus of attention by industry professionals, some of whom have been promoting niche tourism products grounded firmly in outdoor locations varying from constructed parks to the so-called wilderness. The third part of this collection deals with the natural environment and tourism; it covers a broad range of contemporary issues as well as diverse regions including Costa Rica, Malaysia and the UK. Contributions range from a general critique of rural tourism, an analysis of niche markets and products reliant on the natural environment, especially walking, through to firm advice on how to manage a destination: throughout these chapters the importance of sustainable tourism is emphasised. Furthermore, there are detailed examples and case studies examining the broader context of sustainable tourism as a developing idea and as a political and practical reality in Costa Rica. This is followed by a revealing study of the development of ecotourism in Malaysia that exemplifies how this niche tourism product has captured the imagination of people around the world and is being implemented as a development tool. Finally, a closing chapter reviews ideas and examples of nature-based tourism and relates them to contributions in this volume. Moreover, it uses current developments in Dumfries and Galloway to give specific substance to arguments.

Despite the fact that much of the tourism activity is taking place in a rural environment it is, nevertheless, culturally determined by values, representations, perceptions, fashion; in short, the entire experience of living in a specific culture will largely determine an understanding of the natural environment. In their critical analysis of rural tourism, Lesley Roberts and Derek Hall draw the reader's attention to the meanings attached to actions, including consumption, and point out that such consumer behaviour is as much about the perceptions of the consumer as it is about the objects being consumed. However, much contemporary marketing practice is modernist in style; it assumes rationality, consistency, organised behaviour; whereas consumption is more about defining images and demarcating social relationships thereby 'constructing' (culturally) the world. Roberts and Hall argue that tourism in general (and rural areas in particular) represent contexts that challenge the traditional modernist approach to marketing. The essential characteristics of niche tourism markets are established and the complex nature of tourism is analysed identifying a homogenisation of demand in the postmodern markets for tourism. The potential dangers of labelling tourism in rural areas as a market niche is emphasised.

Roberts and Hall draw attention to the top-down approach to markets that characterises segmentation, whereas, in contrast, they argue that niche markets develop from the bottom upwards in that they are started by identifying the needs of a few individuals. A wider sociological approach towards tourism studies is advocated – for example, in order to understand the changing ways that people are consuming the countryside. Furthermore, it is argued that rural tourism is not small-scale low impact (as often believed) and it is not a niche within tourism markets – rather this view of it as a niche can divert from critical issues of management. It is suggested that a more human-oriented research methodology, such as ethnography, could be employed to understand emerging consumer issues. There is a risk that niche marketing could lead to more competition, whereas it is collaboration that is needed.

A broad analysis of the cultural construction inherent in rural tourism activities, together with a reminder of the need to preserve the assets utilised lead neatly into the most topical of issues: sustainable tourism. This has become a subject attracting interest across the spectrum of academic disciplines and the industry.[4] Other bodies, Non Governmental Organisations among them, have developed a strong interest in issues of sustainability, especially environmental conservation and biodiversity. The Tourism and Environment Forum aims to promote greater sustainability in Scottish tourism; it highlights the link between tourism and the natural environment. Sandy Dear outlines some of this work and the general situation in Scotland, and considers general themes including: what it is that people want from Scotland; the competitiveness of tourism in a global context; the emergence of a more experienced and demanding tourist, and the increasing fragmentation of tourist markets leading to the growth of niche tourism. He emphasises the need to understand what tourists want in order to attract them, and the fact that the natural environment features very high on the list of attractions for those people that visit Scotland (for 47% of tourists the landscape and scenery was the main reason for their visit). There is consequently a necessity to market the environment properly to ensure better access and to sustain it. Visitor impact needs to be controlled, especially in the areas of transport, accommodation and attractions: all should be made sustainable.

But what is this concept 'sustainable tourism development' really about? In his chapter on tourism and sustainable development Phil O'Brien traces the genesis of the concept and places it into its historical and international context. There has been a distinct growth in interest, activity and discussion since the Rio conference of 1992, and tourism is likely to remain one of the great drivers of the global service sector in the future. Tourism will probably become a catalyst for sustainable economic and environmental development, and the final declaration of the Johannesburg Declaration (Section 41 on tourism) deals with sustainable tourism development. However, there remains the existence of 'greenwash' within the tourist industry – and the creation by the UN of a Global Compact to guide businesses on sustainable practices is only a voluntary agreement - whilst the influence of big business on the sustainable development conference in 2002 was strong.

There are definite positive signs regarding international political

---

[4] Sustainable tourism has produced an increasing flow in academic publications: witness Bramwell *et al* (1998), Mowforth and Munt (2001) and the *Journal of Sustainable Tourism* (Channel View Publications).

recognition of the value and potential of ecotourism and the UN environment programme recognised that it can contribute to poverty alleviation and environmental protection. Nevertheless, problems of definition remain regarding ecotourism, and more generally O'Brien suggests that the tourism industry is not sustainable in its approach to the environment, development and human rights. In some respects the case of Costa Rica might act as a micro-model of the global scenario, a place whose image as an ecotourism destination has been successfully promoted, but where the broader agenda has been wanting in terms of genuine sustainability and good practices. O'Brien notes the biodiverse wealth possessed by Costa Rica: here tourism is a key activity and Costa Rica has boomed since 1988 after being sold as 'an ecotourism haven'. Yet the tourist industry is relatively unregulated and usually it is economic gains that determine decisions. For Costa Rica its natural heritage remains the 'jewel' in its collection of assets; but there is a strong risk of degradation. Meanwhile, the present government is actively seeking to improve controls over natural resources and this could be beneficial for the sustainability agenda and the country's future.

As with Costa Rica, Malaysia also has a rich natural environment, but it has only recently begun to exploit this heritage through the niche of ecotourism. Rosazman Hussin gives an overview of the development of ecotourism in Malaysia and records the initiative begun in the 1990s to orient the country towards 'sustainable tourism development' rather than simply higher growth rates in tourist arrivals. He explores why this change of direction occurred and how the plans make sense. The decline in tourism arrivals is analysed in detail and it seems that serious criticism of the impact of tourism within the country, together with uneven tourist arrivals, led policymakers to search for a new icon: the niche market product that is ecotourism. In 1995 Malaysia formulated an Ecotourism Master Plan to assist development. However, it concentrates on the natural environment somewhat to the detriment of local community participation. A case study of a village in Sabah region demonstrates this weakness and illustrates the need for a fairer approach to the distribution of costs and benefits. Hussin gives a list of essential and controversial issues to be addressed relating to this ecotourism project, varying from the conflict of interests, the destruction of forests, community participation in projects and the issue of carrying capacity management – all of which have some universal relevance. Ultimately the Malaysian government needs to ensure that ecotourism development benefits local communities and other stakeholders in a sustainable manner.

Returning to Scotland and the broader issue of niche tourism markets reliant on the natural environment, Rory MacLellan offers a strong criticism of the use of niche product and marketing, noting its divergence from marketing theory: market profiles were created after the actual niche had been identified. So which comes first, the product or the market? This problem goes to the heart of the tourism industry in Scotland, and he gives examples of the complexity and confusion surrounding tourism and the natural environment. Continuing the theme of sustainability, the issue of impact is highlighted, including the economic and environmental effects of tourism and the need for a holistic understanding of this phenomenon. This is supported by statistics showing the various contributions of different types of activities to the economy, with walking featuring as a major contributor.

Using walking as an exemplary activity, MacLellan illustrates the varieties of motivation among tourists and their differing profiles. The point that walkers are not homogenous is well made and relevant to other groups, as is the fact that walking has repercussions far beyond the fundamental act, in terms of access, management and impacts. Equally, responsibility for provision and maintenance is not clear-cut. Overall there is a need to connect suppliers and managers of nature-based tourism with promoters and ensure that visitor management and countryside protection is uppermost in the minds of those involved. The natural environment is both an attraction and the foundation for much tourism activity in Scotland, and more work should be done to achieve its sustainable development.

The issue of visitor management is something that has been referred to as of prime importance by many contributors, including MacLellan, and this is addressed directly by Bill Taylor *et al* in their examination of the concrete and specific practicalities of implementing sustainable rural tourism management. In considering the practical realities of managing sites in rural areas, they present a systematic approach to visitor management that is driven by new directions in countryside and access policy that has been increasing public expectation and the broader sustainability agenda. They propose a Sustainable Visitor Management System (SVMS) that is cyclical, and involves an iterative planning and management process. It is presented as a menu of procedures and tools that can be used at a range of visitor sites. Key issues to be addressed by SVMS include the following: gaining acceptance (by the management) of a systematic approach; clear objectives; stakeholder participation and decision-making structures; suitable staff time and resources; regular data gathering; cost-effective methods for measuring 'quality'. This chapter provides a clear theoretical approach to and description of the SVMS: a plan that is to be put to the test in Scotland during 2003.

Finally, Mhairi Harvey and Steven Gillespie offer a critical assessment of ecotourism, nature-based tourism and the niche market. As such they provide a thought-provoking finale for the third part of this volume and use examples from Dumfries and Galloway in Scotland as well as referring to other contributors in support of their ideas. They argue that the promotion of nature-based activities (as products) without reference to their actual regional location can be confusing for potential visitors, and that such activities should be contextualised. This is a challenge to contemporary niche product marketing in Scotland and concrete examples are given of recent projects in the south of Scotland that promote nature-based tourism without targeting a niche market. Further, it is suggested that ecotourism should be utilised as a guiding principle (in the manner of an ethical template) rather than thought of as a product.

This introduction has been written as a form of journey through the central points made by the contributors in this volume, and it has given a glimpse of the breadth and depth of the subject matter dealt with. We have ranged from the highly abstract and theoretical to the pragmatic reality of implementing ideas. Moreover, we have moved from the high arts and metropolitan centres to the naturalists' concerns in the rural periphery. This is a fair reflection of the scope of niche tourism and hopefully will lead the reader into considerate and constructive work in future.

References

Alpine, L. (1986) Trends in special interest travel, *Speciality Travel Index*, Fall/Winter: 83-84.

Bramwell, B., I. Henry, G. Jackson, A. Goytia Prat, G. Richards, J.Van der Straaten (eds) (1998) *Sustainable Tourism Management: Principles and Practice*.. Tilburg: Tilburg University Press.

Burns, P. and A. Holden. (1995) *Tourism: A new perspective*. Harlow: Prentice Hall.

Cooper, C., J. Fletcher, D. Gilbert, S. Wanhill and R. Shepherd (1998) *Tourism: Principles and Practice* (2nd Edition). New York: Longman.

Hall, C. M. (1989) Special interest travel: A prime force in the expansion of tourism? In R. Welch, (ed) *Geography in Action*. Dunedin: University of Otago.

Hall, C. M. and B. Weiler. (1992) What's Special about Special Interest tourism? In B. Weiler and C. M. Hall (eds). *Special Interest Tourism*. London: Belhaven Press.

Mowforth, M and I. Munt. (2001) *Tourism and Sustainability: new tourism in the Third World*. London: Routledge.

Read, S. E. (1980) A prime force in the expansion of tourism in the next decade: special interest travel. In D. E. Hawkins, E.L. Shafer, J.M. Rovelstad (eds) *Tourism Marketing and Management Issues*. Washington D.C: George Washington University.

Sharpley, R. and D. J. Telfer. (2002) *Tourism and Development: Concepts and Issues*. Channel View Press.

WTTC. (1996) *Progress and Priorities 1996*. World Travel and Tourism Council, Brussels.

Chapter 2

Niche Tourism in Question:
Keynote

Derek Hall

This short preamble to the conference aims briefly to set the context for subsequent papers and to raise a number of questions for discussion. In pursuing these aims the paper has four objectives. First: to revisit the definition of 'niche' and to briefly note its origins. Second: to pose questions concerning the recognition or otherwise of 'niche tourism'. Third: to draw out some inconsistencies or paradoxes which appear to surround the term. And finally, to briefly draw on ideas flowing from the above in order to reflect on the role of 'niche tourism' in the conference's geographical context of southwest Scotland.

Niche tourism in question

Dictionaries tell us that the word 'niche' is derived from Old French *nichier* to nest, and this in its turn is taken from Vulgar Latin *nidicare*. It can mean:

- a recess in a wall especially one that contains a statue;
- in an ecological context: the status of a plant or animal within its community, which determines its activities, and relationships with other organisms;
- but most appropriately for the current context, it can refer to a position particularly suitable for the person occupying it.

But when we turn to the tourism literature for more specific, applied enlightenment, we find that this is less than forthcoming. In both recently published encyclopaedias/dictionaries of tourism (Jafari 2000; Beaver 2002), there is no specific entry for *niche tourism* nor reference to it in the index. In Rik Medlik's (1996) earlier *Dictionary of Travel, Tourism and Hospitality* again *niche tourism* does not appear, although *niche marketing* does feature in the index, albeit minimally, and then with directions for the reader to refer to the *target marketing* entry.

Echoing this paucity in our reference sources, many key tourism texts seem not to recognise the term 'niche tourism' at all. Yet probably most of us employ the term regularly and think we know what we mean by it, even if we may use it with little thought to its precise definition.

Undertaking a web search for this holy grail, depending on the search engine employed, the investigator is likely to be faced with little more than disparate 'examples' of declared niche tourism, accompanied by little conceptual clarification and certainly little evidence of a critical evaluation. Thus, from this author's web search, a report from the Indian *Express Travel and Tourism* (Sisodia 2002) was found to tell us that the Tourism Authority of Thailand has been looking to what it refers to as *the Indian niche market* to promote tourism products such as spas, religious tours and locations for 'Bollywood' filming; while the *Jordan Times* discusses how private hospitals in the country have "filled a niche" with 'medical tourism' (Dajani 2002). Indeed, this latter arena is one in which the Cuban authorities have found considerable success as a concomitant to the high output of qualified medical staff which the country's education and training system – and national sense of priorities – has provided (e.g. see Feinsilver 1993; Directorio Turistico de Cuba 2000).

Closer to home, at least in terms of the conference venue, the Scottish tourism strategy (Scottish Executive 2000) strongly emphasises niche development, and the VisitScotland *Scotexchange.com* (2002) website lists some seventeen 'niche markets', ranging in scale and specialisation from city breaks to equestrian activities and English as a foreign language. But these are often clearly no more than tourist market super-segments, their very diversity of scale and complexity significantly reducing the utility of the term 'niche'.

Of course niche tourism is not just about marketing in a narrow sense, but is generally considered to concern:

- identifying and stimulating demand, segmenting consumers into identifiable groups for targeting purposes, and
- providing and promoting supply, by differentiating products and services from those of competitors.

But this raises a number of further critical questions, such as the extent to which a niche is real, manufactured or imagined. The extent to which the identification of niches in tourism is actually subjected to interrogation may vary considerably. Indeed, the assumptions that the following conference papers make will equally vary.

For example, the 'cycling tourism niche market' is in fact comprised of a series of groups with potentially very different aspirations, activity patterns and impacts. Sustrans (1997: 7) recognises four market segments – infrequent, occasional and frequent leisure cyclists, and cycling enthusiasts – each with distinctive activity interests and product requirements. To these four segments one might add mountain bikers, racing cyclists and no doubt one or two other groups (e.g. see Lumsdon 1999, 2000, 2001).

From niche to mass

Staying with a transport theme, the assumed image of steam railway enthusiasts, viewed as a niche market in almost pejorative terms, needs substantial revision. In the UK there are over 140 restored railways in addition to countless static museum exhibits (Butcher 2002). Steam railways, as visitor attractions, might best be described as a niche in reverse, a particular attraction appealing to what might at first appear to be an esoteric market segment that promoters have sought to broaden by diversifying attraction bases. Certainly the traditional image of steam railway enthusiasts ('anoraks', 'gricers' etc.) has been of predominantly male, often unmarried, socially restricted individuals with interests in engineering and transport, interests which have never appealed to fashion-conscious adolescents and young adults. However, wider market developments in the 1970s and 1980s saw the growth of appeals to nostalgia and application of the ubiquitous term 'heritage' to steam railway attractions. This began to generate a broader appeal to families. Upon this foundation have been developed much more concerted efforts to broaden the customer base of such attractions. In addition to the usual gift and catering facilities, this has been most notably pursued by:

- combining the steam railway with a starkly different yet complementary experience, such as a farm park, as at the Almond Valley Heritage Centre, Livingstone, West Lothian (Almond Valley Heritage Trust 2002), or a garden centre, such as

Bressingham's 'Steam and Gardens' in Norfolk (Bressingham Steam Preservation Company 2002), to provide, in combination, a full day's experience appealing to family groups;
- providing shopping experiences to explicitly appeal to women;
- offering explicitly family-oriented special activity weekends, such as the Brecon Mountain Railway's family history weekend and Halloween special weekend;
- providing evening attractions, such as August Saturday music evenings held by the Gwili steam railway near Carmarthen;
- running *Thomas the Tank Engine* (a copyrighted brand) days and other special events aimed at children, especially during school holidays and at weekends;
- providing 'Santa specials' and 'mince pie specials' to extend the family season through December and into the new year;
- offering professional training facilities such as 'footplate' training for aspiring engine drivers. This reflects the fact that few opportunities now exist anywhere in the world for steam engine driver training;
- offering train hire for special events such as weddings and anniversaries; and
- promoting themselves as potential film set locations, particularly for cinematic experiences emphasising a nostalgia dimension, with the ultimate aim of generating more custom through recognition in and association with particular films. Perhaps the UK model for this was the Keighley and Worth Valley Railway, situated in 'Bronte Country' (West Yorkshire), which featured heavily in the sentimental 1970 film *The Railway Children* (Carlton Online, 2000).

Thus, the case of steam railway attractions offers an example of a niche interest that has explicitly sought mass appeal through the accretion of complementary activities to attract non-traditional, non-niche markets.

Pursuing the cinematic theme, the experience of places that have employed cultural motifs as attractions (e.g. Herbert 1996, 2001, 2003), and particularly of those harnessing popular, media-driven, culture, has shown that niches, however defined, can be susceptible to the range of problems and conflicts associated with mass tourism.

As part of strategic place marketing (Kotler *et al.* 1993), locations are promoted through the construction or selective tailoring of particular images. The exploitation of popular culture with which to construct such images has quickly shifted from appeals to particular audiences to the generation of attractions deriving from mass media appeal. Film and television studios have for some time recognised the popularity of visits to the places where films and television programmes are made, such as Universal Studios in Orlando and Granada Television in Manchester. But only relatively recently have tourism authorities and promoters taken advantage of the popularity of particular locations because of their inclusion in a film or television series. Before this, film companies were encouraged to locate films in particular areas because of the economic benefits which would be gained from increased demand for goods and services (including local residents as film 'extras') from the local area during the filming, not from visitors coming to see where the film was made. This has changed in the last two decades, and has been interpreted by some commentators as a reflection of the way in which television, film and video have overtaken the role of the written word as key vehicles for reaching mass audiences with place images (Butler 1990, 1998).

The place-specific nature of popular media-led tourism is a potentially powerful tool if harnessed for policy purposes. Such harnessing is currently being pursued in at least two ways:

- inducing filmmakers to employ particular locations or regions for shooting on the assumption that a successful film will assist image projection and the attraction of tourists and/or inward investment. Thus the role of Scottish Screen (2002) is "to establish Scotland as a major screen production centre and project our culture to the world" (e.g. see McCubbin 1999; see also Blandford, 2000);
- publicising and promoting the locations featured in film and televisions: for this reason, in 1999 the British Tourist Authority set up a 'movie map' website providing details, on a cross-referencing basis, of films and soaps shot in the UK, and their locations (BTA 1999; Buncombe 1999).

Locational attractions can be prolonged with very successful films, which may be screened for several months in cinemas, and then made available on video, DVD, and later shown on television and cable networks. Television 'soaps' can run for decades. Tooke and Baker (1996) found for four UK movie locations that visits increased in the first year by 30-90%, while Riley *et al.* (1998) identified that the effect of movies on locations in the USA could last for at least four years and increase visits by 40-50%. The extent to which subsequent

tourist activity at such locations reinforces media images or helps to
generate new identities is not well researched. Many attractions
visited as a result of film-induced tourism may not have been
attractions before, and their promotion may have been predicated on
the assumption that specific interest markets would be attracted.
However, such apparent niche appeals can generate mass problems,
and the long-running nature of television soaps appears to be able to
sustain such problems over a significant period. Thus the village of
Esholt, to the north of Bradford in West Yorkshire, which for several
years was the location for the long-running and widely popular rural
television soap opera *Emmerdale,* was host to over 750,000 visitors in
the last full year of filming there (Davidson and Maitland 1997).
Mass problems that have been shared by many popular media-
induced tourism attractions include:

- congestion and carrying capacity problems,
- excessive merchandising, including the production of cheap, poor
  quality souvenirs,
- local price inflation,
- demand for of natural or man-made associations with the film or
  programme (e.g. Watson-Smyth and Garner 1999), to the extent of
  vandalism and theft,
- imitative behaviour (even attempted and successful suicide has
  been identified: Riley *et al.* 1998; Willan 2000), and
- the development of multiple websites that can depict confusing
  and possibly contradictory images of a particular location.

Competitive yet collaborative?

A number of further conceptual and practical inconsistencies and
paradoxes relating to employment of the term 'niche tourism', are
taken up particularly in the chapter by Roberts and Hall (2003) within
the context of rural tourism. One critical issue, for the coherence of
'community' and regionally based tourism is the potential problem
that niche marketing, with its emphasis on distinctiveness for
competitive advantage (e.g. Thomas and Long 2000), may act to
encourage local competition rather than collaboration between
businesses and even neighbouring public agencies. This is of course
contrary to current conventional wisdom which tells us that tourism

businesses should pursue local and regional co-operation and networking (e.g. see Richards and Hall 2000). Certainly there are several factors that would seem to suggest the need for small businesses to collaborate in the development of niche tourism. These include the difficulty for small businesses to identify niche markets in their infancy, and the potentially high cost of actual niche marketing.

Taking these considerations and applying them within the context of south-west Scotland, there appear to be at least two ways of conceptualising how tourism businesses in relatively sparsely populated areas can pursue meaningful collaboration within the pursuit of niche markets.

The first is through 'functional complementarity': collaboration within the same niche theme can be pursued in different but adjacent local areas in order to gain wider regional benefit. For example, despite a recent festival and reinvigorated efforts to raise quality and promotion (e.g. Hamilton 2002; Peterkin 2002), the Burns product of south-west Scotland still appears relatively fragmented and unfocused, perhaps due to the different approaches taken by authorities in Dumfries and Galloway and Ayrshire. Yet given the global network of Burns Associations and the Scots diaspora (e.g. Brander 1997), the Burns heritage in and around Ayr and in Dumfries would seem to demand a regional approach to development, promotion and marketing requiring stronger co-operation and co-ordination. In short, the whole can, and should, be much greater than the sum of the individual parts.

Second, collaboration in pursuit of niche markets can take place through 'spatial complementarity': developing and building upon the initial advantage of geographical clusters of similar 'niche' activities by pursuing complementary diversification from those activities within the same location. Wigtown, in Galloway, provides a good potential example of this where book town designation and the establishment of a critical mass clustering of bookshops and related literary activities has also helped to stimulate and support such activities as food fairs. Yet there is much untapped potential here for perhaps a genealogy centre and a focus for military history. For example, the nearby Baldoon airfield was an important training centre for air crew from a number of Allied countries – notably Australia, Canada, New Zealand and Poland, as well as the UK - during the Second World War, and the RAF war graves at Kirkinner reflect the high casualty rate experienced in the Wigtown area particularly resulting from air crashes and target practice accidents (Hall nd; Murchie 1992). The heritage – indeed archaeology – of these exploits may appeal to different yet complementary diaspora markets to those who may seek out their genealogical roots in the area. The survivors who served at the base, their relatives and acquaintances, and those interested in military history provide a potentially diverse market for the 'product' to attract.

Conclusion

In conclusion, 'niche tourism' would appear to be in question for a number of contrasting reasons. First, like tourism itself, it is a concept we think we all understand yet we may not agree on how to define or operationalise it. Thus there may be multiple conceptual niche tourisms as well as multiple operational tourism niches.

Second, rather like use of 'eco-', 'sustainable' and 'community-based' prefixes, the term 'niche' when used to precede 'tourism' has been adopted in some cases as a strictly marketing – even propagandist – term which may not necessarily accurately reflect the *actualité* of the nature, context and ethos of the product being promoted.

Third, the very explicit presence, recognition and extolling of 'niche tourism' within the industry, whether real or imagined, does nonetheless appear to have been a major driving force in tourism's recent global growth, in the generation and regeneration of destinations, and in the range of products made available. Yet with

• markets which may not be distinctive, but dynamic and overlapping,
• a lack of consensus and precision on definition, and
• a product and its ethos which may be more illusory than real,

is it a healthy sign that the industry should appear to be being driven by 'niche tourism'? Or is it actually the case that this is an over-hyped, politically correct and convenient delusion? After all, global mass tourism is still growing in absolute terms, and with more developing countries raising their living standards and entering the mass tourism market, is not this likely to be the real industry driving force - and source of major global access issues and tensions - for much of the rest of the twenty-first century?

References

Almond Valley Heritage Trust, The (2002) *Welcome to Almond Valley*, Edinburgh: Almond Valley Heritage Trust (http://www.almondvalley.co.uk).

Beaver, A. (2002), *A Dictionary of Travel and Tourism Terminology*, Wallingford: CAB International.

Blandford, S. (ed.) (2000), *Wales on Screen*, Bridgend: Seren/Poetry Wales Press.

Brander, M. (1997), *The World Directory of Scottish Associations*, Glasgow: Neil Wilson.

Bressingham Steam Preservation Company (2002) *Bressingham Steam and Gardens*, Bressingham: BSPC (http://www.bressingham/co.uk).

BTA (British Tourist Authority) (1999), *Movie Map*, London: BTA (http://www.visitbritain.com/moviemap/moviemap.htm).

Buncombe, A. (1999) "TV locations to star in UK tourism push", The Independent (27 February).

Butcher, A.C. (ed.) (2002), *Railways Restored*, Hersham: Ian Allan Publishing, 23rd edn.

Butler, R.W. (1990), "The Influence of the Media in Shaping International Tourist Patterns", *Tourism Recreation Research*, 15:2, 46-53.

Butler, R. (1998), "Rural Recreation and Tourism", in *The Geography of Rural Change*, B. Ilbery (ed.), Harlow: Longman, 211-232.

Carlton Online (2000) *The Railway Children*, London: Carlton (http://therailwaychildren.carlton.com/1970production).

Dajani, D. (2002), "Private Hospitals Fill Niche with 'Medical Tourism'", Jordan Times (5 March) (http://www.jordanembassyus.org/03052002007.htm).

Davidson, R. and Maitland, R. (1997), *Tourist Destinations*, London: Hodder and Stoughton.

Directorio Turistico de Cuba (2000) *Health*, Havana: Directorio Turistico de Cuba (http://www.dtcuba.com/eng/salud.asp).

Feinsilver, J. (1993) *Healing the Masses: Cuban Health Politics at Home and Abroad*, Berkeley: University of California Press.

Hall, R.L. (n.d.), Unpublished Recorded Recollections, Holland-on-Sea, Essex.

Hamilton, J. (2002), "Rabbie Who? Why Burns Country is Brushing Up On the Bard", Sunday Herald (Glasgow) (12 May).

Herbert, D.T. (1996), "Artistic and Literary Places in France as Tourist Attractions", *Tourism Management*, 17:2, 77-85.

Herbert, D.T. (2001), "Literary Places, Tourism and the Heritage Experience", *Annals of Tourism Research*, 28:2, 312-333.

Herbert, D.T. (2003), "Literary Places and Tourism", in *Niche Tourism in Question*, D.V.L. Macleod (ed.), Dumfries: University of Glasgow Crichton Publications.

Jafari, J. (ed.) (2000), *Encyclopedia of Tourism*, New York and London: Routledge.

Kotler, P., Haider, D.H. and Rein, I. (1993), *Marketing Places: Attracting Investment, Industry and Tourism to Cities, States and Nations*, New York: The Free Press.

Lumsdon, L. (1999), "Integrating Transport and Tourism: Recreational Cycling", *Countryside Recreation News*, 7:2, 2-5.

Lumsdon, L. (2000), "Transport and Tourism: Cycle Tourism – a Model for Sustainable Development?", *Journal of Sustainable Tourism*, 8:5, 361-377.

Lumsdon, L. (2001), "Cycling Tourism", in *Rural Tourism and Recreation: Principles to Practice*, L. Roberts and D. Hall, Wallingford: CAB International, 173-174.

McCubbin, S. (1999) "Scotland the Movie Playing to Full Houses in the Film Industry", Scotland on Sunday (1 August).

Medlik, R. (1996), *Dictionary of Travel, Tourism and Hospitality*, Oxford: Butterworth-Heinemann.

Murchie, A.T. (1992), *The RAF in Galloway*, Wigtown: GC Book Publishers.

Peterkin, T. (2002), "Ayrshire Cabbies Do the Burns Knowledge", Daily Telegraph (13 May).

Richards, G. and Hall, D. (eds) (2000), *Tourism and Sustainable Community Development*, London and New York: Routledge.

Riley, R., Baker, D., and Van Doren, C. S. (1998), "Movie Induced Tourism", *Annals of Tourism Research*, 23:4, 919-935.

Roberts, L. and Hall, D. (2003), "The Niche Pastiche: What Rural Tourism is Really About", in *Niche Tourism in Question*, D.V.L. Macleod (ed.), Dumfries: University of Glasgow Crichton Publications.

Scottish Executive (2000) *A New Strategy for Scottish Tourism*, Edinburgh: Scottish Executive (http://www.scotland.gov.uk/library2/doc11/sfst.pdf).

Scottish Screen (2002) *Who are We?* Edinburgh: Scottish Screen (http://www.scottishscreen.com/index.taf?_P=ABO).

Sisodia, R. (2002), "TAT Aims to Target the Indian Niche Market", Express Travel and Tourism (New Delhi) (1 June) (http://www.expresstravelandtourism.com/20020615/globetrot3.shtml).

Sustrans (1999), *Cycle Tourism Information Pack TT21*, Bristol: Sustrans (http://www.sustrans.org.uk).

Thomas, R. and Long, J. (2000), "Improving Competitiveness: Critical Success Factors for Tourism Development", *Local Economy*, 14:4, 313-328.

Tooke, N. and Baker, M. (1996), "Seeing is Believing: the Effect of Film on Visitor Numbers to Screened Locations", *Tourism Management*, 17:2, 87-94.

VisitScotland, (2002), *Know Your Markets,* Edinburgh: VisitScotland (http://www.scotexchange.com).

Watson-Smyth, K. and Garner, C. (1999), "Location Groupies Force Sale of the UK's Second Most Famous Front Door," The Independent (17 November).

Willan, P. (2000), "Death in Venice is Big Tourist Attraction", The Guardian (20 November) (http://www.guardianunlimited.co.uk/Archiv/Article/0,4273,4093385,00.html).

PART II

TOURISM AND CULTURE

Chapter 3

Culture and the Construction
of a Niche Market Destination

Donald Macleod

Introduction

This chapter considers the way that the region of Dumfries and
Galloway (D&G) has been constructed, in the sense of presented to
the general public, as a tourist destination and latterly as somewhere
with niche market qualities. An underlying premise is that all places,
as they appear to the human mind, are created by people, not
necessarily in the material sense, but in the sense of being described
and interpreted: an image is made and an idea is imparted about
somewhere specific. This process of imagining a place is particularly
interesting when we consider the business of tourism, where
specialists are employed to draw attention to a place and entice others
to visit it. The study examines the concept of culture and the
construction of place and analyses how the process of construction
has been undertaken within tourist guide brochures, revealing changes
in style and emphasis over a short period and suggesting a deeper
continuity generic to the brochure industry. It will also highlight a
contemporary branding campaign within a market town that is
seeking to promote itself through its produce.[1]

Culture and tourism

Culture is a term that has numerous interpretations. Some of the
broadest come from anthropologists, one of whom defined it as:

---

[1] According to the STEAM survey for 1999 D&G received some 922,000 ' staying tourist trips'
(minimum one night stay) that generated £118.5m in revenue. A different survey for 1998 showed
there to be 19.2m 'leisure day visits' to the region, generating £117m. It also estimated that 10%
of the workforce was involved in tourism-related employment (UKTS, IPS, UKDVS). Clearly
tourism is very important to the area, and efforts are being made to boost it. An indication of the
relevance of cultural tourism is that out of the top twenty visitor attractions in the region, 15 were
cultural in a broad sense, including museums, castles and art centres (Dumfries and Galloway
Tourism Strategy: 2001-2006).

Culture and civilisation, taken in its widest ethnographic sense, is that complex whole which includes knowledge, belief, art, morals, laws, customs, and any other capabilities and habits acquired by man as a member of society. (Tylor, 1871)

This is an embracing perspective, illustrating the holistic approach of anthropology – seeking to combine aspects of culture often regarded as separate. More recently, a subjective, phenomenological approach has found popularity, with Geertz, one of the most influential anthropologists of his generation, describing culture in the following way:

Believing with Max Weber, that man is an animal suspended in webs of significance he himself has spun, I take culture to be those webs, and the analysis of it to be therefore not an experimental science in search of law, but an interpretive one in search of meaning. (Geertz 1973: 5)

More succinct definitions are given of culture as:

A system of ideas, beliefs and behaviours. (Macmillan Dictionary of Anthropology)

The way of life of a people. (Social Science Encyclopaedia, Kuper and Kuper 1985: 178)

Bearing in mind these definitions, we can understand that for some thinkers cultural tourism might feasibly embrace almost everything, as the human mind interprets the world about it in a culturally determined way, strongly influenced by the social surroundings in which it develops.

In comparison with these expansive understandings of culture, the meanings we find in tourism 'literature' are quite confined. Robinson notes that:

The definition of cultural tourism (and by definition cultural tourists), particularly as used by the tourism industry, is unfortunately dogged by the dominant perspective of culture in the high-arts sense. Thus cultural tourism is often reduced to a form in which the focus is upon an experience of museums, theatre, architecture and the like. (Robinson 1999: 4)

For example, a look at advisory strategies, in particular the 'D&G Tourism Strategy 2001-2006', shows cultural tourism as a niche product nesting among others including walking, cycling, golfing and gardening. This cultural niche is broken down into constituent parts – visual arts, theme towns (Kirkcudbright Artists and Wigtown Books), the Robert Burns Trail, Arts Audience, Art and Craft businesses, Film-tourism, Music Unit and Literature projects. It is assumed that people, the potential tourists, will be attracted to these niche products like specific butterflies to distinct flowers. Indeed, the anticipated tourists are described in some detail: 'SKI (Spending Kids' Inheritance) Brogues' and 'Empty Nesters' (mature adults whose children have left home). They are regarded as 'tourers' and 'potterers', often members of the National Trust, RSPB and AA/RAC.

The inherent problem here is that there is an intrinsic inflexibility within this approach – an assumed stasis among the customers - whereas in reality the audience's tastes may change, may be more divisive and be more expansive. In addition, the differentiation of separate markets as niche products may not reflect the audience's desires, or the actual behaviour of tourists on the ground – who seek out varied and integrated experiences. This paper examines the construction of cultural tourism and shows the artificiality, complexity and occasionally arbitrary nature of this phenomenon. And in so doing it will indicate the future potential and diversity of a tourist destination.

The cultural construction of place

Cultural construction implies the deliberate manufacturing of a product, an activity that is strongly determined by the values and desires of those actors engaged in the process. This fundamentally arbitrary process can illustrate the broad range of creativity in which places and their identities are transformed. Tourism, and the divergent and varied forms it can take, offers an example of the endless capacity of humankind to find interest, enjoyment and entertainment in the world. Tastes may be determined by cultural factors, time, place, personal experience, gender, education, religion and so on, yet such determinants are but factors in the complex make-up of an individual. Fashions change and are influenced by ideas and concepts that are not immediately apparent. The transformation of places, determinable over extended periods of time, and the change in tourism patterns, usually occurring over shorter periods, alert us to the process and possibilities for reconstructing, remodelling and reinventing an image. Places are but constructions of the human imagination

One scholar who has described these processes of change and highlighted the central cultural construction of place, especially in relation to tourism, is John Urry (see also MacCannell 1976). His seminal work on 'the tourist gaze' (Urry 1990) drawing on Foucault's notion of the professional gaze, showed how tourists and their cultural backgrounds determine largely how things are seen within the context of the vacation experience. In his work 'Consuming Places' he states that 'Cultural industries are concerned in part with the re-presentation of the supposed history and culture of a place' (Urry 1995: 154). He gives an example of how places can be transformed: 'It is worth pointing out that twenty years ago no one in Britain would have contemplated visiting industrial Lancashire by choice' (ibid: 158). Liverpool now attracts 20 million visitors a year and most British towns and cities seek to attract visitors through repackaging their history and culture. There has been a huge growth in heritage and a vast 'collective nostalgia' for the past, such that a new museum opens every fortnight (ibid: 159).

Similarly, in a paper examining the national identity of Iceland and the impact of tourism, Einarsson highlights the historical changes and the powerful impact of visitors to Iceland on the development of the country's image:

> For travellers coming before the eighteenth century, Iceland represented a strange place with strange people at the periphery of the world. Gradually the position of Iceland changed in the view of the foreign travellers, who came to look at the world through the lenses of the Enlightenment and romanticism....
> 'The national identity is supported though major practices throughout the year, such as the Christmas season and the tourist season, creating images for Icelanders to nourish and for tourists to gaze at. (Einarsson 1996: 233)

The development of romanticism in Europe was also crucial for the image of D&G and the Lake District in England, with their association with untamed nature, spiritual enrichment and artistic inspiration. Scotland, Iceland and the Lake District experienced a remarkable transformation within the broader public perception through fresh intellectual and artistic interpretations: a reinvention of place, the cultural construction of a destination. Nineteenth-century tourism in D&G was boosted by a number of factors including the new railway connections, the fashion for escaping the urban industrial environment, and the influence of Victorian romanticism on the middle and upper classes. This romantic influence included the cult of medievalism and the Gothic revival in literature, art and architecture.

> Victorian tourists, inspired by Scott's romantic view of Scottish history, came in search of the actual settings and scenery – the abbeys (like Dundrennan and Sweetheart), the castles and tower houses (like Caerlaverock and Threave), and the sea coasts and caves of the smugglers and raiders. (Donachie and Macleod 1974: 130)

The Lake District is a region that bears obvious comparison with D&G because of its proximity, geographical similarity, agricultural character and increasingly important tourism based economy. It is a distinct success as a tourist region, with some 17 million visitors in 1990 (Urry 1995). More interestingly, it had an income from tourism of £600 million in 1999 (Cumbria Tourist Board), many times greater than D&G. In Urry's opinion it has a 'coherent identity' that makes marketing it relatively straightforward in the UK and overseas. However, in the 1630s the area was described as 'nothing but hideous, hanging hills', and Defoe wrote about Westmoreland as 'the wildest, most barren and frightful of any that I have passed over' (ibid: 193). Urry points out that the Lake District was 'discovered' then interpreted as appropriately aesthetic. After this it was transformed into managed scenery suitable for millions. He spotlights the 'place-myth' that grew around the Lake District, with its association with literature (Ibid: 194).

This particular place-myth sought to join a literary shrine, akin to Stratford-upon-Avon, with a shrine to nature. Behind individual perception of the Lake District there are more systematic discourses of landscape, countryside, scenery and sight. These have authorised and legitimised specific activities and ways of seeing, for example walking and quiet recreation in the open air. Leisure activities have therefore been constructed, and we must not forget that the concept of a holiday itself is wholly culturally determined.

To put this into a global cultural perspective, for the fishermen on the Canary island of La Gomera the notion of a holiday away from home was alien until the 1990s; the nearest they came to this was relaxing on a religious festival day (the original holy day). Furthermore, the idea of leisure walking in the mountains was anathema, partly due to its association with backbreaking journeys carrying fish. Other non-industrialised cultures did not even have the concept of a holiday let alone the work ethic: it is reported that certain hunter-gatherer societies spent more time relaxing than carrying out subsistence tasks.[2]

Dumfries and Galloway: the view from the brochures

Bearing in mind the points that Urry and others have made about the influence of romanticism in the construction of place, we can turn to D &G and analyse the way it is represented and interpreted through tourism literature. Much of the cultural construction of place comes through promotional literature in the form of tour brochures that often aim to create in the mind of the reader a specific set of images.

> The brochure is probably the most conspicuous element of the commodification process and recognised as vital in communicating the tourist product across geographical and cultural distances. (Robinson 1999: 12-13)

> The images define what is beautiful, what should be experienced and with whom one should interact. (Dann 1996: 79)

A review of tourism literature for D&G, in the form of specific brochures over the past nine years, is an exercise that serves a number of purposes.[3] It reveals common and consistent themes that run throughout the course of time. It shows the transformation in emphasis, style and content. It pinpoints underlying intentions of the writers, possible hidden designs, those unspoken values and expectations. It draws attention to the cultural construction of place

---

[2] See Macleod (2001) on National Parks and indigenous peoples; Sahlins (1972) on 'The original affluent society'; Croll and Parkin (1992) on human relations with the natural environment, and see Robinson (1999) on the search for difference as a culturally determined issue.

[3] The literature chosen comprises: The Dumfries and Galloway Tourist and Accommodation Guide 1993; First in Scotland Spring 1994; First in Scotland Autumn 1994; High Days and Holidays, June 1994; Dumfries and Galloway Holidays and Accommodation Guide 1997; Dumfries and Galloway Holiday Accommodation Guide 200; Dumfries and Galloway Holidays and Short Breaks 2002. Inevitably there were differences in focus relating to the target audiences: for example, the First in Scotland guides incorporated a shoppers guide and included numerous advertisements for local traders.

thereby unveiling key elements of those agents creating the image.

Recurring themes in tourism brochures

Attractions mentioned in the brochures include the following: Caerlaverock Castle, Sweetheart Abbey' The Mare's Tail waterfall, Robert Burns Statue, the Good Neighbours festival, Dumfries Bridge and Caul, The Brow Well, Annan, Robert The Bruce Statue, Dumfries Leisure Centre, Threave Gardens, Kirkudbright, Wigtown, Whithorn, The Solway Coast Heritage Trail, The Galloway Forest Park, Gretna Green, and The Riders on the Marches. Out of these listed items, the following appear in all the pamphlets – Caerlaverock Castle; Robert Burns Statue; Sweetheart Abbey. This suggests that the heritage of the region is perceived as a strong attraction and the physical remains of ancient buildings are in themselves popular sites and evocative symbols of the region.

There are other more general themes apparent in the literature, including the common use of photographs illustrating the scenic beauty, portraying landmarks, historic buildings, statues, as well as people pursuing outdoor activities. Of these, sailing in dinghies is a popular feature, as are pictures of rivers, hillsides and unpopulated landscapes. These images tie in with other themes which recur: the notion of the South West Coast as *'The Riviera of Scotland'* - the region as *'Scotland's best kept holiday secret'* - and the region as *'Scotland in Miniature'*, possessing everything that the rest of Scotland can offer but on a smaller scale. These notions offer instant comparison to the potential tourist, but at the same time don't reveal the specific assets/attractions which the region possesses, and furthermore, may even diminish the region because it becomes merely *similar* to another place but not *actually* that place. It becomes everything and nothing. One paragraph from the 1993 Guide demonstrates this:

> High and low. Severe and dramatic. Remote and accessible. Wild and tamed. As you explore Dumfries and Galloway's countryside you'll discover a hundred different lands which mingle and blend to give South West Scotland its special character.

Perhaps this mixture is a bit too much like blended whisky. It seems the 1997 Guide learnt from this and moved on, providing headings that were regionally specific and stirring: *'Murder and Mayhem: the Border Reivers'*. An examination of changes over the period will highlight the potential variety of the region and the ways in which it can be promoted.

Discernible changes over time

A comparison between the Dumfries and Galloway guide of 1993 and that of 1997 is fruitful, comparing like with like even though it is over a short period. The most obvious difference is one of format. The 1993 Guide used a double page feature to cover a specific theme (e.g. 'A land of contrasts') in which the printed text was surrounded by small supporting photographs. In contrast, the 1997 Guide chose to have a double page spread photograph, with small insets of other pictures on which the printed prose were superimposed. Furthermore, the headings in the 1997 Guide were more provocative and challenging:

> What shall we do today? / Celebrating a saint, several sinners and a sailor / The West, sub-tropical gardens and 4000 years of history / The heart of Galloway, hills, heather and a warm welcome / Down Nithside to Dumfries, the home of Robert Burns / Murder and Mayhem: the Border Reivers.

In contrast, the 1993 Guide headings seem pedestrian and merely descriptive:

> A land of contrasts / The Riviera touch / Highland and hinterland, from rocky mountains to new forest / The past in our present, over 6000 years of tourism / From eventful past to event-full present / Making tracks and blazing trails / Anything you can do – you can do better in Dumfries and Galloway / Where there'll always be a welcome.

The transformation to the more sensationalist representation of 1997, one which deliberately engages the reader through emotive communication, may be due to numerous factors including new writers, the influence of other more successful products, the changing times in journalistic fashion, a general decision to market more aggressively and so on.

As well as a detectable transformation in textual communication means, the material of the 1997 guide focuses on some items that were not emphasised in the 1993 guide. One of these is the Reivers article on the Borders raiders and their activities, given a very high profile, with a double page spread photograph of men in period costume galloping towards the observer, swords drawn. The Reivers do also appear in the First in Scotland Guides, with some considerable coverage, but they are barely mentioned in the 1993 guide. In a similar vein, the spread on saints and sinners in the 1997 guide includes a full-page portrait of two galleons fighting at sea, presumably supporting the small mention of John Paul Jones, founder of the US Navy. He is described as the man *'who led a life that makes most blood and thunder novels seem tame'*. Further on we learn of a civil war at Castledykes: *'based around the story of the Covenanters' part in those bloodstained pages of our history'*. Clearly the guide has been designed to stir the reader by reference to exciting and dangerous aspects of the region's past.

Writing style and presentation in the brochures

The development of a more aggressive, bloodstained history reaching out from the pages of the 1997 guide illustrates the variety of the styles and presentation that may be found in the different literature. The headings of this guide were provocative, questioning, personal and challenging: a sense of spontaneity pervaded the pages. An easy-going manner was also present in the earlier 1993 guide, with its humorous puns and playful wording. However, the actual prose of the 1997 guide becomes evocative, descriptive, poetic, when employed to describe the natural charms of the region:

> Galloway is a land of colour, daubed with the purple of heather, the yellow of the whins – that's gorse in English – and every shade of green from the artist's palette.

Similarly, when recalling the history of the area (particularly the more violent times) the language turns to highly charged imagery:

> You may find it hard to believe that this was a land that once rang to the clash of sword on helmet, to the clatter of charging hooves and the cries of victors and vanquished.

For other purposes, the prose style is sparse and descriptive, listing details, although it may be in the form of a friendly advisor:

> Start at the highest village in Scotland, Warnlockhead. Call in
> at the lead mining museum, where you can make your way
> underground, see the mineral seams and learn how the miners
> lived.

The guide becomes an invisible hand on the tourist's shoulder. More
commonly the description is straightforward but exaggerated, with
continual reminders of the exceptional nature of certain attractions.
History is proudly portrayed, but compressed into sound-bites without
reflection:

> Arriving at Whithorn in the 4th Century, St. Ninian founded
> Scotland's first Christian church. During the Middle Ages this
> became a famed centre of pilgrimage. Scottish kings and
> queens made the long journey south – among them Mary
> Queen of Scots.

And why does the 1993 Guide mention '6000 years of tourism' (from
the Neolithic farmers onwards) whereas the 1997 Guide talks of
'4000 years of history' (the Standing Stones of Torhousekie)?
Perhaps this shows that material proof, in the form of clearly visible
artefacts, is needed to support such historical claims, even in a tourist
brochure.

The region has been reinvented and is being represented as a
potentially exciting, vigorous, ancient and surprising place. By
changing the focus of a proportion of the material and intensifying the
appeal to raw emotions, utilising violent imagery, the writers have
produced a view of history, and consequently a presentation of place,
which is markedly different from that evoked by the 1993 brochure.[4]

However, a further (possibly retrogressive) development is seen in
the Dumfries and Galloway Accommodation Guide 2001 with a
determined effort to establish an image for the region as a place
where people can relax. The 'strapline' used is *'The natural place to
unwind'* and it appears on the cover. A full page photograph of the
river Nith reaching its estuary back-grounded by the Criffel mountain
adorns the cover, intended to give the viewer a sense of peace. The

[4] As Selwyn (1993: 129) notes, sites, as portrayed in tourist literature, have become 'centres of
physical and emotional sensation from which temporal and spatial continuities have been
abolished'.

content headings inside the brochure maintain this sense of calm - *'Escape from the crowd at any time of the year / Time out in unspoilt scenery / Discover our heritage / Inspiring landscapes / Explore our tourist trails'*. The brochure writers appear to have returned to the earlier style of the 1993 Guide, with even less emotional content, although the subsections occasionally catch the eye with headings reminiscent of the gory 1997 Guide: *'Early visitors, saints and sinners / Castles, murder and mayhem'*.

Further into the brochure a page is devoted to outdoor activities, the niche market products: golf, cycling, bird-watching and walking. The environmental assets of the region have been placed in primary position, followed by a heritage theme with articles on abbeys, standing stones, castles and mills, and finally articles on the internationally renowned literary giants and less well-known artists of the region.[5]

The cultural construction of place in context

The main point remains that tourism brochures do not merely inform the reader about aspects of the place to be visited, they describe and interpret the place, in a conscious, deliberate way. They display detectable transformations over short periods of time, reflecting fashions and other influences. Furthermore, and on a deeper cultural level, they remain reflections of the values and preoccupations of the society from which they were produced – the broader cultural context. The writers of the brochures dealing with D&G will have been influenced, often in an unacknowledged sub-conscious manner, by their socio-cultural environment at numerous levels: their home culture, such as Scotland with its westernised outlook; their education, both formal and informal, will have shaped them. And professionally, the type of industry in which they work, with its codes of behaviour, language, idiosyncrasies and objectives will inform their public communication patterns. In addition, factors such as the operating budget, the potential visitors and their propensity to read brochures, and the desires of the membership of a particular regional tourist board all form constraints.

These elements go towards the sum of experiences that underpins the presumptions and preconceptions of the people writing the

---

[5] Such a focus on nature and serenity, utilising straplines like 'The natural place to be' and 'Naturally you'll like it' is partly explained by the focus on target markets including short-break visitors from urban areas and the more mature population.

brochures and shape the final product. Added to this are the demands of the client and the changing patterns of the market. It is the latter qualities that become more easily discernible in a comparison of brochures over a short time period, but these are mere ripples on the surface of deeper water.

Castle Douglas Food Town

We now move from an analysis of the written description of a region with its potential for creativity dependent upon the use of a phrase and the choice of emphasis and style, and turn to the actual creation of a brand image. This is not the work of professional writers, but the labour of a group of people who have decided to promote such an image, and intend to back this newly created brand image with real, tangible assets. The efforts to establish Castle Douglas as a Food Town is an example of a small-scale development, an exercise in branding, and offers an insight into the inclusion of cultural, social and political factors in an economically motivated promotional event.

A general overview will be useful and we might consider the formation of social identities:

> Social identities emerge out of imagined communities, out of particular structures of feeling that bind together three elements, space, time and memory, often in part in opposition to an imagined 'other' such as a neighbouring country. However, massive amounts of mobility may transform such social identities formed around particular configurations of space, time and memory. (Urry 1995: 166)

This view is particularly relevant to our paper in its examination of D&G where initiatives to brand specific towns are now underway: Wigtown Book Town, Kirkcudbright Artists' Town, and Castle Douglas Food Town. These three towns exhibit different qualities in relation to their recently acquired branded identities. Wigtown won a competition in 1997 and was awarded the 'Book Town' title from outside planners looking to create such a town in Scotland. Kirkcudbright has developed into a haven for artists over the past 100 years, initially summer visitors escaping the city: the town has now become a magnet for artists and related persons from outside, launching itself as Kirkcudbright Artists' Town in 2000. In contrast,

Castle Douglas has been a trading centre throughout its existence, 200 years or so, and has been renowned regionally for its butchers' meat, its fish and dairy products.

While the towns use 'space, time and memory' to accentuate their respective identities, they have not developed their identities in opposition to others, rather, they sought to distinguish themselves, rise above the crowd and draw attention to specific assets. In terms of their identities, Castle Douglas was 'born' with its food-based asset; Kirkcudbright has 'achieved' its artists' town identity over the years, and Wigtown has had its book town identity 'thrust upon it' (see Macleod 1997 on the acquisition of identity). These respective product-based identities (commodities) are in the earliest stages of development and Castle Douglas Food Town was eventually launched in June 2002.

Castle Douglas is a planned town, founded in the 18th Century by Sir William Douglas, a wealthy merchant. He wished to establish a centre of commerce in his native Galloway. The original idea was to develop the cotton industry and the town became an important market with regular cattle and horse fairs. It remains today a centre for the local farming area and is the home of the annual Stewartry Agricultural Show and the D&G Horse Show, as well as housing a modern auction market. The town is well known in SW Scotland for selling good quality meat and attracts shoppers from outside the region. Other major attractions in the vicinity include Threave Gardens (56,000 visitors/year) and the Lochside Camp Site (30,000 visitors/year). Currently Castle Douglas has a population of 3,800 and some 160 businesses are based in the town.

During the year 2001 Castle Douglas had been in the process of developing and promoting itself as Castle Douglas Food Town. In this sense it will be following the route pursued by Wigtown Book Town, and more recently Kirkcudbright Artists' Town, in creating for itself a brand image, a strong, product-based identity. The origins of this initiative have been described as beginning with the Soil Association and its 'Food Futures' project, intended to develop sustainable local food economies throughout the UK in 2000. This idea was reinforced during the Galloway Food Festival, where a display panel, composed of shops that dealt with food in the town, emphasised the association of Castle Douglas with food. A local man who worked on the display wrote to the Galloway News suggesting the idea for promoting Castle Douglas as a Food Town (personal communication, A. Livingston). It seems that others were thinking along similar lines and by the autumn of 2000 the Community Council had arranged a meeting on the Food

Town proposal: a press release was followed by a Border TV item and the idea gained more coverage and a wider public awareness. Eventually an Action Group was formed to deal with the promotion. The official launch of the project was planned for the Stewartry Show on August 2nd 2001, but was postponed due to the Foot and Mouth Disease (FMD) crisis, and was eventually held in June 2002. A booklet promoting Castle Douglas as a Food Town has been widely circulated. One press release in 2001 stated:

> Food is the bridge linking the productive and recreational, natural and cultural qualities of this landscape. By promoting Castle Douglas as the 'Natural Place for Food' we will encourage visitors attracted by the quality of local food to discover the countryside and the town, the foundations are in place. Building the bridge simply requires strengthening links which already exist.

The statement makes the profound point that food, as a product of a specific human culture, does indeed provide a direct link between the natural environment and human society, between nature and culture. Furthermore, we must remember that food is a fundamental element of a society's identity, its social organisation, and of course, its sustenance. It is easily overlooked that for tourists, food is an important part of their experience while on holiday.

An essay report circulated in the region examines the natural heritage of the area, and the overlap between farmed landscape and wild landscape.

> What is being suggested is that from a situation in which farmers and farming represented Galloway as an essentially conservative (and Conservative) locality, a different set of actors are emerging who are actively engaged in the construction of a new representation of 'Galloway'. Significantly, food processors and retailers are leading players, although they are supported by a range of other players in newer businesses and communities. (Livingston 2000: 8)

Conclusion

Throughout this chapter the driving theme has been the reinvention of place through cultural construction. Examples from the Lake District, Iceland, Dumfries and Galloway and Castle Douglas have been offered as supporting evidence to this view. If we accept that places are indeed cultural constructions – most plainly when they are being represented to others – then we can conclude that the possibilities for representation are only limited by the human imagination. The same potential for development might be said for the process of attracting visitors. In this way, the assets that D&G possesses, in natural and cultural heritage forms may be considered as so many treasures which may be displayed and polished in as many different ways as the owner pleases. Moreover, these are not, by any means, the only assets possessed. There are others that can be realised, appreciated and used to attract, again depending on cultural values and propensities.

Nevertheless, the focus on niche market products becomes paradoxical. It draws attention to specific elements and attractive qualities, highlighting them and occasionally creating them. But simultaneously it creates boundaries. The processes of essentialising and delineating a site both attract and repulse. Identities and products may intermix strongly, but may give an overall false representation of a region and its qualities. The construction of culture in tourist brochures and marketing is unavoidably limiting, for the purpose of comprehension and expression. It must be borne in mind that such construction of place is never final, is contextually determined and may prove inhibiting for future development. Similarly, the branding of a town brings problems of over-identification with a product, the under-representation of other qualities, and creates the risk of delimiting the identity of a town. What happens when the product is no longer desirable?

There are similar dangers with the stereotyping, through categorisation, of tourists. Assumptions are made and limitations developed about behaviour, needs and interests. More efforts should be made in finding out what these tourists want. They must be envisaged in a more holistic way and perceived as people with a far larger set of interests and desires. As a consequence, the clustering of diverse attractions will make more sense and predictions can be made as to the possible interconnection of attractions and the utilisation of assets.

Those involved in tourism should pay attention to broader trends beyond the confines of their main focus of interest. They must realise that culture is something inherently non-discrete, forever changing and infinite in potential. This makes the marketing of products both risky and rewarding.

References

Abram, S. Waldren, J and D.V.L. Macleod (eds) (1997) *Tourists and Tourism: Identifying with people and places*. Oxford: Berg.

Croll, E. and D. Parkin (eds) (1992) *Bush Base, Forest Farm: Culture, Environment and Development*. London: Routledge.

Dann, G. (1996) The People of Tourist Brochures. In Selwyn, T. (ed).

Donachie, I and I. Macleod. (1974) *Old Galloway*. London: David and Charles.

Einarsson, M. (1996) The Wandering Semioticians: Tourism and the Image of Modern Iceland. In *Images of Contemporary Iceland: Everyday Lives and Global Contexts*. G. Palsson and E.P.Durrenberger (eds), 215-237.

Geertz, C. (1973) *The Interpretation of Cultures*. London: Fontana Press.

Kuper, A and J. Kuper (eds) (1988) *The Social Science Encyclopaedia*. London: Routledge and Kegan Paul.

Livingston, A. (2000) *Marketing Galloway*. Unpublished paper.

Macleod, D.V.L. (1997) 'Alternative' tourists on a Canary Island. In Abram, Waldren and Macleod (eds).

...   (1999) Tourism and the globalisation of a Canary Island. Journal of the Royal Anththropological Institute. Vol 5 (3).

...   (2001) Parks or People? National parks and the case of Del Este, Dominican Republic. *Progress in Development Studies*. Vol 1 (3): 221-235.

MacCannell, D. (1976) *The Tourist: A New Theory of the Leisure Class*. London: Macmillan Press.

Macmillan Dictionary of Anthropology. (1986) C. Seymour-Smith (ed.).

Robinson, M. (1999) Cultural Conflicts in Tourism: Inevitability and Inequality. In Robinson and Boniface (eds). *Tourism and Cultural Conflicts*. Oxford: CABI Publishing.

Sahlins, M. (1972) *Stone Age Economics*. Chicago: Chicago University Press.

Selwyn, T. (1993) Peter Pan in South-East Asia: views from the brochures. In *Tourism in South East Asia*. Hitchcock, M., King, V. T., and Parnwell, M. J. G. (eds). London: Routledge, 117-137.

Selwyn, T. (ed). (1996) *The Tourist Image: Myths and Myth Making in Tourism*. London: John Wiley Ltd.

Tylor, E.B. (1871) *Primitive Society: Researches into the Development of Mythology, Philosophy, Religion, Language, Art and Culture*. London: John Murray.

Urry, J. (1990) *The Tourist Gaze*. London: Sage Publications.

...   (1995) *Consuming Places*. London: Routledge.

PART III

TOURISM AND THE NATURAL ENVIRONMENT

Chapter 4

Developing Cultural Tourism:
Strategic Thinking and Opportunity
(Abstract)

Murray Pittock

Context

In the increasingly homogenous economic environment brought about by globalization, culture (defined in an inclusive sense as in the UNESCO definition which stresses its role as a denominator of identity at every level) is one of the key ways in which the particular identity (or brand) of a small country can profile itself in the world. As the *Charter for the Arts in Scotland* put it in 1993, culture (and here multicultural sensitivities also have a profound importance) is 'the key component in defining human identity', and with that our profiling of ourselves to each other and to others.

Such a profiling has an impact in at least two ways. It creates a recognizable international identity, which can aid both tourism and development (cf. the 90% rise in overseas tourists to Glasgow on the back of a culture-led regeneration in the 80s and 90s and the integration of cultural questions into the Executive's National Tourism Strategy), and it enriches the lives of the citizenry both through their passive enjoyment of culture and its imaginative expression in the arts, and also through the confidence-building effect of participation in artistic endeavor. 93% of participants in arts events report an increase in self-respect, with 80% agreeing that the experience has improved their capacity to work with other people and 72% reporting improved communication skills. The visual arts can help tackle important issues such as social exclusion, poor health and learning difficulties: they are critically important for maintaining an environment in which people can develop confidence and feel positive about themselves. Culture increases self-respect.

Culture is also an important part of enterprise, for its promotion not only underpins the importance of personal creativity, but also promotes allied social goals such as tourism, inward investment, national branding and opportunities in training and employment: Ireland is the obvious example in this context. In UK terms, the arts give back £3 in NI, VAT and income tax for every £1 of investment, while only banking, tourism (a linked activity) and shipping produce more invisible earnings. In Scotland, Edinburgh's various festivals contribute at least £20m to the economy of the city; with the Edinburgh Hogmanay festival alone supporting over 700 FTE jobs from the 91 000 estimated to be generated by the creative economy as a whole.

Argument

'Developing Tourism' examines ways in which better development of heritage and arts tourism in particular can improve both the internal consumption of Scottish culture and its external promotion, finishing with two case studies. Recent research has revealed the reputation of Scotland internationally to be a small country of spirit and integrity, but also one that is stuck in the past. Some of this stereotyping undoubtedly descends from the eighteenth and nineteenth-century romanticization of Scotland which still draws many people to visit the country; and in this aspect, it is not unwelcome. It is important not to de-mythologize tartan to too great an extent. On the other hand, it is important for the development of the image of Scottish culture that the need for change is recognized, both in the development of a greater range of the country's potential, and also in an awareness of the need for specifically regional development.

There are some very helpful signs in the latter area. The new Burns festival and other efforts to promote the South West, the greater development of Angus tourism (both 'Pictish' and otherwise) since 1980, and the growing awareness of the need for regional branding (Grampian as 'whisky and castles' country: though we should beware of overly limiting a brand). Theatre, music and other contemporary art can also be linked to tourism, as in the 1998 Argyll TinCAN (The International Contemporary Arts Network) festival.

On the other hand, the very terms in which these welcome changes are expressed can continue to display a degree of internal imprisonment by the Romantic paradigm of a rural Scotland of ruined castles, clan warfare, game and malt. The apparent bias complained of by some towards rural tourism at the expense of the major central belt cities (*Herald*, 20/3/02) is matched by an apparent unwillingness among the public branding agencies to sell the built heritage effectively. Nor is this the only example of a missed opportunity.

Missed opportunities

- Architectural tourism

- Reliable timetabling and good publicity for historic re-enactments; a lack of 'living history' (storytellers of Scottish stories, distinctively Scottish mediaeval markets: contrast English Heritage). Timetabling is increasing, but still often via Scottish press (cf. *Sunday Herald*, 17/3/02).

- Limited visual, animatronic and audio guides

- Lack of focus on famous writers, artists, events: now improving, but still considerable regional difference: the sophistication of Skye and Lochalsh is in Scotland

- The audio and multimedia potential of Scottish music: the audiences for Cappella Nova and others indicate a real appetite not matched (except slightly at Stirling Castle) by music's role in promoting heritage. More generally, there is a lack of attention to sound and smell in cultural tourist facilities (cf. Jorvik, The Oxford Story)

- Lack of stress on investment for repeat visitors, particularly in National Trust for Scotland properties like Culloden, whose visitor numbers subsidize the other Highland properties; contrast New Lanark, where there has been a synergy of funding and interpretive skills from different bodies. Does this indicate the importance of cross- corporate cultural collaboration?

Two case studies

- NTS Culloden: 120 000 paying visitors pa (falling slightly); 250 000 on battlefield. Profit-making site, insufficiently commercialised for culturally sensitive reasons. No video; no audio guide; limited living history in season: not effectively advertised. Recent management consultancy report, but no fundamental action on display area: not upgraded since 1984. Artifact collection: haphazard and arranged in old museum style; too valuable to touch.

- Worcester Commandery: much lower-profile site, but more sophisticated in every way. HQ of Charles II; animatronics; 17th Century texts recorded; interactive weapons systems videos; visitors judge in trial of Charles I; scheduled living history days for tourists and schools; general videos; targeted acquisitions; model battlefield; weapons that can be handled by children.

A Way Forward

While most tourism suppliers are not governmental agencies, it is important that good best practice advice and understanding of these issues is emplaced in Executive cultural policy. In particular, opportunities are beginning to be taken to respond to rapidly increasing North American interest in Scottish history, culture and roots (150% increase in Americans claiming Scottish ancestry in recent census) both through innovations in the areas listed above, and also via the comprehensively organized publication and digitization (and even possible relocation) of major genealogical archives, since the tracing of Scottish ancestry is a major tourist interest. Some of this kind of work is already beginning: ancestralscotland.com is fronted on the Visitscotland site. It remains the case, however, that Scottish use of cultural tourism as a means of boosting visitor numbers and enhancing the guest experience has a great deal of unexplored potential, from things as simple as automatic room upgrades through more developed information channels for cultural tourist events to better site development.

There are other related issues, such as public-private or public sector collaboration that might include the development of Executive best practice guidelines in the commissioning of arts and crafts for capital projects or environmental development. In this context, the national branding of public space found elsewhere in the EU (for example, in the green/environmental theme in the Netherlands, a country of course built on pioneering land reclamation) represents an opportunity for which plenty of scope exists in Scotland: the public projection of 'national brand' features can be useful both for community self-respect and international profile. They can also be used to overcome harmful stereotypes: arguably the Keating 'Creative Nation' strategy in Australia was an example of this. In these ways, tourism will gain from the renewal of public infrastructure in Scotland and the UK. In this context, however, we must proceed with caution, for there is a lack of central will to proceed with best practice evident in some quarters, as witness the attack by 'the new director of the Scottish Arts Council' on 'the Scottish Executive for the low priority it has given to arts and culture' (*Herald*, 1 May 2002). Culture has been called an 'afterthought' in current policy, and whether or not that is an exaggeration, there is plenty of scope for the development of cutting-edge ideas in an international context. Public art's role in social inclusion remains a major opportunity, but the greatest and most immediate need is to align cultural tourism with the range of Scottish achievement in the arts, with its diversity and with its cultural specificity to a greater degree, and more rapidly, than is at present evident. The world is moving on, and we must learn from it as well as contribute to it.

Chapter 5

Literary Places and Tourism

David T Herbert

Introduction

There is little doubt that literary places have exceptional qualities that set them apart from other tourist attractions but they also share more general qualities with the broader group of heritage places. Literary places are the products of associations between places and writers; they are constructed as tourist attractions. The questions to be explored revolve around the meanings with which they are endowed by custodians and visitors. What are the custodians seeking to present? How do the visitors read the texts of literary places and how do they interpret them? What are the qualities that set literary places apart and what are the issues that they raise?

There are many literary places (See Figure 1). More significant literary places stand as attractions in their own right and are the hubs of tourist travel, others prosper as convenient stopping points along a well-recognised tourist itinerary. This dichotomy prompts further questions. What kinds of tourists come to literary places and what do they seek there? Literary pilgrims come with a great deal of knowledge of the writers and their works, more general visitors with only a passing interest in the literary connections and attractions are more general and aesthetic. This division is simple and uncritical but it does raise the issue of different types of visitors with varying expectations. It also suggests that literary places have roles to play for a wide range of tourists and are worth promoting and developing.

The qualities of literary places

Literary places often possess qualities such as easy access, scenic attraction and good facilities, but there are other special features that set them apart. Firstly, visitors come to literary places because of the connections that they have with the lives of writers. Former homes of

writers can inspire awe, reverence or nostalgia. Marsh (1993: xi, xv)
expressed this well when she described the homes of writers in
England:

> In these places, a visitor can still walk out of a house and into
> landscapes that have barely changed since the writer drew
> breath from them and breathed literature into them ...We
> walk in our writers' footsteps and see through their eyes
> when we enter these spaces.

In some ways these qualities of literary places are not exceptional.
They are shared for example with the homes of statesmen or artists;
fame and notoriety are not exclusive to writers. George
Washington's home at Mount Vernon, Virginia and the Claude
Monet house at Giverny, Normandy are now major visitor
attractions.

   Secondly, tourists may be drawn to literary places that form the
settings for novels. Imaginative literature may be set in the locations
that writers knew and the landscapes of the novels and specific sites
or buildings may have significance. *Jamaica Inn* on Bodmin Moor is
the title of a novel by Daphne du Maurier but is also a real place built
as an eighteenth century coaching inn. The region and the hotel
promote the du Maurier connection and there is a Daphne du Maurier
room with a collection of memorabilia. Sker House in South Wales
was built by the monks of Neath Abbey in the twelfth century and
became a country house that has recently been restored. When R.D.
Blackmore, author of *Lorna Doone*, wrote *The Fair Maid of Sker* he
based the novel on Sker House; another real place with a literary
connection. It is in this context that some of the special qualities of
literary places begin to emerge. The place is inhabited by characters
from both the real life of the writer and the imagined world of the
novels. It is this merging of real and imagined that gives literary
places a special meaning. For any reader of Thomas Hardy, the
landscapes of Dorset and Hardy's Wessex are suffused with the
imagery of the journeys of Tess of the D'Urbervilles. Fictional
characters, such as Tess, and events from the novels often generate
the strongest imagery. Pocock (1987: 138) argued that tourists to
Haworth sought out the moors, which formed the settings for the
novels and the home of the Brontës, but emotions they experienced
when crossing them were stimulated 'Less with the excitement of
treading in the Brontës' footsteps than with the thought that
Heathcliff might appear'. It is the fact that the places were significant

within the novel that gives them a special meaning. Butler (1986) argued that some readers visit such places because it gives them a greater insight into the novel as a work of literature. A visit to Laugharne, for example, might still help to capture the mood of a place that contributed to Dylan Thomas's *Under Milk Wood*; the Cobb at Lyme Regis might yet engender the image of *The French Lieutenant's Woman*.

Thirdly, tourists may be drawn to literary places that are capable of acting as a catalyst for memories or some long standing affective attachment to an ideal or image. The former response is reminiscent of Marcel Proust and his many examples of the ability of specific items or events to resurrect emotions from a barely remembered past. Squire (1993, 1994) exemplified this with her research into Hill Top Farm, former home of Beatrix Potter who wrote the *Peter Rabbit* stories for children. For many of the visitors that she interviewed the main experience was one of evoking childhood memories and emotions; their recall was of the telling of the stories and their bonds with home and family. Children's stories are a particular genre likely to lend themselves to these kinds of reactions and in some ways the whole range of Disneyland phenomena as tourist attractions originate in this way. Squire also noted other emotional reactions from her Hill Top Farm visitors. There was for some a reminder of the traditional rural way of life and for others of the English countryside of earlier times. In a similar way, Davies (1995) noted the significance of the Evangeline story, as depicted in Longfellow's epic poem, to the Acadian people of eastern Canada. For them the story was one of lost territory and places and identity. Some writers, such as Burns or Yeats, act as symbols of national identity and their places have that significance.

A fourth reason for visiting a literary place may have less to do with the literature than with some event in the writer's life. Van Gogh was an artist rather than a writer but Millon (1993) commented that many people visited Auvers-sur-Oise near Paris because of its association with the manner of the artist's death rather than with his art. It was at Auvers that Van Gogh died, supposedly after a suicide attempt, and is buried with his brother Theo in an ivy-covered grave.

The reasons that tourists visit literary places are various. If they are drawn there because they are interested in the imaginative world of the writer, this is a motive that sets literary places apart. The lines between real and imagined are blurred. Hardy described Wessex as a place made up of 'The horizons and landscapes of a partly real, partly dream country' (Birch, 1981: 355). Writers have licence. The places may provide the settings and inspirations but the dominant force is the plot and the facts are properly manipulated to serve its needs. To some extent then the literary place may have the qualities of a dream world and that forms part of its attractions.

Types of literary places

Many literary places take the form of small museums or collections based in a house formerly occupied by a writer. Some elements of the original dwelling have usually been preserved and there are artefacts that can be dated to the author. One such example is the former home of Jane Austen. The writer and her family occupied the dwelling at the village of Chawton in Hampshire from 1809 to 1817. The cottage was divided after 1845, though the arrangement of rooms is basically unaltered, and now the Jane Austen Memorial Trust administers the house as a small museum. There are items of original furnishings and displays of the family history along with direct memorabilia of the writer that includes the donkey cart in which she used to visit local friends. Even though this is simply the place where Jane Austen lived, visitors are still capable of reading it as part of her imagined world:

> No enthusiast could ask for a plot more evocative of Jane Austen. ... It is a house from which any Austen heroine might aspire to higher things – yet to which she might safely retreat from life's vicissitudes. (Jenkins, 2001: 18)

Dylan Thomas and his family from 1938 to 1953 occupied the Boat House at Laugharne. Standing on the cliff overlooking the Tâf estuary, the Boat House has a spectacular setting. The house contains many items from the writer's day and is a small museum under the custodianship of the Carmarthen District Council. There are tape recordings of the poems and a video display of the writer and his life. There is also his writing shed described by Ferris (1977: 844) as his 'word-splashed hut', which is still a major attraction. These are writers' houses but there is some difference in kind between the two examples. Whereas Jane Austen's House is clearly a literary place because the writer lived there and none of her novels were set in Hampshire, the Boat House has that quality but adds another. The aspect of the Tâf estuary and much of the nearby town of Laugharne has the ability to evoke the imagined landscapes and characters of

Under Milk Wood. The literary place combines real and imagined worlds.

Another type of literary place is that which arises purely from the imagined world of the writer. Some take the form of a simulacrum or a place that never existed. A good example of this is the Sherlock Holmes Museum in Baker Street, London. A wall plaque marks 221b Baker Street even though that part of the street did not exist when Conan Doyle named it as the lodgings of Sherlock Holmes in the period 1881 to 1904. The Museum consists of rooms containing the great detective's chair, desk, hat etc., even though of course this is a fictional character invented by the writer. The visitors still come undeterred in many thousands to have their photographs taken sitting in the chair, smoking the pipe or wearing the hat.

Other literary places are regional. Catherine Cookson Country occupies part of South Tyneside and has links both with the home of the writer and the settings for her novels. Brontë Country in South Yorkshire is a favoured literary tourist attraction as is George Eliot Country around Nuneaton, Warwickshire. Many of these labels are used as part of a promotional or marketing exercise for the tourist industry with the aim of attracting more visitors. Places will actively use their association with a writer as part of their place promotion, often incorporating the literary connection into a logo. Some of the place promotions are contestable in their foundations. Cabourg, Normandy, for example, uses its connections with Marcel Proust and portrays itself as the model for his fictional seaside town of Balbec. In reality, Proust did spend summer holidays with his grandmother in Cabourg and some of his 'remembrances' of places and characters, such as the promenade and the Grand Hotel, are reminiscent of that place. He did however holiday at other places in Normandy and Balbec is most probably an amalgam of remembered places. Attempts to use literary linkages have increased with the stronger thrust towards cultural policies. As the industrial city image fades, the cultural city is a worthy substitute, albeit partial. Glasgow benefited enormously from its designation as a European City of Culture. Many other cities have looked towards heritage of some kind, including literary heritage, as a means of new image building. Swansea has used the Dylan Thomas connection as part of a strategy of inventing a new image for a former industrial city. The approach can only be partial and it was clear at Cabourg (Herbert, 1996) that although Marcel Proust added something to the town's appeal he was marginal to its other attractions.

One variant of this kind of literary place is the literary tour. The literary tours of Dublin (Igoe, 1994), including the tour of literary pubs in the city, cater for the visitor experience in a number of ways. Firstly the sites have some real life connection with the writer, such as the pubs frequented by Brendan Behan or James Joyce. Secondly, some of the sites will present sessions of readings of prose or poetry that relate to the writers and help cultivate the literary ambience. Actors may lead the tours and it is their interaction with audiences and clientele that sets the scene. Publications, such as Costello's (1998) *Dublin's Literary Pubs,* assist the literary tourist and allow him or her to follow in the footsteps of James Joyce, W.B. Yeats, Brendan Behan, Anthony Cronin and Patrick Campbell, often introducing fictional as well as real figures. The *Paris Literary Promenade* is a walking tour based on the places connected with writers who made their homes in Paris. From Gertrude Stein to Janet Flanner, James Joyce to Samuel Beckett, Ezra Pound to George Orwell, writers migrated to Paris and its heady atmospheres. Part of the *Promenade* takes in the cafés of Paris linked with French writers such as Sartre, Camus and Simone de Bouvoir; the cafés of central Paris have always been of great significance as the meeting places of writers, artists, intellectuals and radicals. Literary tours of this kind are created and amplified to attract visitors and fall easily into the list of literary places.

Another type of literary place is that associated with a festival or celebration of literature or with an exceptional promotion of books and literature. Hay-on-Wye in Herefordshire, England has become a major centre for book sales and accessible collections of second hand publications. Every year the small town serves as the centre for a major festival at which there are seminars and talks by well-known writers and a variety of prestigious literary events. Hay-on-Wye has some fair claim to be regarded as a literary place. The city of Swansea was the focus for a Year of Literature in 1995 and the year long festival attracted many literary figures in an expansive programme. Other places hold exceptional collections of books and famous libraries, or host festivals of literature and have some claim for designation as literary places.

Literary places in the landscapes of tourism

As tourism has grown in its avaricious way, so the demand for attractions has multiplied. In modern tourism, literary places add to the typology of attractions and fit into the growing array of tourist places. As with all typologies of places there are strong variations. Different literary places will cater for different types of tourists. Those who are attracted to the Dublin Literary Pub Tour, for example, may be different from those drawn to Hill Top Farm in Cumbria. There are 'different strokes for different folks', a dictum that summarises the diversity of tastes for many kinds of visitor experiences. Are there still literary pilgrims, the 'travellers' of the tourist round, versed in scholarship and with the cultural capital to gain most from the visitor experience? There is evidence to support the contention that many visitors to literary places have at least a good working knowledge of the writer whose home they have come to see; further they have read at least some of the works. Essentially, the value of visiting a literary place is greatly enhanced by good awareness of the writer or the novels or both. At Chawton in Hampshire, where Jane Austen lived, over 85% of visitors interviewed had read at least one of her novels; just fewer than 30% had read all six (Herbert, 2001). At Laugharne, home for many years of Dylan Thomas, almost 80% had heard of, read or seen a performance of *Under Milk Wood*. Poetry is a less popular medium but about 40% of the Laugharne visitors were aware of at least some of Dylan Thomas's poems such as *A Child's Christmas in Wales*. A large number of visitors to literary places are on this evidence at least literary aware and other studies (Squire, 1993; Pocock, 1987) provide similar confirmation.

It is probably fair to claim that around this majority with some level of literary awareness are a large minority with little or no knowledge of literature at all and very small minority of literary experts. The latter would tend to visit specific places linked with their specialist writer, to be more interested in the real lives of the writer than with the fiction, and to be well read in literary criticism and biography as well as in the novels. They might look to the visit to satisfy an interest but perhaps also to gain some greater insight into the writer or some facet of the work. The former would have only a passing interest in the writers and their works but are drawn to an attractive and accessible place that fits conveniently into the visitor itinerary. One transformation of the literary place is that which occurs when a novel becomes a television presentation or a film. Awareness grows rapidly among those with some knowledge and makes inroads into the least well-versed groups. Numbers of visitors to a place will rise and literary places previously neglected may become visitor attractions. More strikingly, places that have no more claim to authentic links to a writer than the fact that they were chosen for the setting of the television or film presentations are transformed into hot spots of the tourist trail. Stamford in Lincolnshire, where the television film of George Eliot's *Middlemarch* was made in 1994 became a tourist attraction even though it had no connection with either the writer or the novel. Tours in Seattle are now arranged to include the house occupied by Tom Hanks on the waterfront for the making of *Sleepless in Seattle*. The simulacrum, or invented place, is also part of the landscape of literary places.

Who are the literary tourists?

Visitors to heritage sites, historic houses, art galleries and museums tend to be drawn disproportionately from groups with higher socio-economic status and above average educational qualifications. Surveys of visitors to literary places confirm this kind of visitor profile. At the Jane Austen House in Chawton, 60% of visitors could be classed as managerial, professional or skilled white collar; at the Boathouse in Laugharne, 49% fell into these categories. A further 30% at each of these places were students, housewives or retirees; people in low skilled occupations were very thinly represented. The dominant group was what Thrift (1989) termed the service classes. Visitors also tended to be adult with 41% of Chawton visitors falling within the 35 to 54 year-old age band and to be first time visitors to the site. 82% of those interviewed were visiting Chawton for the first time (Herbert, 2001). Well over 80 % of visitors at both Chawton and Laugharne had come on a day trip from a relatively short distance though many were on holiday in the area. Both Chawton and Laugharne were clearly parts of a wider tourist itinerary in their respective regions. At Chawton, visitors had typically also visited the historic towns of Chichester, Salisbury and Winchester, sites such as Stonehenge and Arundel Castle and houses such as those inhabited by Gilbert White and the Duke of Wellington. Laugharne visitors had sometimes followed the Dylan Thomas 'trail' in Swansea and had been to local towns such as Tenby and Carmarthen and to sites such as St David's Cathedral, Pembroke Castle and the Aberglasney Historic Garden. They were largely inquiring and interested tourists with eclectic tastes rather than focused and dedicated literary *aficionados*.

The idea that there is a broad dichotomy of visitors to literary places was confirmed at both Chawton and Laugharne. On the one hand there were visitors who emphasised their literary interests and some knowledge of the writer, on the other were those who claimed primarily to be seeking relaxation and more ephemeral pleasures. The two parts of the dichotomy are not however discrete and there are clear possibilities of many visitors coming for both those types of reasons. The 'why' of tourism remains a question about which there is limited understanding. Many people arrive with ill-defined reasons but the visit invokes reactions that can include a sense of nostalgia and a perceived association with the world of the writer. Generalizations are possible but each visitor has some particular chemistry with the place and its presentation. This is especially so at literary places where the fusion of real and imagined worlds engenders a unique set of emotions. Chawton and Laugharne offer an interesting contrast. Jane Austen lived in Hampshire but the county did not serve as the setting for any of her novels. Chawton visitors were interested in the life of Jane Austen and the house in which she lived. Her fictional worlds were elsewhere, Box Hill in Surrey where Emma took part in the picnic party, the Cobb at Lyme Regis where Louisa had her accident. Visitors to Chawton are unlikely to gaze out on the streets with Emma Woodhouse or Elizabeth Bennett in their mind's eye. Yet that seems exactly what visitors to Haworth experience in their walks on the Yorkshire moors where Heathcliff and Catherine Earnshaw walked in the imagined world of Emily Brontë. It is also possible at Cabourg where the knowing tourist looks down the promenade and envisages the advance of a group of young ladies that include Albertine, with her brilliant laughing eyes and plump matt cheeks. Indeed, a presented quotation on a plaque facing the green space in front of the Grand Hotel encourages the visitor to do just that. The Boathouse at Laugharne transgresses into the fictional world of the novel. Rightly or wrongly, many saw Laugharne as the foundation of *Under Milk Wood.* They gaze across the Tâf estuary and imagine the 'sloe black, slow, black, crow black, fishing boat bobbing sea'. They transpose Milk Wood into Laugharne:

> This timeless, mild beguiling island of a town with its seven public houses, one chapel in action, one church, two billiard tables ... three rivers, a visiting sea ... and a multitude of mixed birds. (Cited in W. Davies, 1991: 91-2)

This is the real magic of literary places. They have the ability to touch human emotions and to evoke memories in powerful ways. Whether they serve as a means of reliving or enhancing an enjoyment of the story, of an attachment to the character or a remembrance of the situations in which the story was told, they add immeasurably to the tourist experience.

Presenting literary places

Presentation of a literary place in many ways defines its character and its attractiveness to visitors. The owners or managers of literary places will use presentation or the range of interpretive techniques to convey a particular kind of message or establish a particular kind of ambience. Interpretation is a powerful instrument. Even in its pioneering days in the United States National Parks Service it was introduced to achieve a specified impact on visitors to sites of natural heritage. Freeman Tilden (1977) used the phrase:

> Through interpretation, understanding,
> Through understanding, appreciation,
> Through appreciation, protection.

That message remains a dominant theme for the public agencies, which, as custodians of heritage sites, present them to a visiting public. For many types of visitor places, however, the aim of interpretation will vary. For some the entertainment aim is dominant and the site is essentially interpreted as a tourist place, for others the 'heritage' site may be modified or 'antiqued' to increase its entertainment value. There may be other kinds of messages, political, nationalistic, cultural, or materialistic, that interpretation seeks to convey to visitors. In summary, the presenters of heritage sites are empowered to create and sometimes invent a visitor attraction through the methodologies of interpretation. The qualifier to this argument is the potential for interaction between presenter and visitor. Interpretation may convey specific messages but the visitors may read them in various and perhaps unintended ways; the text is capable of a variety of interpretations. Figure 2 summarises these relationships well and is adapted from Johnson (1986).
    These principles of interpretation apply to literary places and the imaginative dimension that is present enhances the scope for imaginative presentation. Many visitors seek entrance to the fictional worlds of the novels and their central characters. The Web Site for the writer of the Narnia children's stories is titled *Into the Wardrobe*

invoking a key element of C.S Lewis's magical stories. The power of children's stories has already been mentioned in connection with Squire's (1994) studies of visitors to Hill Top Farm, the home of Beatrix Potter. Harris (2001) described the first steps towards the invention of a literary place. J.K. Rowling, author of the Harry Potter stories, had bought Killiechassie House in Perthshire, Scotland. The Times writer first mentions that it 'Bears a passing resemblance to Hogwarts School where Harry Potter learns the art of wizardry'. A local resident is quoted as saying, 'this is the perfect place to conjure up stories and mysteries. The countryside around here really feeds the imagination'. The process of inventing a '*Harry Potter Country*' has begun. Another powerful figure in children's literature, Lucy Laud Montgomery, the author of *Anne of Green Gables*, has similar status. Fawcett and Cormack (2001) describe three literary tourist sites in Prince Edward Island, Canada that are associated with the writer. At these sites the presenters had many elements to choose from, the real place, biography, fictional settings and characters from the novel. Lucy Montgomery lived at the Cavendish house for much of her childhood and early adult life. Interpretation at the Cavendish house relies on a small number of simple devices, signage, a bookstore and a recorded orientation talk. This is where the writer lived and the aim is to create an atmosphere of sincerity and respect. Green Gables House, the model for the stories, is located within the Prince Edward Island National Park. It moves the visitor from the real world of the author to the fictional world of her novels. The orientation film at the site 'weaves together images of the author' (696). Visitors are encouraged ' To move between fantasy and reality in Lovers' Lane, the Haunted Wood, and the house that inspired Green Gables' (696) and again, to use their imaginations and catch a glimpse of the spirit of Anne of Green Gables. The Anne of Green Gables Museum at Silver Bush presents artefacts, books, photographs, letters and articles associated with Lucy Montgomery and her work. Again, fact and fiction are merged as visitors are invited to view the enchanted bookcase that appears in the novel. Artefacts are introduced with citations from the text of the novel. 'The teapot is all that is left of Grandmother Mac Neill's fluted set' (699).

The study by Fawcett and Cormack (2001) is interesting in its portrayal of the significance of a writer to the tourism potential of a specific part of Canada. It also reveals the varying ways in which presenters of sites portray their products. At Cavendish House there is little attempt at invention but some attempt at faithful restoration and an overall aim of creating the aura of the writer's presence at the

home where she once lived. Green Gables House and the Museum at
Silver Bush trespass significantly into the fictional worlds of the
novels and seek unashamedly to establish a visitor experience that
draws largely on the imagined and the emotional. The contrasts
demonstrate clearly the range and diversity possible at literary places.

They also illustrate the complex ways in which literary places can
address the issue of authenticity. Some sites, like the Jane Austen
House and the Cavendish House stay close to the demands of
authenticity, others such as the Green Gables House take major steps
into the imaginative arena. The wider debate on authenticity in
heritage tourism resolves into compromise. Samuel (1994) argued
that the problematic nature of authenticity is not particular to heritage.
There is, in his view, no such thing as the authentic past, memory
changes and is historically conditioned, history and memory are
inherently revisionist. He argued that historians, in common with
heritage managers, re-invent the past, reconciling past and present,
memory and myth, written record and spoken word. A heritage place
may be presented as authentic but will inevitably, to a greater or
lesser extent, be a social construction. Schouten (1995) held the view
that none of this mattered. Visitors are looking not necessarily for
historical reality but for an experience that is rooted in the past rather
than a faithful reproduction of it

There is a range for literary places from the very specific
historically verifiable building, landscape feature or artefact to
imagined worlds of the stories. For tourism, the key tests are whether
they are what they claim to be and whether they provide visitors with
the kinds of experiences they seek. For some that may be touching the
desk at which the writer worked, for others it may be the power to
transport them into the world of the novel. The value of literary places
as affective places is very high. They can stir the emotions, evoke
memories and invite nostalgia. They belong as much to a subjective
as to an objective landscape, their roots are in culture rather than
economy.

Conclusions

Literary places fit easily into the list of visitor attractions and will
rarely be ignored by place promotion or tourism marketing agencies
whose imperative is to add to the overall profile of a region. At this
level they can be viewed in relatively straightforward ways, they are
just one more type of attraction for visitors that provide volume and

diversity to what is on offer. In some situations, such as the Anne of Green Gables places on Prince Edward Island, literary places rank among the main attractions. More commonly, they are useful adjuncts to a more compelling list of attractions. Beyond this level of just adding to a list or itinerary, literary places become more complex to understand and present to a visiting public. Their exceptionality affects many aspects of literary places. It affects the reasons why visitors come in the first place, it affects the meanings they attach to the experience of the visit, and it affects the way in which the place is presented in terms of interpretation. The exceptionality also draws any analysis into consideration of some of the key issues in heritage tourism such as authenticity. Exceptionality does not imply uniqueness. There are other types of visitor places that share some of the qualities most clearly expressed at literary sites. As Samuel (1994) reminded us, historical sites are variously remembered, revised and re-invented. Hughes (1992: 38) noted:

> A blurring of boundaries between fiction and history that is characteristic of tourist promotional literature.

Authenticity becomes a malleable concept almost by definition at literary sites. Even at those sites where the link is only with the life of the author, the recurrent issues surrounding authenticity are present. Was the house actually like this? Have the landscapes changed beyond recognition? At sites where the fictional world of the novels is built into the presentation, different yardsticks must measure authenticity. Authenticity has been a contested concept since Mac Cannell initiated the debate in the context of tourism (MacCannell 1973; 1976). Wang (1999) provided a recent review and argued that the concept of existential authenticity allowed a focus upon the reality of the visitor experience regardless of whether the toured object was authentic or not. 'What tourists seeks are their own authentic selves and inter subjective authenticity'. (Wang, 1999: 365-6). This stance has resonance with that developed by Crang (1996) in his account of re-enacted heritage. Crang argued that the participants turned to the past as a strategy to find an authentic experience that they grounded in the present:

> The authenticity was not so much found in the past as in the comunitas felt with others equally both trying and admitting the impossibility of ever achieving it. It is (a) reflexive construction. (Crang, 1996: 428)

These views on authenticity help make sense of the experience of visiting a literary site. It is the experience that is the central concern for visitors, who bring to the visit a multiplicity of prior knowledge and attitudes that affects their individual experiences. The experiences are various and encompass objects with some claim to be verifiable and imaginative portrayals that are clearly not. The success of the literary place is assessed in terms of its ability to allow a multiplicity of expectations to be satisfied and to provide new dimensions to their experience of the writer and the works. Hopefully, that experience will spill over into and enrich other aspects of the visitors' lives.

The managers, custodians and presenters of literary places clearly have significant roles. They seek to promote a visitor attraction and can range between all points of the spectrum between real lives and imagined places, characters and events to do so. Place promotion is an accepted part of tourism marketing and the availability of a literary connection offers an additional dimension to what is available. Many places are only literary places and the variations in presentation will depend upon what is available and what can be invented to create the ambience of the writer. For other places, the literary connection may be just one facet of the diverse attractions of a tourist destination.

References

Birch, B.P. (1981), "Wessex, Hardy and the nature novelists." Transactions, *Institute of British Geographers*, 6, 348-58.
Butler, R. (1986), "Literature as an influence in shaping the image of tourist destinations." In J.S. Marsh (ed.) *Canadian Studies of Parks, Recreation and Tourism in Foreign Lands*, Trent University, Ontario.
Costello, P. (1998), *Dublin's Literary Pubs*, Mc Gill/ Queen's University Press, Montreal.
Crang, M. (1996), "Magic kingdom or a quixotic quest for authenticity." *Annals of Tourism Research*, 23.2, 415-31.
Davies, G. (1995), Rewriting the Acadian Evangeline myth: Roberts, Saunders and Nova Scotia popular culture, Paper presented to the *Canada in its Literature* conference, University of Wales Swansea.
Davies, W. (1991), *The Loud Hills of Wales: Poetry of Place*, Dent, London.
Fawcett, C. and Cormack, P. (2001), "Guarding authenticity at literary tourism sites." *Annals of Tourism Research*, 28, 686-704.
Ferris, P. (1977), *Dylan Thomas.* Penguin: Harmondsworth.
Harris, G. (2001), "Mansion to be Rowling's magical retreat." *The Times*, November 22, 11.
Herbert, D.T. (1996), "Artistic and literary places in France as tourist attractions." *Tourism Management*, 17, 77-85.

Herbert, D.T. (2001), "Literary places, tourism and the heritage experience", *Annals of Tourism Research*, 28.2, 312-33.

Hughes, G. (1992), "Tourism and the geographical imagination", *Leisure Studies*, 11, 31-42.

Igoe, V., (1994), *A Literary Guide to Dublin.* Methuen, London.

Jenkins, S. (2001), "England's best houses", *The Times Weekend*, December 1: 18.

Johnson, R. (1986), "The story so far: And further transformations", in D. Punter (ed.) *Introduction to Contemporary Cultural Studies*, Longman, London, 277-313.

MacCannell, D. (1973), "Staged authenticity: arrangements of social space in tourist settings", *American Journal of Sociology*, 79, 589-603.

MacCannell, D. (1976), *The Tourist: A New Theory of the Leisure Class*, Shocken, New York.

Marsh, K. (ed.) (1993), *Writers and their Houses,* Hamish Hamilton, London.

Millon, C. (1993). Unpublished letter from the Office de Tourisme, Auvers-sur-Oise.

Pocock, D.C.D. (1987), "Haworth: the Experience of a Literary Place", in W.E. Mallory and P. Simpson-Housley (eds) *Geography and Literature*, Syracuse: Syracuse University Press, 135-42.

Samuel, R. (1994), *Theatres of Memory: Past and Present in Contemporary Culture*, Verso, London.

Schouten, F.F.J. (1995), "Heritage as historical reality", in D.T. Herbert (ed.) *Heritage, Tourism and Society*, Mansell, London, 21-31.

Squire, S.J. (1993), "Valuing countryside: reflections on Beatrix Potter tourism", *Area* 24, 5-10.

Squire, S.J. (1994), "Gender and tourist experiences: assessing women's shared meanings for Beatrix Potter", *Leisure Studies*, 13, 195-209.

Thrift, N. (1989), "Images of Social Change", in C. Hamnett, L. McDowell and P. Sarre (eds) *The Changing Social Structure*, Sage, London, 12-42.

Tilden, F. (1977), *Interpreting Our Heritage*, University of North Carolina Press, Chapel Hill.

Wang, N. (1999), "Rethinking authenticity in tourism experience. " *Annals of Tourism Research* 26, 349-70.

Figure 1. Writers' houses in the United Kingdom . Derived from information contained in Marsh, K. (ed.) (1993) *Writers and their Houses*, Hamish Hamilton

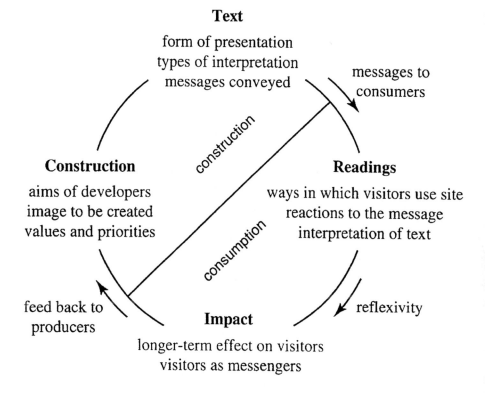

Text

form of presentation
types of interpretation
messages conveyed

messages to
consumers

construction

Construction

aims of developers
image to be created
values and priorities

consumption

Readings

ways in which visitors use site
reactions to the message
interpretation of text

feed back to
producers

Impact

longer-term effect on visitors
visitors as messengers

reflexivity

Construction and Consumption of Heritage Places

Figure 2 Construction and consumption of heritage places (Adapted from Johnson, R. (1986) "The story so far: And further transformations", in D. Punter (ed.) *Introduction to Contemporary Cultural Studies*, Longman, London, 277-313.

Chapter 6

Eye of the Beholder
Transcending Scottish icons,
with particular reference to bagpipes

Mike Paterson

By any standard, Scotland is icons-rich. To the extent that it is recognised in target markets, Scotland's distinguishing imagery promotes differentiation. A study by MORI for the British Council found that only six per cent of the wealthier, better educated young adults in 13 countries who made up the survey's samples were at a loss to associate some predictable image with Scotland, with whisky, kilts and bagpipes topping the list (MORI, 2000).

An aspect of many national and cultural icons — not just Scotland's — is the ambiguity with which they present themselves to the world: New Zealand's flightless kiwi bird, Scotland's skirt for men, France's bubbling wine, Venice's watery thoroughfares, alpenhorns, igloos…. In each case, there are measures of the oddly familiar, the familiarly odd. It is not because they conform to everyday expectations that the towers at Pisa and Paris are so widely recognised. Such images seem peculiarly able to become repositories of ranges of meaning which arise and are maintained in the minds of the people who find the images alluring or intriguing. They accommodate stereotypes, memories, evocations and impressions drawn from experiences and narratives which need not be consistent or necessarily positive, but which become increasingly resistant to contradiction or revision.

The British Council, in its *Through other eyes* surveys of 1999 and 2000 (which asked young professionals and postgraduate students in 13 countries "which two or three sources of information" were "most important when forming an opinion specifically about the United Kingdom"), made clear the potency of local cultural filters through which information from outside the community must pass (see appendix). Icons are a part of this, evoking, not the reality, but the meanings with which they have been suffused.

Within the communities or countries that are associated with them, icons can become limiting, even prescriptive forces. The iconised image of bagpiping, for example, is typically stuffed with romantically overdressed Victorian imperialism: an anachronistic figure making Highland hills ring with longings for ancient days of tartan-swathed glory, or striding into battle on some foreign field. After all, "what could be more gallant and heroic than a man unarmed advancing intrepidly in the face of an enemy, encouraging his comrades on to deeds of hardihood and glory, by those martial strains, so congenial and animating to the feelings of every Highlander?" That is how it was put by Sir John Murray, chairman of the judges panel, to a "large and enthusiastic" audience at the Highland Society of London piping competition in Edinburgh, in 1816 (*Caledonian Mercury*, 1816: 3 August).

When, a full 182 years later, Dr Angus MacDonald won the prize for ceòl mór (piobaireachd) at the 1998 Royal National Mod, *The Scotsman* carried a photograph of a lone piper on the shore silhouetted against the setting sun. Dr MacDonald described the experience of the icon acting prescriptively:

> The photograph was taken the next day (the day after winning the trophy). One of the photographers got hold of me, and he wanted a photograph. … he starts off: 'well, we'll use this background' … then he says: 'let's jump in the car and we'll go down here', and you get led on a bit. … I had no idea. … He'd wanted me to go out to Dunvegan Castle and do this silhouette beside the castle. A couple of them had it all arranged for the next day so I stayed in my bed and refused to answer the phone and didn't actually do it. But … they got hold of somebody else and did a silhouette and used it in some of the papers — like the *GP News*, and so on, 'GP wins prize' — and put my name against it, but it wasn't me at all. They wanted to see the usual stereotype… Most of the time that you see anything in the papers, it's a bit of a laugh … it's a joke.[1]

Stereotyped images of the sort abound in Scotland's promotional iconography and are central to an event like the Edinburgh Tattoo, which really has less to do with Scottish culture than it has with the emotions peculiarly evoked by British military-imperial nostalgia. It is a small step on to the spectacle of massed pipe bands: on 6 April 2002, some 8,000 pipers, most of them American, massed in New York for Tartan Day.

---

[1] Personal communication, 1 February, 1999.

Images of the sort dominate. Said John Hutchison, director of a 250,000-image Edinburgh-based photo library: "most of the traditional music pictures we send out are of pipers and pipe bands."[2] Largely defined by demands outside of Scotland (predominantly from publishers in the south of England), these images constantly confirm the misleading stereotype.

> The historical community roles of piping in Scotland have long been overlooked. And the reality of piping activity today could hardly be more at odds with the icon. The great Highland bagpipe produces a powerful, complex and distinctive sound that is widely, if not universally, thought of as being declaratively Scottish.[3]

This is despite the pipes having been widely co-opted by British (as distinct from Scottish) commercial, military and diplomatic interests abroad. Even when non-Scots play the pipes — and despite the pan-European, Balkan, Middle Eastern and North African historical provenance of bagpipes and, in many cases, the survival or revival of these traditions[4] — the bagpipes still speak predominantly of Scotland.

The constrictive and prescriptive powers of the icon, however, have led many Scots to seriously underestimate or ill judge the potential piping has as the substance of international attractions, as value-adding support for other events, and as a strongly differentiating and value-adding marketing tool. Thus, putting 8,000 pipers and drummers into Times Square, and all for a good cause, is an

---

[2] Hutchison, John: Then director of the Still Moving Picture Company, Edinburgh: Interview. 23 February 1999.

[3] Bagpipes were identified as the one image that "best sums up Scotland" by 11 per cent of respondents in a 17-nation survey of young achievers by MORI for the British Council in 2000. It was the third most frequently mentioned identifying image, after kilts and whisky.

'— MORI. *Through other eyes 2 — How the world sees the United Kingdom: The findings of a second round of research into attitudes of young professionals and postgraduate students in seventeen countries carried out by MORI on behalf of the British Council* (British Council) http://www.britcoun.org/work/survey/sec_society (8 October 2000).

[4] For example, Paris-based independent film maker Christian Rouaud, working on a five-part television series on piping in Europe, spoke of a new surge of piping interest across Europe:

It's a second revival. There was a first wave in the 1970s, and there is another wave now. ...I think it's a reaction against the '80s when the only idea was economic efficiency and you had to be a winner — now I think people want something different and they are turning to tradition to find something (through which) to exist as people, not only a manager or worker, or future Americans, whatever.

— Rouaud, C. Interview, 26 July, 2000.

achievable goal, even if it obscures the pipes' musical value: several thousand ill-rehearsed musicians of mixed ability simultaneously playing ANY instrument are bound to challenge most concepts of musicality. Those who saw the massed pipers in New York as a cost-effective Scottish promotion could perhaps have been more reflective, particularly when it is remembered that many New Yorkers — thanks to their own heritage and St Patrick's Day parades — are likely to associate massed pipe bands with Ireland.[5]

In Scotland, piping is on the brink of a revolution driven by an onslaught of internally and externally generated influences. If few of the developments afoot are widely documented, and the piping literature has generally presented a more stable picture of piping, it is because most of the real and potential influences have yet to radiate across the piping interests that exist within Scotland. Their combined impact, however, will strengthen for decades yet. They present pipers with new opportunities, challenges and needs. Together, the changes afoot will radically reshape the musical experience of today's young pipers.

Widely acknowledged improvements made over the past 20 years to reeds, bags, moisture control devices and instruments generally have helped players of good ability to attain more consistent high standards of performance.[6] More reliable instruments also make piping more approachable and more quickly satisfying to learn.

Implementation of the Scottish Arts Council's *Traditional Music in Scotland* report (1999) promises to steadily widen awareness of traditional music in Scotland's schools. There is already a strong and growing demand for piping tuition in most areas, which often goes un-met. Pipe bands, the TA and Cadet Forces, individuals and instructors to schools all provide opportunities to learn, though provision varies from one area to the next.[7] Fèisan nan Gàidheal,

---

[5] Brian Meagher, for example, is a fourth-generation Irish New York piper who teaches piping at the University of New York, instructs the New York City Fire Department Pipe Band and has various other piping connections. He said: "I would say the majority of New Yorkers see pipe bands as Irish."

— Meagher, B. Interview, 13 April 1999.

[6] Broadcaster and piper Iain MacInnes, for example, has made this point:

The quality of performance is fantastically good, the quality of the instruments is as never before … You have to give credit to the people who have developed synthetic drone reeds and various synthetic bags. These developments have allowed average to good players to produce a consistently excellent sound.

— Paterson, M. (2000b).

[7] Piping tuition has been available to interested students at a varying number of Scottish state schools since 1976. The majority of older instructors locate their background within the oral tradition, the competitions and pipe bands contexts and the structures of what might be called the

formed in 1988, and its member groups are bringing considerable numbers of young Highlanders into a closer awareness of their culture and provide an impetus that moves beyond the National Mod. Alongside this, concerns to maintain Gaelic and Scots languages are helping to provide more positive contexts for traditional music.

A reform of the Institute of Piping standards in 2001 introduced a more objective set of assessments for pipers pursuing generally recognised qualifications. This is likely to encourage greater standardisation of teaching across a diversity of institutional and individual providers. The three-year National Schools Piping Project, operated by The National Piping Centre, 1999-2001, proved a highly successful outreach to young pipers nationally[8] and led to the launching in 2002 of the National Youth Pipe Band of Scotland — a concert band. The National Centre of Excellence for Traditional Music at Plockton High School, with piping as an option, had its first intake of students in 2000.

The Royal Scottish Academy of Music and Drama's BA (Scottish Music) degree produced its first graduates in 1999, and led on to the establishment of a BA (Scottish Music — Piping) degree in 2001, taught by The National Piping Centre and the Academy. As well as opening a new avenue of progression for the most talented pipers, and ensuring they have a good musical grounding, this qualification gives pipers a route to qualify as fully certificated teachers of music.

A shift in military priorities, along with the vigour of civilian pipe bands, has seen a decline in the relative influence of military piping and drumming. Major Gavin Stoddart, director of Army Bagpipe Music, was reported in *The New Reed*, a publication of the National Schools Piping Project:

> The emphasis has changed, purely for career management, onto the military role. ...When I joined, piping and drumming

---

traditional piping establishment. Increasingly, however, as the availability of opportunities widens (as, for example, with the implementation of the Scottish Arts Council's 1999 report by David Francis, *Traditional Music in Scotland — education, information, advocacy*), and where retiring instructors are replaced, posts are increasingly likely to be filled by graduates of, for example, the Royal Scottish Academy's BA (Scottish Music) and (as certificated teachers of music) from the new National Piping Centre -RSAMD BA (Scottish Music — Piping) degrees. Not only will graduates have proficiency on a second instrument, but also they will have been exposed to the wider contexts of piping, musicology and the traditional music scene. The longer-term implications of this for piping are considerable.

[8] "From every point of view, this imaginative and far-reaching project has been an unqualified success and an exemplary use of public funds."
— Colvin, Sheila (Scottish Arts Council's project monitor). *Final project monitoring report:* Scottish Arts Council: 2002.

came first and the military side took the back seat. ...My
memory goes back to a time when it was great to sit all day
playing pipes and drums. We don't get a chance to do that
now. Every piper and drummer has to have a career structure
... and has to do serious career courses.[9]

The "civilianising" of pipe bands has brought with it changes in pipe
band uniforms, repertoire and styles, although the founding of the TA
and Army Cadet Force Pipes and Drums Centre at Redford Cavalry
Barracks, Edinburgh, in 2001 may reassert the Army's influence by
promoting piping in the Army Cadet Force and Territorial Army. Said
Colonel Robert Patterson, the Centre's Officer Commanding: "We are
working to help make instruction on our national instrument more
accessible to young people, regardless of where they are and whatever
their circumstances."[10] The progress of cadet pipers is managed in line
with civilian Institute of Piping qualifications, through which the
cadets can earn a recognised musical qualification. Regular force
piping and drumming instruction has been centralised at Inchdrewer
House, Colinton Road, Edinburgh, from which the Army School of
Bagpipe Music and Highland Drumming is likely to elevate the
profile of military piping again but with less pervasive influences on
civilian piping than in earlier decades.

It is worth noting, too, that the gender balance in piping and
drumming has improved over the past 20 years, although there is still
considerable progress to be made.[11]

Scholarly research and publication relating to Scottish piping are at
last taking some sort of hold. A growing body of scholarly research
and a minor publishing boom (e.g. Buisman, Cannon and Wright,
2001; Cheape, 1999; Donaldson, 2000; Gibson, 1999 and 2002;
McDonald, 2000; Mackenzie, 1998; Seattle, 1995, etc.) are helping to
make piping "ideas rich", and energising debate over issues of
musical interpretation and piping history. Scholarly work will
increasingly help to resource teaching, contributing to a deeper
popular understanding and appreciation of Scotland's piping
traditions.

The traditional music revival from the 1950s impinged little on

---

[9] Paterson, M. (2000a.)

[10] Patterson, Col. R.M. Interview, 2 April 2002.

[11] For example, of 146 cadets (12-18 year-olds) attending at a week-long cadet forces piping and
drumming course at Cameron Barracks, Inverness, 30 March-6 April 2002, 61 (42 per cent) were
female, 85 (58 per cent) were male.

piping at first (Munro, 1996) but, from the 1970s, amplification technology has enabled Highland pipes to be recruited into traditional music groups: internationally touring bands such as Ossian, Alba, Battlefield Band, Tannahill Weavers and Ceolbeg led the way. The opportunities this exposure created (more in markets like Germany than at home) helped to bring forward a few "star" pipers, people like Gordon Duncan, Iain MacDonald, Fred Morrison, Rory Campbell and Martyn Bennett. At the same time, pipe tunes have been widely adopted by other musicians, especially fiddlers. This is helping to open the repertoire to wider audiences.

The 20-year-old Scottish small and bellows pipes revival is slowly helping to diversify styles and repertoire as, for example, through the activities of Lowland and Border Piping Society. It is also extending the awareness that Scottish piping embraces a number of traditions, and inflections of those traditions, some of which have been lost. As instruments that are more ensemble-friendly than the Highland pipes, the smallpipes (pitched in various keys) give Highland pipers an alternative but not unfamiliar instrument that lets them participate more fully in the Scottish and wider "Celtic" musical revival, helping to form new, wider links, broaden experience and shift outlooks.

The perceptions young people have of the wider music industry, and the increasing likelihood of their being taught in non-traditional contexts, is encouraging young pipers to play in public and with other musicians. Performance, as opposed to competition, is a strengthening priority. Opportunities for this are widening, helped undoubtedly by the Irish-led "Celtic" music boom. International interest in bagpipes is considerable[12], growing and takes a variety of forms.

A widespread European piping revival promises to restore bagpiping to its medieval range, with revivals actively being pursued in Italy (especially in Isernia, Bologna, Sicily and Sardinia), France, Galicia, Asturias, Norway, England, Britanny, Ireland, Italy, Hungary, Bohemia, Bulgaria, Slovakia and elsewhere. Quite startling has been the provincially funded and promoted bands movement in Galicia.[13] The basis of a new pan-European musical forum is in place,

---

[12] For example, some 40 countries have been represented by students attending The National Piping Centre since 1997; in 2000, three postgraduate students were conducting piping related postgraduate research at the School of Scottish Studies, Edinburgh: all were overseas students.

[13] *Notes*, published by The National Piping Centre, reported in Autumn 1999:

Musician and composer Xosé Lois Foxo, director of the Real Banda and the provincial Escola de Gaitas (piping school) in Ourense, said that the school began with 60 pupils and now (in 1999) has 15,000. It employed 60 instructors paid by the government. 'In the province we have about 80 pipe bands and all get money from the Deputacion (provincial government). I can't say exactly how much it costs each year, but it is very significant support. People in school pay only 1,000

with the proliferation of a diversity of international festivals and events, large and small, including Le Festival Interceltique de Lorient en Bretagne (France), Celtic Connections in Glasgow, the Festival Internazionale della Zampogna (bagpipes) in Scapoli, Italy, the annual Galician gaita (bagpipes) competitions, Ireland's William Kennedy Piping Festival, the biennial Strakonice Bagpipers Festival in southern Bohemia. There are scores of such festivals, opening new forums for Scottish and Irish piping traditions in new contexts, and widening creative possibilities as the various traditions mature, develop and interact. Often related to tourism as well as to local musical and cultural interests, these events are creating performance opportunities outside of the traditional Highland games circuits (in Scotland and abroad). On a different front altogether, Scottish musician Lindsay Davidson is finding respect and regular radio air time in Poland for exploratory compositions which feature the Highland pipes in orchestral and choral arrangements as a classical instrument.[14] Scottish promotional interests would do well to heed the pipes' potential to help raise Scotland's profile in Europe.

Cultural vigour in descendant and expatriate communities overseas (such as those in Canada, United States, Australia, New Zealand and South Africa) persists. As well as providing definitive experiences of "Scottishness" in these countries, this interest continues to help lift Highland piping standards, expand the repertoire and exercise creativity. At the same time, new communities of interest in Highland piping are springing up (Scandinavia, Germany, Latin America, Czechoslovakia, Italy, etc, provide examples), resulting in a still-widening internationalisation of Scottish-style Highland piping, particularly in the form of pipe bands and popular concert music. Mainstream piping repertoire has undergone some remarkable shifts, and an even wider variety of repertoire and styles is likely to be explored in the years ahead. Musicality is a key issue and, as pipers seek to reach new and wider audiences, this is likely to be increasingly defined in many of piping's contexts by non-pipers.

The persistence of piping activity in post-colonial nations (including Hong Kong, South Asia and the Middle East) is also evident. The bases are laid here for the emergence of new, distinctive

---

pesetas (about £4) a year for piping tuition. ...It's very important to have these young people working in something cultural. The streets are no good for the young people, drugs, a lot of problems, television is not interesting. I think it's one of the best ideas of our government to have money for young people for music, for tradition...' .

— Paterson, M. (1999).

[14] Davidson, Lindsay. Interview, 8 April, 2002.

piping cultures as these countries move beyond colonial contexts, taking piping with them. Beyond this, there is evidence that the Highland bagpipe is beginning to be more or less strongly indigenised into other cultures in several parts of the world, in South Asia and Brazil, and potentially in Hong Kong.

It need not stop here. The related traditions of North Africa have yet to be drawn into the widening exchange of ideas, for example, and we might well see opportunities arise to open cross-cultural contacts and conduct musical explorations involving reed pipe traditions in other parts of the world, including mainland China.

Employment opportunities for pipers are still limited, but there has been a marked increase in the number of top-level pipers who support themselves partly or wholly in ways directly related to piping, and performance can contribute usefully to the earnings of a person who is a reasonably versatile traditional musician.[15] Pipe-making, repairs and reed-making are now also supplemented by increasing teaching and performing opportunities.

Information and multimedia technology and musical notation software, separately and together, have helped to extend the rapid dispersal of new composition, widen spheres of dialogue and influence, and establish new opportunities for distance education. New recording technologies have made it easier and cheaper for artists to produce their own compact discs, communicate by the Internet and set up websites, and to share repertoire, styles and interpretations. These are fledgling fields of technology, opportunities are growing, and piping-related initiatives are bound to proliferate.

The icon of piping clearly needs rehabilitation — but rehabilitation is a need that applies with equal strength to many of Scotland's other icons. It would be unwise to discard the goodwill with which the familiar icons have been invested, but it has to be recognised that

---

[15] Pipers such as Rory Campbell, Finlay MacDonald, Simon McKerrell and others are making a living from performing internationally. Finlay MacDonald, for example, says:

I don't think you need a (regular) job. ...I paid my way through college by playing for weddings, funerals, bar mitzvahs and, okay, it's not musically what I want to do, but it's paying the money for it. I'm a year out of the Academy (RSAMD) and it's been good. I've been busy, and when I've not been away touring or playing, I'll write music, I do my books, I'll write away sending demo cds — there's a lot to do. Festivals abroad, with the folk band has been where most of my work has been; you can always teach as well. I've played with orchestras, house bands for radio, I still do weddings, flute and whistle accompaniment for singers, session work, ceilidh work ...I've had a lot of work from the musicians union, people phone up. There's an endless list if you do the work in the first place. I'm lucky in a way — I've got flute, uillean pipes and whistle and the folk band to get work with. I don't know how it would be for a piper who was only a piper ...There's money to be made. it's not like a degree in law where after a couple of a years you can count on 30 grand a year — that's not the life of musician but it's not what I want. I've seen the world.
— MacDonald, F. Interview, 26 July 2000.

iconography is a dangerous craft. An icon, once established, acquires a life of its own and, as the Caterpillar told Alice: "One side will make you grow taller, and the other side will make you grow shorter" (Dodgson, 1986. p.53). It is important to know which is which and choose with discernment.

Nor are icons forever. Christie Johnstone — effectively forgotten these days — was the creation of a prolific Oxfordshire playwright and novelist Charles Reade (Hammet, 1986). He completed the playscript *Christie Johnstone* by 1850 but it was the 1853 novel published in London that found a popular market, with a first American edition in 1855. Reade's idealisation of the fishwives of Newhaven in a book awash with class-bound sentimentality undoubtedly made its contribution to Scotland's tourism industry. There was a time when Edinburgh's tourist shops bulged with Christie Johnstone dolls, prints and souvenirs. Before Reade's book, the fishwives were appearing on postcards and in advertisements as distinctive Edinburgh characters, but it was Christie Johnstone who provided the inspirational icon that impelled another English author of the day, the Rev. Edward Bradley, to set off in search of what he would refer to as "perambulating fish-shops".

Bradley's response to the fishwives of Leith is predictable: "Half-a-minute's actual experience had disillusioned me of all my Christie Johnstones…". But he then went to some lengths trying to find reasons to agree with Reade. He devoted nearly 20 pages of *A Tour in Tartan-Land* to the subject — admiring the fishwives' "costume", for example, if not their drinking habits (Bradley, 1863. 301-319). If anything, he managed to add to the fascination that the icon erected by Reade already offered middle class period interest.

Christie Johnstone was doomed, despite the best attentions of Edinburgh souvenir sellers, but not by her fictional status, nor by the advent of fish shops, chippies, health and trade regulations, or radical changes to the fishing industry. Were icons so vulnerable to their own fallacies Scotland's image might not still be adorned with a Bonnie Prince Charlie, a Loch Ness monster or quite so many encastellated ghosts. She died with the society inhabited by the likes of Reade and Bradley. This was the society that produced Reade's readers and primed their imaginations; it fired desires to discover and experience Christie Johnstones in particular ways. To discern a Christie Johnstone among the fishwives of Newhaven was to confirm one's own preconceptions and wishful thinking, and affirm one's own identity.

An icon has meaning only because people have poured meaning into it for reasons that arise from their own values, attitudes and culture. When the vested meanings no longer move or excite people, the icon dies. Editions of *Christie Johnstone* were produced into the early part of the 20th century.[16] In 1922, Norman MacDonald directed a 56-minute film version for Broadwest Films (Bruce, 1996: 22) and that was about the end of it. After the First World War, Christie Johnstone's appeal quickly faded.

The unreconstructed image of piping cannot confidently be expected to last indefinitely. Scotland is ill placed to generate new icons on an international scale Thus far, many of the old icons have managed to endure. They live on in the hearts and minds of millions of Scotophiles and Scotophobes alike. The most interesting of these is possibly Robert Burns: an adroit mythmaker who shaped himself into an icon that nicely met the intellectual and artistic measure of his times — although his poetry continues to pay the price.[17]

He set about constructing the "heaven-taught ploughman" identity well before he was published (Burns, 1969: 1). His masquerade as an untutored rustic was one that many Scots were happy for him to play — and they became active collaborators. Thus a young man who was deeply and widely read, a voracious devourer of ideas, and a complex individual, was reduced to a stereotype. Along the way, the greatest poet in the Scots language became firmly welded to a haggis. A sillier image of literary genius is difficult to imagine.

Conclusions

Time and again, we see Scotland's most widely recognised icons burdened with decrepit and unhelpful meanings. They have been weakened because the narratives that first informed their meanings no longer correlate with the experiences and the contexts of today — fewer and fewer people identify with them in ways that also engage them with contemporary Scotland. The meanings that suffuse an icon can exclude as potently as they include. An icon stirs expectations which an associated event or product must address. Wider access may be curtailed for people whose values clash with those that have

---

[16] For example, Chatto and Windus, London, brought out editions in 1905 and 1905, and J. M. Dent and Sons (London) in 1912 and 1929.

[17] See, for example: Bold, 1997. p. 43-52.; Daiches, 1997, p. 18-31; Morgan, 1994,. p 1-12; Simpson, 1994, p 70-91.

become attached to an icon.

If Scotland's icons are to be reinvigorated, it will not be by technical boasts or marketing assertions. It will be by providing experiences and narratives, born of Scotland's diverse, contemporary cultural realities that penetrate the cultural filters of our target markets, attach themselves to the icons and begin shifting expectations. A way to begin addressing this is, for example, to establish brandings based on actual expressions of some of the activities to which the least moribund icons point (Paterson, 2001a). Piping alone can provide a number of worthwhile narratives — including its European dimensions. Communicating these narratives is a relatively low cost way to raise Scotland's visibility and inject new energies and meanings into the conceptions of Scotland found in our target markets.

Icons can be recruited as triggers to open new discourses and spur our own creative energies. Thus, for example, as a genius of Scots writing, Robert Burns gives the southwest of Scotland in particular opportunities to embrace the whole of non-Gaelic Scottish literature — in Scots and in English, the poetry the prose and the theatre, books, film, theatre, video, the internet... retailing, workshops, summer schools, readings and mini-festivals. Here we can find, not just a bunch of fusty authors and literary critics, but a host of almost universally beloved characters: Toad of Toad Hall, Robinson Crusoe (arguably), Tam O' Shanter, Childe Harold and Don Juan, Peter Pan, Long John Silver, Dr Jeckyll, Richard Hannay, Inspector Rebus, Dangerous Dan McGrew, Prester John, Sherlock Holmes, and Private Angelo, even Harry Flashman (in his later years) and Harry Potter ("birthed", as he was, at Nicholson's Cafe, Edinburgh). As an energetic conservator of Scots music, Burns opens a door to the whole of Scots traditional and contemporary music, to performance, festivals, recording, workshops and master classes. Such activity must first be nurtured locally. It takes time; it must be discerningly seeded and patiently grown within host communities.

Because the icons and the expectations they encourage are already out there, they cannot be ignored, and the choices for dealing with them are few. Uncritically embracing them traduces the reality while speaking to a dwindling market; a posture of cultural and artistic introversion would see Scotland failing to communicate with the potential sources of interest that exist.

It is important, rather, to tap into the interest they arouse but also to consistently exceed the expectations, using quality and creativity to lead the icons forward. This way, Scotland would stand to grow its markets and stimulate its arts at the same time. Research as well as marketing is required to lead Scotland into new concepts of its tourism and export marketing potential, and to formulate strategies to tap it. But, if a Canadian pipe band can fill venues like Carnegie Hall and the Sydney Opera House (as the Simon Fraser University Pipe Band has done) surely, as the proprietors of such a culture, Scots might dare to aim as high. Icons ought not be conceptual gin traps.

APPENDIX

TABLE (1): Sources of information about the United Kingdom (overall averaged percentages) mentioned by respondents to the 1999 and 2000 MORI polls: *Through other eyes 1&2 — How the world sees the United Kingdom: The findings of a second round of research into attitudes of young professionals and postgraduate students in seventeen countries carried out by MORI on behalf of the British Council.* Thirteen countries were surveyed in 1999, 17 in 2000.

	Year	
	1999	**2000**
LOCAL SOURCES		
Word-of-mouth (family/friends)	5	14
People who have visited the UK	27	16
Word-of-mouth (work colleagues)	8	—
Acquaintances from the UK	14	7
Local Media		
National TV news	19	31
Local press	26	37
Local radio	4	5
(Totals:	*102*	*110)*
BRITISH SOURCES		
Visiting the UK	12	16
British press	16	16
BBC World Television	20	23
BBC World Service	11	13
Embassies/consulates	6	—
Tourist authorities	7	*mentioned*
Other official U.K. sources	2	—
(Totals:	*74*	*68)*
INTERNATIONAL SOURCES		
Internet	4	21
Other international TV	14	8
Other international press	15	11
Other international radio	5	*mentioned*
(Totals:	*38*	*40)*
OTHER		
Books	27	25
Films	13	12
Academic sources	*mentioned*	8
(Totals:	*40*	*45)*

— MORI. *Through other eyes: How the world sees the United Kingdom — The findings of research into the attitudes of young professionals in thirteen countries carried out by MORI on behalf of the British Council October 1999* (British Council, October 1999).

and:
— MORI. *Through other eyes 2: How the world sees the United Kingdom. The findings of a second round of research into attitudes of young professionals and postgraduate students in seventeen countries carried out by MORI on behalf of the British Council October 2000* (The British Council, October 2000).
— British Council. http://www.britcoun.org/work/survey/sec_society (8 October 2000).

References

Bold, V. (1997), 'Inmate of the Hamlet: Burns as peasant poet'. in: Simpson, Kenneth (ed.), *Love and Liberty: Robert Burns a bicentenary celebration*: Tuckwell Press. 43-52.
Bradley, Rev. E. (writing as "Cuthbert Bede") (1863*), A tour in Tartan-land:* Richard Bentley.
Bruce, D. (1996) *Scotland the Movie*: Polygon.
Buisman, F., Cannon, R., and Wright, A. (ed). (2001), *The MacArthur-MacGregor Manuscript of Pibroch:* 'Music in Scotland Series', Universities of Glasgow and Aberbeen in association with the John MacFadyen Trust.
Burns, R. (ed. Lamont-Brown, R.), (1969), *Robert Burns' commonplace book*: Wakefield S. R. Publications.
Cannon, R. (1995), *The Highland bagpipe and its music*: John Donald.
Cheape, H. (1999), *The book of the bagpipe*: Appletree Press.
Colvin, S. (2002), Final project monitoring report (National Piping in Schools Project): Scottish Arts Council.
Daiches, D. (1997), 'Robert Burns: the tightrope walker' in Simpson, Kenneth (ed.) *Love and Liberty: Robert Burns a bicentenary celebration*: Tuckwell Press. 18-31.
Dodgson, C. (writing as "Lewis Carroll"} (1986), *Alice's Adventures in Wonderland*: Methuen.
Donaldson, W. (2000), *The Highland pipe and Scottish society 1750-1950*: Tuckwell Press.
Gibson, J. (2002), *Old and New World highland piping*: McGill-Queen's University Press.
... (1999), *Traditional Gaelic bagpiping, 1745-1945* (NMS, Edinburgh, and McGill-Queen's University Press.
Hammet, Michael (1986), 'Introduction and notes' to *Plays by Charles Reade*: Cambridge University Press.
McDonald, Patrick (1784, republ. 2000), *A collection of Highland vocal airs never hitherto published. To which are added a few of the most lively country dances or reels of the north Highland and Western Isles: and some specimens of bagpipe music, new edition*: Taigh na Teud.
Mackenzie, B. (1998), *Piping traditions of the north of Scotland*: John Donald Press.
Martens, M. (2000), 'Continental Europe sees piping gain ground', *Notes No. 12*, (Spring), The National Piping Centre. 17-18.

Morgan, Edwin (1994), 'A poet's response to Burns' in Simpson, K. (ed.) *Burns Now*: Canongate Academic. 1-12.

MORI (2000), Through other eyes 2: How the world sees the United Kingdom. The findings of a second round of research into attitudes of young professionals and postgraduate students in seventeen countries carried out by MORI on behalf of the British Council: The British Council.

...   (1999), Through other eyes: How the world sees the United Kingdom — The findings of research into the attitudes of young professionals in thirteen countries carried out by MORI on behalf of the British Council October 1999: British Council.

Munro, Ailie. (1996), *The democratic muse, folk music revival in Scotland*, (rev. edition): Scottish Cultural Press.

Murray of Lanrick, Sir John, quoted addressing the audience at the Highland Society of London Piping Competition in the Theatre Royal Edinburgh, 31 July, 1816: *Caledonian Mercury* (3 August), 1816.

Paterson, M. (1999), 'Galicia's gaitas are cutting a dash', *Notes No. 10* (Autumn), The National Piping Centre. 11-12.

...   (2000a), 'Pipers soldier on': *A New Reed No. 5*, (Spring), The National Schools Piping Project. 3-4.

...   (2000b), 'It only gets better...' *Notes No. 12*, The National Piping Centre (Spring).

...   (2000c), *A Scottish National Youth Pipe Band: a feasibility study*: The National Piping Centre (unpubl. manuscript).

...   (2001a), *Selling Scotland: towards an intercultural approach to export marketing involving differentiation on the basis of 'Scottishness'* (unpubl. PhD. dissertation): University of Glasgow.

...   (2001b), 'Institute of Piping adds value to its qualifications': *Notes No. 16* (Spring), The National Piping Centre.

Seattle, Matt (ed). (1995), *The master piper — nine notes that shook the world, a Border bagpipe repertoire prick'd down by William Dixon AD 1733*: Taigh na Teud.

Simpson, Kenneth (1994), 'Robert Burns: 'heaven-taught' ploughman?' in Simpson, K. (ed.), *Burns Now:* Canongate Academic. 70-91

Chapter 7

The History of Musical Tourism in Dumfries and Galloway

Lesley Stevenson

Introduction

This paper offers an historical perspective on a niche tourism product which is currently a particularly topical issue in Scotland, having recently been the focus of a number of tourism initiatives and the subject of both parliamentary and media debate. The particular niche in question here is musical tourism in general, and that related to Scottish traditional music in particular. The aim is to determine to what extent it is desirable or indeed appropriate for music to be considered a 'niche' form of tourism. Indeed musical tourism appears to currently be considered a niche within a niche, for it is a subset of what VisitScotland terms the 'cultural tourism product'. The implication of such terminology is that music is a tourism product to be directed at and consumed by a target market of enthusiasts. Such an understanding may however, cause us to underestimate the profound influence which music can exert on the motivations and expectations of tourists in general, including those outwith the target market in question. In order to develop this argument, current efforts to market music as a niche tourism product will be contrasted with the historic role which music played in shaping visitors' perceptions of Dumfries and Galloway. By reference to travel literature dating from the eighteenth century onwards, it will be demonstrated that Dumfries and Galloway's rich heritage of traditional song was inextricably linked to the tourist image of the region. Traditional music was historically a vital source of 'cultural capital' for the region.

Music and tourist promotion

Music is indeed instrumental in formulating the images which people hold of particular places; to use Urry's (2002) term, music has a fundamentally important role to play in constructing the tourist gaze. Thus, the respective musical traditions of New Orleans and Liverpool evoke the distinct sense of place, or 'cultural capital', so essential to succeed in today's competitive tourism marketplace (Abram and Waldren, 1997). Similarly, for cities such as Nashville and New Orleans, music is at the very basis of their tourism promotion efforts, while Cape Breton Island in Nova Scotia markets itself with the slogan "In New Orleans They Mardi Gras, In Cape Breton We Ceilidh" (Feintuch, 2001). The rationale underlying such efforts is that music can function as a particularly potent signifier of place; as DeWitt (1999: 62) notes, "For music to serve as an index for a place, no physical experience aside from hearing the music is necessary for an association to be created."

Indeed, VisitScotland has recently acknowledged that Scotland's indigenous musical traditions are a rich source of cultural capital. Its recent publication, Soundtrack for Scottish Tourism (VisitScotland/ SAC, 2002: 3) notably identifies traditional music as "one of the truly unique assets that Scotland can offer as it seeks to differentiate itself in the world travel market."

Although active attempts to harness traditional music for tourism purposes are comparatively recent in Scotland, music has played a fundamentally important role in the historical development of the nation's tourism industry. Indeed, Byrom (1997) argues that the Scottish Tour, as it evolved form 1760 onwards, had its roots in, *inter alia*, popular collections of Scottish balladry. Glendening (1997) similarly notes that interest in balladry was one of a number of features of Romanticism that advanced Scottish tourism. The Dumfries and Galloway of the late eighteenth and early nineteenth centuries was well-placed to capitalise on this interest, for it has much history, legend and lore which has been commemorated in ballad form. Moreover, as home to some of Scotland's most prolific and renowned song collectors its musical traditions have been well chronicled in the ballad collections for which there was so much Romantic enthusiasm. This rich traditional song heritage was instrumental in forging visitors' perceptions of the region, constructing an image of a picturesque land steeped in history and romance.

Travellers' accounts of the area are accordingly peppered with references to particular ballads, and characterised by pilgrimages to sites associated with famous songs. Similarly, guidebooks have historically employed references to ballads, thereby both inspiring and reflecting the popularity of musical pilgrimages. Eschewing practical advice regarding details such as directions (Haldane, 1990), guidebooks frequently invoked song references as a form of crude promotional tool, designed to describe the romantic, historic or picturesque nature of certain places.

Music and the picturesque

In seeking to promote and describe the picturesque nature of Dumfries and Galloway in particular, guidebooks invariably employed quotations from the poetry and song of Robert Burns. Through his work Burns did much to foreground the scenic aspects of Dumfriesshire and in so doing influenced prevailing attitudes towards beauty. The pervasive effect of Burns' songs in directing and manipulating the tourist gaze is described most succinctly by Burke (1983: 149), who contends that, "We shall always visualize 'Ye Banks and Braes o' Bonnie Doon' through his eyes, and walk with him beside 'The Banks of Allan Water'".

Indeed, if we are to inspect travellers' accounts from the eighteenth century onwards, it is evident that Burns' songs certainly had this effect on travellers gazing upon the river Nith in Dumfries. Upon visiting Dumfries in 1722 Daniel Defoe's reaction to the river "Nid" was characteristically uncomplimentary, for Defoe was typical of the neo-classical age in that he regarded the wild, majestic scenery so beloved of Victorian travellers, as chaotic and therefore dangerous (Squire, 1988). Thus, detailing the Nith's tendency to flood, he described a destructive river which left its banks strewn with sand and stones, thereby 'spoiling' and 'beggaring' the soil. Defoe's description contrasts sharply with those recorded by Victorian travellers, however; for Bogg (1898: 344), for example, the sight of the swollen river was a "magnificent", rather than a dangerous, sight. Indeed, from the turn of the century onwards many travellers were inspired to visit the Nith, in search of the 'lovely', 'winding', 'sweeping' river which Burns had described in songs such as 'Adown Winding Nith', 'The Banks of Nith' and 'As I Stood by Yon Roofless Tower'.

Many visitors to the Nith in the early nineteenth century exhibited the romantic tendency to gaze upon places selectively, studiously avoiding those features which could spoil the poetic scene (Squire, 1988). Thus although in 1838 Dibdin (1838: 448-9) praised the "broad, beautiful and weedless Nith", with its "translucent waters", the supposed purity of the river is a matter of some dubiety. By this time the constant clamour of the tweed mill, which was in operation at the side of the Nith would have disrupted the scene, polluting both the air and the river.

It is significant that Burns wrote 'The Banks of Nith' in 1788 while living at Ellisland Farm, some 6 miles north of Dumfries. The river that Burns described, with its "fruitful vales", "bounding hawthorns" and "lambkins", thus referred to the rural prospect that he experienced from Ellisland. Nevertheless, visitors in the following centuries invariably took his vision to refer to the part of the river which flowed through Dumfries and which was increasingly marked by the trappings of industrialisation. Indeed, it appears that the influence of Burns' songs was so pervasive that many travellers were able only to view the river through his eyes and to describe it using his language. Thomson (1930: 96), for example, described how he "walked on the Sands where sweeter flows the Nith between its bridges", thus directly quoting 'The Banks of Nith'. A later traveller was more explicit regarding the impact which Burns' song had on his own perception of the river, noting that: "Winding Nith too, has more than mere beauty to commend it, because Robert Burns has given it a place amongst the classic streams." (Cuthbertson, 1938: 72).

The impact of Burns' songs in constructing the tourist gaze was undoubtedly compounded by the manner in which guidebooks capitalised upon their commercial potential. In 1904, for example, The Glasgow and South Western Railway (1904b: 3) was advising its customers that those in search of charming picturesque scenery would be amply rewarded by the sight of the "sweet Afton" and the "winding Nith". In so doing it actively participated in the perpetuation of Burns' vision of both rivers.

Music and history

Although a prolific folksong collector, Burns did not exhibit a substantial degree of interest in traditional ballads (Hodgart, 1962). Other collectors such as Sir Walter Scott, however, did much to bring the region's rich heritage of traditional balladry to the attention of the Victorian public and in so doing fore-grounded the historic and romantic associations of Dumfries and Galloway. Indeed, it can be argued that Scott's ballad collection, *Minstrelsy of the Scottish Border*, functioned as a guidebook. With its extensive annotations, detailing the respective origins and location of each ballad, the *Minstrelsy* served to direct "would-be ballad tourists" to sites of musical interest (Byrom, 1997: 333). Divided into three sections –

'Historic Ballads', 'Romantic Ballads', and 'Imitations of the Ancient Ballad' – the very structure of Scott's volume helped construct an image of Dumfries and Galloway that appealed to Victorian tourists. Moreover, the ballads themselves and Scott's commentary were intrinsically linked to the manner in which such tourists gazed upon their respective sites.

Thus in 1838 Dibdin visited Caerlaverock Castle, noting that it was the subject of a ballad by Charles Kirkpatrick Sharpe, published in Scott's collection. The ballad, 'The Murder of Caerlaveroc', recounts the dramatic tale of a murder that is recorded as having taken place in the castle in 1357. With its supposed basis in historical fact, dramatic narrative and heroic themes, the ballad appealed greatly to Romantic sensibilities.

Although the ballad itself refers to the castle long since destroyed and replaced by the one which Dibdin saw, for many visitors of this era it would have been impossible to disassociate their personal view of the castle from that evoked by the ballad. As Dibdin (1838: 457) recounts, the "venerable guide" insisted upon reciting the verses while conducting visitors around the ruin. Indeed, the language which many visitors used to refer to the castle is often evocative of the ballad's descriptions of "proud Caerlaveroc's towers", with Bogg (1898: 358), for example, talking of the castle's "commanding presence" and its "hoary towers". Thus his view of the scene appears to some extent to have been constructed by a ballad that actually referred to a castle that no longer existed.

Similarly, ballads concerning the region's notorious Border reivers appealed particularly to the Romantic fascination with history, for they often bear particularly strong links to recorded incidents and characters. Such ballads glorify these freebooters, depicting them as heroes while presenting custodians of the law as criminals (McAlpine, 2000). This romanticisation of their lawless acts had an evident effect on the manner in which tourists gazed upon places associated with the ballads. In 1898, for example, a notable musical pilgrim named Edmund Bogg (1898: 311, 314) sought out places associated with the eponymous reiver of the ballad 'Johnie Armstrong', terming him a "true Border king" and describing his "splendid retinue".

Bogg did not only glorify Armstrong's character, clan and deeds, however: he also described scenes associated with such ballads in the most romantic of terms. Thus, speaking of Gilnockie Tower, Johnie Armstrong's place of residence, Bogg (1898: 314) noted that the sight of its neighbouring woods, meadows and river "imparts tuneful melody and lulls the soul into reveries of ballad romance." For Bogg (1898: 316), nearby streams were "musical with song", which caused his memory to be cast back to "half-fabled ballads". Thus, the manner in which he viewed the scene appears to have been inextricably linked to the ballads which he came in search of: for the scene which he viewed was not that of the late 19th century, but his conception of the 16th century debatable land.

Music and romance

Tourists such as Bogg also travelled in search of the sites of the romantic ballads and love songs of the region. Praising Galloway for its romantic associations, Cuthbertson (1938: 72) noted that: "Two songs known to every Scot from childhood days are 'Annie Laurie' and 'Helen of Kirkconnel Lee', and both ladies were natives of the shire." These two love songs in particular appear to have captured the imagination of the travelling public and the respective locations of each accordingly became the object of many a tourist pilgrimage.

Bogg, for example, appealed for his readers to follow him to "a beautiful nook of ballad land" (1898: 322) rendered classic by its association with the latter song, also known as 'Fair Helen of Kirkconnell'. The tale of a celebrated beauty murdered by a jealous suitor, the song is a particularly popular one, being found in a number of ballad collections including Scott's (1931) *Minstrelsy*. Incorporating the popular themes of chivalry and heroism, 'Fair Helen of Kirkconnell' particularly appealed to romantic sensibilities, and accordingly provided poetic inspiration for many poets of the era.

For later visitors such as Bogg, the pilgrimage to the churchyard at Kirkconnell Lee - where Helen was killed and where her grave is still visible - was a patently profound and moving experience. His language is particularly poetic, and paradoxically intent on describing the scene of a tragedy in musical terms. Thus, the "song of happy birds, the rhythmic murmuring of the tiny rivulet" and "the mystic melodies, echoes of the past": are all the objects of his praise (Bogg, 1898: 325).

Guidebooks such as Todd (1904) and GSWR (1904b) capitalised upon the popularity of 'Fair Helen of Kirkconnell', exhorting readers to visit Kirkconnell Lee and experience the pathos and tragedy expressed in the ballad. Similarly, Dickie's *Guide to Dumfries and Round About* (1898: 150) advocates that readers visit the site associated with the aforementioned love song, 'Annie Laurie', claiming that it "ranks for range and intensity of popularity with 'Auld Lang Syne' and 'The Banks o' Doon'". Indeed, accounts left by twentieth-century visitors to the region reveal a common preoccupation with 'Annie Laurie', and a desire to pay a form of musical pilgrimage to the 'Maxwelton' which is referred to in the first line of the song:

> Maxwelton braes are bonnie,
> Where early fa's the dew.

'Maxwelton' refers to Maxwelton House, near the Dumfriesshire village of Moniaive, where Annie Laurie was born in 1682. Many 20th century visitors to the region who visited the house actively sought out the braes of the song, invariably anticipating that they would be as 'bonnie' as the song proclaims. In a 1947 tour around Galloway, for example, M'Carter (1947: 25) proclaimed upon reaching Maxwelton House that "All around us are the braes of the famous song.... Bonnie indeed they are."

A common mistake made by many travellers, however, was to assume that the song actually referred to the Maxwelltown area of Dumfries. Invariably this did not deter them from seeking to gaze upon the braes of which the song boasts. Edwin Muir was particularly notable for making this mistake in his 1935 tour of Scotland, for upon his arrival in Dumfries he announced that Annie Laurie's braes were "covered with tasteless council houses" (Muir, 1979: 69). That Muir spoke of this song in most derogatory terms, yet still actively sought out the place to which it referred, is to a large extent indicative of the potency which songs have historically possessed in directing the tourist gaze.

By the turn of the century ballad references still proved to be convenient and potentially lucrative promotional tools, even though the tourist market had by this time changed from one consisting solely of the upper classes to one dominated by the middle classes. Thus, both Dickie's (1898) guidebook to Dumfries and Glasgow and South Western Railways Company's (1904a) guide to *The Land of Burns and the Clyde* exhorted potential clients to visit Caerlaverock Castle, citing the aforementioned ballad as evidence of the castle's tragic and historic credentials. Similarly, the 1898 Portpatrick and Wigtownshire Joint Railway's guide to tours in Galloway, pointed to Kenmure Castle on the shores of Loch Ken, as a site of interest, emphasising that it was the seat of the family to which the ballad 'O, Kenmure's On and Awa, Willie', refers.

Indeed, touring the region for its literary and musical associations continued unabated well into the next century, with Smout contending that it reached its apotheosis in the years preceding the First World War (Byrom, 1997). Even as late as the 1950s border ballads recounting the exploits of the border reivers evidently maintained some small degree of appeal for potential tourists. The 1955 *Official Guide to the County of Dumfries*, for example, advocated Langholm as a base for exploring the neighbouring districts of Eskdale and Liddesdale, noting that they had been "made famous in border minstrelsy." (CCD, 1955: 53). However, whilst the introduction to the 1955 edition proclaimed the area to be "renowned in song and story", the 1962 *County of Dumfries Official Guide* contained no similar references, preferring instead to concentrate on the activities which the region has to offer. Thus, Caerlaverock Castle is recommended, yet not for its association with the erstwhile oft-cited ballad. For both editions, the musical associations most actively promoted are those related to Burns, and the song, 'Annie Laurie'. Indeed, together with the region's various Burns-related attractions, the song 'Annie Laurie' is one musical attraction that continues to be of significance to the region's tourist industry to this day. Guided tours are conducted around Maxwelton House, and on the Moniaive village website it is advertised as the home of the heroine of "Scotland's best-known love song".

Whilst the other ballads already discussed have long ceased to be featured in tourist literature, recent years have seen music achieve increased prominence as part of the region's tourist offering. Today, however, it is the musical activity, rather than the musical traditions of the region, which functions as the tourist attraction.

Gaelforce

The explicit recognition that the region's wide range of music festivals may serve tourism purposes came with the 1997 establishment of the 'Gaelforce' festival series. Running annually throughout August, September and October, Gaelforce consists of a diverse programme of music, dance, art, theatre and film events, bound together loosely by the common theme of the Celt. Founded with the intention of attracting visitors into the region after the peak tourist season, Gaelforce is a "ground-up" initiative, based on the ideas of local event promoters, rather than being dependent on outside intervention (McNeill, 2002). Many of the events in the series were in existence long before Gaelforce's inception, yet have benefited from the extra marketing power which inclusion in the programme has conferred upon them.

As the scope of the Gaelforce programme alone indicates, there is a great deal of musical activity throughout Dumfries and Galloway. Folk festivals are held annually in Crocketford, Portwilliam, Portpatrick, and Moffat, whilst a Celtic music festival is held twice a year in Water of Deugh. The region is also home to Scotland's largest country music festival, which has been held in Creetown every September since 1997. The Langholm and Eskdale Music and Arts Festival, held annually in Langholm for the past 6 years, also features a diverse bill of folk, classical and jazz acts, together with a variety of other art forms. Traditional music also features prominently in the annual Gatehouse of Fleet Festival, while musical events form an integral part of the Dumfries and Galloway Arts Festival.

The year 2002 in particular has seen an explosion of musical events as communities have drawn upon the cultural resources at their disposal as a means of responding to the economic hardships caused by the outbreak of foot and mouth disease in 2001. This year has, for example, seen the launch of both the first Moniaive folk festival and the Kirkcudbright Music Festival, locally led initiatives intended to revitalise their respective economies and tourism.

Traditional music and tourism initiative

At the regional level there have also been recent attempts to harness the talents of local folk musicians for tourism purposes. The catalyst for this increased interest in music's tourism-generating potential was *The Traditional Music and Tourism Initiative* (SAC/ STB, 2000), a project run jointly by the Scottish Arts Council and the Scottish Tourist Board. This initiative was launched in response to the Scottish Executive's (1999) *National Cultural Strategy* and its *New Strategy for Scottish Tourism* (SE, 2000), the latter having advocated the development of niche tourism products as a means of enhancing the performance of the Scottish tourism industry. Seven regions throughout Scotland received funding from this initiative to develop traditional music based tourism projects.

In Dumfries and Galloway this funding was largely channelled into the 2001 'More Music' initiative. Organised by the Dumfries and Galloway Arts Association (DGAA), this project was intended to ensure that visitors to the region had ready access to traditional music, thereby enhancing the quality of their visitor experience and encouraging a return visit. It consisted of a series of 72 sessions and performances by local musicians at hotels, pubs and visitor attractions throughout the region. Together with providing employment for local musicians and enhancing business for local hospitality providers, this initiative had tangible tourism benefits, with no less than 88% of audience members reporting that such events would encourage them to make a return visit to the region (DGAA, 2002).

The project received marketing support from Dumfries and Galloway Tourist Board (DGTB), for music can be classed as belonging to one of the five niche products that DGTB has identified as possessing the greatest potential to maximise tourist revenues for the region. Together with VisitScotland and the other area tourist boards in Scotland, DGTB has in recent years moved away from a destination based approach to marketing. Niche product marketing has come to be adopted, the rationale being that it is an approach which is focused on the experience rather than the place (DGTB, 2001). Given that the More Music project falls into DGTB's "arts and heritage" niche tourism product, promotional materials were accordingly distributed to musical institutions such as folk clubs, folk festivals, the RSAMD and the Traditional Song and Music Association. Moreover, cultural tourists were targeted using the mailing lists of the Dumfries and Galloway Arts Association and the local council's arts team (DGAA, 2002).

Recent initiatives

Thus, whilst in Dumfries and Galloway music may not be considered a niche in itself, it is certainly regarded as an integral component of the arts and heritage niche that is so fundamental to the area tourism strategy. Within this niche a more sophisticated approach to marketing is evolving, as efforts are currently underway to more accurately profile the region's arts audiences and further develop the arts and heritage tourism product. The local council, for example, is presently devising an *Events Strategy*, designed to develop the region's calendar of events and thereby enhance the image of the region as a tourist destination. It takes as its particular focus events that can be classed as belonging to one or more of DGTB's five niche products. Thus, cultural, heritage and arts events are identified as one of the *Events Strategy's* key priorities: whilst the region's network of traditional music festivals are acknowledged as being an integral part of the existing programme of events.

The *Events Strategy* recognises that there has been a lack of systematic analysis of the market demand for most of the region's events, yet acknowledges that this is presently being remedied by the *Pilot Audience Development Project* (Morris Hargreaves McIntyre 2002). This on-going initiative, commissioned by DGAA and funded by the Scottish Arts Council, is intended to evaluate both the actual and potential market for the arts in Dumfries and Galloway. Over one thousand people are to be surveyed in order to assess how the needs of both local residents and tourists who attend the arts can be better met. Using the information gleaned, marketing workshops will be held in order to help arts promoters target potential consumers more successfully. The implication is that musical events will therefore increasingly come to be marketed most aggressively towards those identified as 'consumers of the arts'.

Music and tourism today

At present, however, the region's attempts to develop a musical tourism product are very much embryonic, and as such there is a notable lack of statistics indicating the extent to which musical events impact upon Dumfries and Galloway's tourism industry. Anecdotal evidence does, however, suggest that musical events in the Gaelforce series such as the Portpatrick Folk Festival, the Langholm Festival and the Galloway Folk Festival, are successful in attracting visitors from outwith the region (McNeill, 2002). Moreover, the report, *A Development Strategy for the Music Sector in Dumfries and Galloway* (Jones Associates, 1999) estimated that annually around 86,000 visitors to Dumfries and Galloway attend music performances as part of their trip. From these figures alone, however, it is impossible to determine the extent to which tourists come to the region specifically to attend such performances.

This report concluded that any attempt to develop the market for musical tourism in the area would require the programming of famous musicians from outwith the area. Given that musicians typically travel to audiences, it was noted that performers of considerable repute would be required if visitors from outside the region are to be attracted (Ibid, 1999). This is a strategy with considerable commercial appeal, as festivals such as Glasgow's 'Celtic Connections' demonstrate.

Paradoxically, however, the report also observed that the most successful musical events are those that are based on assets specific to the area in question. In emphasising the interrelation of music and local identity, yet simultaneously advocating the employment of musicians from elsewhere, the report highlighted the two basic methods by which music may be employed for tourism purposes. As an indicator of place, an area's indigenous musical traditions may act as a valuable source of cultural capital. Conversely, musical events that are not necessarily founded upon the region's musical traditions may be cultivated as a means of attracting tourists.

Conclusions

Music initially was an indicator of place in the development of Dumfries and Galloway's tourism industry, evoking in travellers an image of a land rich in romantic and historic associations. Nowadays, however, musical events, performances and festivals function as attractions: the musical tourism product. Commercial concerns have thus seen performers of international stature brought in from outwith the region and the scope of musical events widened as promoters aim to appeal to as wide a cross-section of the population as possible. This is ultimately the rationale behind much festival programming and the 'Celtic' focus espoused by Gaelforce in particular. This, however, being a strategy that is not dependent on local or regional distinctiveness, is one that is easily imitated, as is evidenced by the proliferation of jazz festivals in Scotland in recent years.

Moreover, regardless of whether those targeted are described as 'arts tourists', 'cultural tourists' or 'musical tourists', the risk in regarding music as a niche product is that one may disregard its potential to communicate cultural capital to a far wider audience. This tension between music as a niche attraction and music as a signifier of place is a particularly salient one in the Scottish context, given the aforementioned product-based rather than geographical orientation of recent niche tourism marketing in Scotland. Such an approach does not accord well with the reality that individual regions in Scotland compete with others for tourists in search of musical entertainment. It is evidently not in the commercial interests of any region to offer a musical tourism product that is indistinguishable from those offered by other areas. Thus, in the marketing of any niche form of tourism, it is incumbent upon individual regions to continue to promote their respective place identities.

Dumfries and Galloway has been home to many of Scotland's

foremost collectors and composers of traditional song and as such has a rich and distinctive musical heritage. Indeed, it was this very heritage that ensured that Dumfries and Galloway was historically understood as a picturesque land of history and romance, an image to which region's tourism industry is much indebted. As the region continues to develop and promote musical tourism, this very heritage may provide a useful means by which Dumfries and Galloway can carve out a distinctive musical identity for itself in Scotland's tourism marketplace. Such a strategy has already been used to great effect in the Borders, where the local tourist board has released a "Ballad Trail cassette", designed to offer tourists travelling by car commentary on local sites made famous by song (Gilchrist, 2002). There is much potential for Dumfries and Galloway to capitalise on its rich musical heritage in a similar fashion, for it is a region in which history, legend and lore are inextricably linked with its music. Indeed, for this reason, music was historically far from being a 'niche tourism product' in Dumfries and Galloway; rather, it was instrumental in the development of 'mass tourism' to the area.

References

Abram, S. & Waldren, J. (1997), "Introduction" in *Tourists and Tourism: Identifying with People and Places*, S. Abram, J. Waldren & D. V. L. Macleod (eds), Oxford: Berg, 1-11.

Bogg, E. (1898), *A Thousand Miles of Wandering in the Border Country*, York: John Sampson.

Burke, J. (1983), *Musical Landscapes*, Exeter: Webb and Bower.

Byrom, J. D. (1997), *The Lure of the Tour: Literary reaction to Travel in Scotland 1760-1833*, University of Aberdeen: unpublished PhD thesis.

County Council of Dumfriesshire (1955), *Official Guide to the County of Dumfries*, Dundee and Edinburgh: W S Fenton Publications.

County Council of Dumfriesshire (1962), *County of Dumfries Official Guide*, Gloucester: The British Publishing Company Ltd..

Cuthbertson, D. C. (1938), *Romantic Scotland: the Story of the Shires*, Stirling: Eneas Mackay.

DeWitt, M. F. (1999), "Heritage, Tradition and Travel: Louisiana French Culture Placed on a California Dance Floor", *The World of Music*, 41:3, 57-83.

Dibdin, T. F. (1838), *A Biographical Antiquarian and Picturesque Tour in the Northern Counties of England and Scotland*, London: C Richards.

Dickie, W. (1898), *Dumfries and Round About: The Land of Bruce and Burns, Of Scott and Carlyle*, Dumfries: J Swan.

Dumfries and Galloway Arts Association (2002), *More Music Live*, unpublished.

Dumfries and Galloway Council (2001), *Events Strategy: Draft*, unpublished.

Dumfries and Galloway Tourist Board (2001), *Dumfries and Galloway Area Tourism Strategy 2001-2006*.

Feintuch, B. (2001), *Music on the Margins*, paper delivered at Crossing Boundaries conference: University of Aberdeen (21 July).

Gilchrist, J. (2002), "Jim Gilchrist Ventures into the Debatable Border Ballad Lands", The Scotsman, (31 January), 12.

Glasgow and South Western Railway Company (1904a), *Summer Tours in the Land of Burns, the Highlands and Islands of South-Western Scotland*, Glasgow.

Glasgow and South Western Railway (1904b), *Tourist Guide: the Land of Burns and the Clyde*, Glasgow: John Miller.

Glendening, J. (1997), *The High Road: Romantic Tourism, Scotland and Literature,1720-1820*, Basingstoke: Macmillan.

Haldane, K. J. (1990), *Imagining Scotland: Tourist Images of Scotland 1770-1914*, University of Virginia History Department: PhD thesis.

Hodgart, M. J. C. (1962), *The Ballads*, London: Hutchison.

Jones Associates Ltd. (1999), *A Development Strategy for the Music Sector in Dumfries and Galloway*, Edinburgh: Jones Economics Ltd.

McAlpine, K. (2000), "Proude Armstrongs and Border Rogues: History in 'Kinmont Willie', 'Jock o the Side' and Archie o Cawfield'", in *The Ballad in Scottish History*, E. J. Cowan (ed), East Linton: Tuckwell, 72-94.

M'Carter, E. R. (1947), "By Scaur and by Ken", *Dumfries and Galloway News Review*, 2, 23-25.

McNeill, R. (2002), Co-ordinator of Gaelforce. Interview, (16 May).

Moniaive website (2002), http://moniaive.com, accessed 01/06/02.

Morris Hargreaves McIntyre (2002), *Pilot Audience Development Project: Revised Proposal*, unpublished.

Muir, E. (1979), *Scottish Journey*, Edinburgh: Mainstream Publishing Company Ltd..

Portpatrick and Wigtownshire Joint Railways (1898), *Tours in Galloway: Where to Stay and What to See*, Glasgow.

Scott, W. (1931), *Minstrelsy of the Scottish Border*, London: George G Harrap and Co. Ltd.

Scottish Arts Council & Scottish Tourist Board (2000), *Traditional Music and Tourism Initiative*, Edinburgh: Scottish Arts Council, Scottish Tourist Board.

Scottish Arts Council & VisitScotland (2002), *A Soundtrack for Scottish Tourism*, Edinburgh: Scottish Arts Council, VisitScotland.

Scottish Executive (2000), *New Strategy for Scottish Tourism*, Edinburgh: Stationery Office.

Squire, S. J. (1988), "Wordsworth and Lake District Tourism: Romantic Reshaping of Landscape", *The Canadian Geographer*, 32:3, 237-47.

Thomson, A. A. (1930), *Let's See the Lowlands*, London: Herbert Jenkins.

Todd, G. E. (1904), *Through Scotland by the Caledonian Railway*, Glasgow.

Urry, J. (2002), *The Tourist Gaze*, London: Sage Publications Ltd.

Chapter 8

The Holy Grail of Film Tourism - or -
How to increase visitor numbers without really trying

Belle Doyle

I am Film Officer for Dumfries and Galloway Council and I have two main responsibilities in my job - running the South West Scotland Screen Commission, and managing the Film Theatre in Dumfries. Around sixty per cent of my job is persuading filmmakers to come to this area, and once they are here, acting as a link between local agencies, location owners, the Council and the community. The primary purpose of the Screen Commission is to attract inward investment to the region. To give you an example of the amount of money involved, the first series of *2000 Acres of Sky* spent nearly a million pounds on location. My annual target is three-quarters of a million pounds per year.

All the Screen Commissions in Scotland are funded through their own local authority and Scottish Enterprise money, though we attend trade events together under a 'Scottish' banner rather than as separate regions. Scottish Screen is the main organisation for film in Scotland, running the locations service, production funding and script development, and training and education. One of its most important jobs is bringing in outside film investment into Scotland; for example, film clips are shown as part of trade missions to New York, with the ultimate result of getting East Coast producers to look at Scotland as a location. The Mission Impossible train stunt was filmed here because the Dumfries-Annan line doesn't have any overhead cables. I don't think that there's been any tourism spin-off, although someone did ring me recently to get the exact map reference for a book on locations.

The film industry in Scotland is of course smaller than England - we still don't have a large studio in Scotland, and many productions rely on hiring skilled personnel and equipment from England. The economic value of filming in Scotland is worth about £20-25 million per year,[1] compared to the UK Film Council's figure of £539 million

---

[1] Figures provided by Scottish Screen, 249 West George Street, Glasgow, G2 4QE, www.scottishscreen.com

of inward investment in 2000:[2] this is the amount spent by incoming companies from overseas and doesn't include indigenous film-making. It is a huge global market and what we are all competing for is the big international pictures that will be screened worldwide, be a box office hit and show off a famous location. One of the best (recorded) instances of film tourism is for the Devil's Tower, which was used in *Close Encounters of the Third Kind*. In 1978, visitor figures rose by 74% simply due to the release of the film.

In 1994 there were three international feature films made in Scotland: *Rob Roy*, *Braveheart*, and *Loch Ness*. A report by Hydra Associates in 1997 (Scottish Screen have copies) analysed the value of this year of film production specifically, and looks at the tourism value of three films all concerned with Scottish subjects, one of which won Best Picture and Best Director in the 1995 Academy Awards.[3] Visits to the Wallace monument in Stirling increased by 52% following the release of *Braveheart*. Visits to the Trossacks increased by 19% following *Rob Roy*. Stirling Castle saw a rise of 16%. The Hydra report says is that if we assume that 5% of visitors to Scotland were influenced by films made here, it represents £7.2 million in additional spending. In fact, customer questionnaires showed that the numbers motivated to visit Scotland by watching films was 14%. One of the ironies of *Braveheart* was that a lot of the battle scenes were filmed in Ireland, as the Irish Army provided extras for a very small fee; nevertheless, Scotland benefited from the visitors, as these were Scottish narratives.

But film tourism is usually the last thing anyone thinks about. A good recent example would be the programme made for Channel 4, 'The Edwardian Country House', which was filmed using a mansion in the Scottish Borders. By the time the programme was transmitted, which was almost a year after the filming, nobody had done a press or marketing campaign about the property itself: the production company and Channel 4 had promoted the programme, of course, but there was no tourist campaign to promote the property. The house itself is a private property that opens to the public two days a week: in the end, Edinburgh Film Focus, who have responsibility for the Borders and who originally found the property, released a press release in conjunction with its owner. That was unusual - if it had

[2] Figure given by UK Film Council's Annual Report 2000, available from UK Film Council, 10 Little Portland Street, London, W1W 7JG, www.filmcouncil.org.uk
[3] *The Economic and Tourism Benefits of Large Scale Film Production in the UK*, Hydra Associates for British Film Commission, Scottish Screen and Scottish Tourist Board (Glasgow and London 1997).

been an Historic Scotland property, the press coverage would have been much more organised.

How do we get filming here? We have a location brochure that was put together recently, and we are currently in the process of sending it out to a number of different production companies all over the world.[4] The brochure highlights some of our best and worst features, and its aim is to persuade filmmakers to come here without looking at anywhere else – like the Highlands and Islands, for example. But the only way to guarantee filming here is to be as helpful as possible, look after visiting crews, and hope that they remember how easy it is to film here: filming brings in other filming.

If the production company can cheat the shot and save some money they will: going out on location is an expensive business. So there are two rival forces at work here - the production budget that dictates where and for how long a shoot will go on, and the Screen Commission's job of getting as much production here as possible. So while I dream of getting a major film here, most of what I do is dealing with documentaries, short films, television material: *The Curious Gardeners* on BBC2 featured a local labyrinth maker. Any coverage means a higher public profile for the region.

So the most important element of my job is to get the filmmakers here; the tourism will follow much later. *2000 Acres of Sky* is filmed on the west coast of Dumfries and Galloway, in a village called Port Logan. When Zenith, the production company, first decided to film there, we met the local people and explained the benefits and problems about having a crew filming in the village all summer. There is now a third series of *2000 Acres* and some of the villagers are still reluctant to advertise the location. This has been discussed in great detail with the whole village and what the BBC offered in the end was a credit on the last episode of the second series that said 'Thank you to the people of Dumfries and Galloway'. This isn't usually done for a BBC series but it was decided that the circumstances were unusual, especially with the region still suffering from the impact of the Foot and Mouth Disease epidemic on visitor figures. The dilemma facing the Dumfries & Galloway Tourist Board is how to say it's filmed here without being too specific.

There are always going to be missed opportunities and unexpected hits. But if you think there might be advantages to being a location for something well known, there are other considerations to bear in mind!

---

[4] Available from SWSSC, 28 Edinburgh Road, Dumfries, DG1 1JQ, www.sw-scotland-screen.com

The Wicker Man was filmed almost entirely on location in Dumfries & Galloway in 1972. The thirtieth anniversary of the film is due, and a new DVD has been released, so there has been a lot of publicity recently. Unfortunately, some of the local people here view *The Wicker Man* as presenting the region in a very poor light, with its subject matter of pagan rituals and the sacrificing of virgins among other things - and consider it to be the type of film that attracts the wrong element to the region. I do get enquiries all the time about *The Wicker Man* so I have started to send out a virtual guide to the locations by e-mail constructed as a two-day trip around the region. Eventually I hope a proper leaflet will be produced.

One of the most useful aspects of both *2000 Acres* and *The Wicker Man* is that they show this region as a place where you can recreate an 'island' feel without actually having to go to any island – the light quality on the west coast here is the same as anywhere in the Western Isles. That is a very great advantage, and something to be exploited in the future.

Our most recent feature film was Peter Mullan's *The Magdalene Sisters*, set in 1950's Ireland but filmed just up the road in an old convent in Dumfries. It's unlikely that anyone watching the film will realise it was filmed in Scotland (unless they watch the credits) because the art department very successfully recreated the 'look' of rural Ireland. So in the nicest possible way, I am working at odds with agencies like the local Tourist Board. It makes no difference to me if somebody films here because they are trying to recreate somewhere else. But you never know what's around the corner – the perfect script that combines a high location spend and a massive tourism spin-off might be being written at this very moment!

Chapter 9

Virtual Tourism
Exploring Scotland by CD-ROM

Valentina Bold

I would like to start this paper by quoting from an interview with the
Douglas Lowe brothers. They are members of the Rastafarian Black
Douglas clan, and I first met these regular visitors to Scotland at the
Braemar Gathering in 1998:

> I like the Highlands, this is where the ancient Moray people
> used to live and we're Moors—Mooray, Moors, we're all of
> them—so that's why we're here, and just to enjoy the
> festivities and the people.... In America [we go to Highland
> Games]. California's a big place you see, we've got 25
> million people there so that's a lotta games!....
>
> All I'm looking to see is different people, and you meet
> different kinds of people here. I guess the highlight to me is
> that the royal family comes here...our other particular reason
> is that we make a presence here which is not normally here,
> which is kind of *reclamation, reclaiming* and restoring our
> presence here at the Games...and that's part of what it is to
> me....
>
> The Games were originally from one of the Black Moors,
> Malcolm Canmore, the Moor, to train his soldiers to do his
> fighting. That's what Brae Moor's all about. *Moor's Land*
> meaning dark skinned and we've got dark skin, we're
> Douglases, right? So that's why we're here! And that's what
> they're missing! [*laughs*]... We have the lion, the heart and
> the crown [of the Douglas crest] and the African symbol of
> Ankh, and you know the ancient Scots came from Africa, in
> Egypt, in Scotia, and we're their descendants, some of them,
> and we're just a thousand years later! (Bold and McKean,
> 1999)[1]

---

[1] An earlier version of this paper is Bold 2001.

I wanted to start with this quotation because it encapsulates the sense of personal engagement that makes us receive tourist destinations in unique ways: this is the underlying theme of my paper. I'd like to consider the potential, and the disadvantages, of using digital media to introduce, and represent the regions of Scotland to individual tourists, and in an individual manner. My premise is that digital tours enable people—whether they come from home or from a distance—to experience places in self-directed and thoughtful ways.

My idea is based on the experience of collecting, editing and producing a CD-rom, *Northern Folk: Living Traditions of North East Scotland*[2], with my former colleague, Dr Tom McKean. *Northern Folk* was developed as a team project at the University of Aberdeen's Elphinstone Institute, which promotes, presents and preserves the cultural traditions of Northern Scotland. The idea came from Professor James Porter, Chair of Ethnology at the University of Aberdeen. Tom McKean and I, then Research Fellows at the Institute, developed the idea, conducted the fieldwork and archival research, did the filming and audio recording, helped to develop the programme, and edited the finished product.

We hoped to produce a pocket-sized and peculiarly intimate heritage visitor attraction that would be useful both for those who knew the region, and for potential visitors, with a particular view to the North American market. We decided at a fairly early age to aim our product at the adult market (upper level school students, undergraduates and cultural enthusiasts). The 5-14 guidelines for schools were too limiting for our aims, and we felt that targeting primary school children would have led to a less challenging, if more entertaining, end point.

Producing a CD-ROM seemed a good way to provide a lively introduction to the living traditions of our area, backed up with materials in video, audio and text format. We liked the idea of giving our users the experience of a guided tour, led by real people from our region. The CD-ROM, based around our field-recorded interviews (video and audio) enabled us to create a simulated experience, allowing users to feel as if they were travelling around and meeting people within a community. The people they meet, of course, were selected by us, but represent the multi-talented tradition bearers of North East Scotland: young and old; famous and less famous. We

---

[2] Copies of *Northern Folk* can be ordered direct from the Elphinstone Institute, University of Aberdeen, King's College, Aberdeen, Scotland, or through their website: www.abdn.ac.uk/elphinstone

wanted to give the sensation of meeting people in different contexts and you'll see people reappear in different sections, coming to prominence in some parts, and quoted in others.

We wanted to reflect the diversity and complexity of North East folk. The CD-ROM features a broad range of people including Carmen Higgins, the fiddler; Stanley Robertson, the storyteller; the Eastons, who are local farmers; the Whytes, fishermen for many generations; Jenny Douglas, an ex music hall worker; the Ballantynes, representing an oil worker's family and the children of Auchterless Sunday School. There's material from throughout the area—from the Moray Firth in the NE to Montrose in the SW—from women and men, and from all ages: our oldest contributor was 95, the youngest 7. All backgrounds, too, are represented: Scots of long standing, whose families could be traced within the area for 400 years, like the Strathdees; new Scots, like Salvatore Vaccarino and the Adrons, from places as diverse as Sicily, Nepal and the SE of England and, as you know, California. New activities, like computer games, stand alongside traditional skills, like long lining.

We also wanted to allow the user to meet people from our area in the past, and people we could not feature in the audio-visual sections. Our format allowed us to intersperse the main sections with quotes from additional speakers from diverse backgrounds. We drew on printed sources, like local histories, and on works of fiction and poetry which we felt imaginatively captured the experiences of living in the North East. Visual materials, too, illustrate and complement what's being said in an aesthetically pleasing way. Materials came from many sources: including photographs we took ourselves and ones that came from contributors' collections, along with images provided by public bodies (including the Regional Archaeology Department, Aberdeen Art Gallery, Elgin Museums & Libraries)

Incidentally, although we did not know this at the time, all these aims are broadly in tune with David Herbert's notion of the stages of interpretation in Heritage Visitor Attractions, as cited in Leask and Yeoman (1999: 84): to relate to experience (educate); seek to reveal (inform); view as art (enhance); seek to stimulate (entertain) and aim for wholeness (manage). The product, in this respect, does work as a miniature tourist attraction by proxy.

As well as its presentation advantages, we decided on the CD-ROM format for technical reasons. We did think about using DVD but, when the project started out in late 1996, the technology was not far enough advanced. We rejected the idea of web-based materials because we wanted the CD-ROM to be a discrete, stand-alone product, although it does have a hot-link to supplementary articles on the Web. Extensive research informed our choice. We spent a couple of months being computer nerds: visiting places such as the digitising unit at the Museum of Scotland: this was a dispiriting experience given its dedicated team of over twenty people, working on much less ambitious projects. There were relatively few contextualised, cultural CD-ROMs available in the late 90s—the Museum of Civilisation in Canada was producing some excellent ones which, unfortunately, were published slightly too late to be of direct use. We did, though, view a variety of CDs forms, including the sort that come free with computers—*Wild Africa* was unexpectedly useful in providing ideas on interfaces—and children's computer games.

We researched in-house options for production (the medical Computer Assisted Learning unit at Aberdeen was making multimedia productions, as was the Department of Biochemistry), but soon realised that, in the competitive software market, we wanted to work with a professional company. We wanted to work with people with strong aesthetically driven goals, to complement our own experience in educational and academically grounded projects. After visiting various production companies, we decided to work with Concept Productions, who had just developed a set of touch-screen displays for Aberdeen's renovated Maritime Museum. When we started, the company had never made a CD-ROM. Like many Aberdeen-based concerns, they specialised in videos for the oil industry. We struggled to bring academic and production values together (from our side, the main issues was how to storyboard and tightly edit a project with almost three-dimensional qualities, anticipating a user coming in from different points; from their side, maintaining didactic integrity). We felt it was important to work with a company with both multimedia and cultural experience, and Concept's experience on our project means they are now a leading company within this area, for a wide group of clients with diverse cultural and commercial interests.

The project, from the start, was a team-based one. Tom McKean, an American based in Scotland for ten years at the time, and myself were the people working most closely on the project. We decided on the content, decided who we wanted to feature, and conducted the interviews, drawing on people we'd met in the course of our own research, and editing their words. Naively, we wanted the CD to feel as un-edited as possible, representing people's own voices, with few interventions from ourselves. We discovered that the CD-ROM is one of the most heavily edited formats imaginable (two to three hours of film is edited on our CD-ROM in every 1-2 minute audio visual sequence).

As well as the intellectual issues, we had to be pragmatic and to consider Aberdeen University's financial interests (the Dean of Arts took some convincing). An important member of our team was the AURIS unit: they administer research income for the University and were very helpful with contractual issues. Even so, we ran over budget in the end, and learnt important (if expensive) lessons about costing. The University of Aberdeen provided support in kind in the form of office space and salaries (from late 1996 to mid 1999 we spent most of our time on the project, particularly in its last 6 months). External funding was secured from a variety of sources; not all of it was in place when we began the project; luckily Concept was patient. Fifty percent of our funding came through the Scottish Cultural Resources Access Network. Grampian Enterprise, now Scottish Enterprise: Grampian, gave us a grant of £20,000. The Moray Trust, a local organisation, gave us £10,000. The Scottish Arts Council provided £250 to record the programme soundtrack.

The programme itself contains the following elements: 300 full screen images; 25 minutes video; 35 minutes audio, including the specially-recorded soundtrack, 300 screens of texts (combining interview material, poetry, prose, extracts from historical works), 97,000 words of text in total. It includes information about a wide range of traditional culture: fishing, farming, storytelling, song, music, belief, custom, domestic life, industry and entertainment.

The CD-ROM opens with introductory slideshow, containing a selection of the images in the programme, and accompanied by the Carmen Higgins soundtrack of fiddle music, some with guitar accompaniment. This also comes into play as the screen saver. The repeat user can skip the slideshow at an early stage of viewing, when the 'start' button appears. Then, the user can choose their language for navigation: we consciously chose to use the three main languages of Scotland, particularly as this was envisaged as part of a series. North East Scots is the default, and there are options for English and Gaelic. After selecting language, the user can choose from four sections: Work, Domestic, Community, Recreation and then choose from three further options in each of these. Once a section has been selected, there are four or five introductory screens consisting of a general introduction to the chosen topic. The user is then encouraged to select 'Fowk': a slideshow of video images, stills and discussions: at this level the user meets the folk featured in the CD-ROM.

Additional navigation options include working through the 'Gallery' section: this allows the user to view the CD images full-screen size, and to read a vast range of interview, archival and book-based extracts. All the sources for all the material in the CD-ROM are identified, and it is possible to listen to additional soundtrack music and song passages. From the Gallery, the user can enter a map section, locating people and places and offering an alternative navigation route. There is, in addition, a 'Further Resources' section, listing bibliography, places to find information (libraries, archives, museums, galleries) in the North East with brief annotations, a listing of related video and audio recorded material and the dates and places of birth of all our contributors. There is also a hotlink to articles, teacher and student notes and resources, based at the Elphinstone Institute's website at the University of Aberdeen. Finally, the user selects 'exit' and is prompted (in Scots) either to 'gang awa' or 'bide'; the former option prompts a showing of credits, listing all our sponsors and all the people involved in the project, before the programme stops.

On completion, and subsequently, we felt that this project had several real advantages. The virtual tour experience, for instance, does allow the user to gain a real sense of engagement, and to enjoy the simulated experience of being 'guided' by real people. The user can travel at her, or his, own speed, focusing on personal interests, and returning to different areas, or navigating by different routes. The project promotes and celebrates a local community and brings together a variety of people and institutions.

There are, of course, disadvantages. The biggest of these is expense: this project cost over £50,000, and had additional costs, hidden at the outset to the inexperienced in digital technology. These included copyright clearance; payments for the digitisation of photos to exact specifications; the hiring of professional standard equipment (digital cameras at this time were not of a sufficient quality and we had to use Betacam equipment which the University did not possess); the use of materials (where some providers, such as Aberdeen Art Gallery, generously allowed us free access to transparencies from their collection for a modest flat fee, others asked for much more). Furthermore, a high degree of professionalism was required: Tom and I had to learn to become professional standard camera crew and required training in production and post-production. Some of these drawbacks, as the technology has now advanced, have disappeared (the latest digital video, for instance, is quite a high enough standard to use on screen).

As well as expenses, there are drawbacks related to the highly technical nature of the project. As with any filming project, you are bringing vast quantities of expensive equipment (hired in our case) into people's houses with the awkwardness of setting up, and the intrusiveness of it all; some people respond well, others (children in particular) can find it daunting. Technical faults can also hamper the process. Filming the section on Piper Alpha, for instance, our front light blew out although this worked out quite well: we continued filming with what turned out to be quite an artful dark background effect.

It is, perhaps, even more difficult to learn to think digital, when you are used to the linear demands of article and book writing: this proved to be a huge learning curve. The nature of the medium partly determined the message: on CD, short, bite-sized sections are ideal, remembering that material can be accessed through any part of the programme. In the end we found the medium leads to extremely heavy editing, rather than the lightness of touch we had hoped for.

The demands of our partners were also heavy: SCRAN, for instance, required detailed documentation of the images provided as part of our contract; finally, we had to renegotiate and repay a small part of their grant, as the demands proved difficult to fulfil. This sort of project, too, requires a good base within the community for success. Fortunately, our own collection work meant we had a network of people to draw on for suggestions and resources. Maintaining community support is crucial in this context, as is fulfilling community expectations: people can feel very let down when material they have freely offered is not publicised; luckily our contributors were happy.

The project was also very time-consuming, taking three years from the initial concept to completion, with six months solid work towards the end. At this stage, we faced long working days, partly to use our hired equipment to its fullest. During filming, a typical day might be: in at 9, off to locate and copy some photographs from a library (with our portable copy stand); an afternoon of filming in the field; back to the office to edit the filming; go for a pizza at 10; home around 11/12 and back in at 9 again the next day to repeat the experience. At the other end of the process, we faced proof reading in three formats: a nightmare!

The competitive nature of CD production was equally daunting: we wanted our product to look good on the shelf alongside something produced by Sony. We realised professional marketing was also essential, and used a local distributor and on-line sales: this seemed the right decision at the time but, in retrospect, was not the right way to proceed. In future projects, I would always seek a mainstream publisher who specialises in CD-ROM titles.

Having said all this, I still think the CD-ROM could be a model for promoting tourism and educating people abroad, and at home, about South West Scotland. I do, of course, have some reservations: funding must be in place, and considered at a detailed level before engaging on the project. At the moment I am working on a new project, and receiving assistance in securing funding from the Research and Enterprise team at the University of Glasgow, where I now work. My current bids will, hopefully, secure us high quality digitisation resources, to cut the high production costs we will still need to meet. Glasgow University has a unit dedicated to digitisation in areas of heritage, linked to the Hunterian museum, HATTI, and I shall be drawing on their help. I may also go back to Concept for assistance as, having developed this programme, they can complete a follow-up for considerably less. Local resources in Dumfries & Galloway are also of a very high standard: I have access, for instance, to a significant number of high-quality field-recorded interviews generated, and permission-cleared, by Crichton students, usually with transcripts (we were not able to generate these in bulk at Aberdeen) and there are, of course, wonderful resources in the Dumfries Archives; the Dumfries Ewart Library; Broughton House (Hornel's collection in Kirkcudbright) and elsewhere. I think that the idea of a series helps. My new project will have links to the first CD-ROM: as a teaching aid I have found it immensely useful and, as my students are now tired of North East Scotland, this provides an incentive to complete a CD on the South West. There are new models, of course, to view, as the CD-ROM medium has advanced considerably since 1999.

There are a few things I shall do differently this time. For a start, I plan to be much more focused in the early stages. I shall start by filming, decide what intriguing issues emerge, and interview around them. We went in as traditional folklore researchers, hoping our ideas would emerge from extensive collecting in the area. With a project like this, we wasted time. In future, I plan on a week or two of intensive filming with people I know well; then I shall edit the clips and conduct additional interviews around these clips, to complement the audio-visuals. I also plan to adopt a different thematic approach. Given the backup at the Crichton Tourism Research Centre, it makes sense to focus on links between the environment and cultural traditions, lending a different flavour to the project. My own role, too, will be different: directing rather than all parts. As Head of Scottish Studies at Crichton, I do not have the research time I did at

Elphinstone. One reviewer commented that:

> On the CD sleeve, McKean and Bold are described, too
> modestly, as editors—they have clearly been far more active
> than that word suggests, as energetic researchers, finding
> fascinating archive materials, and also as very active and
> imaginative field-workers, interviewing and filming the length
> and breadth of the North East. They deserve their editorial
> credit, however, because they have synthesised their diverse
> materials skilfully, and organised them so that they are both
> accessible and entertaining. (Milton 2001)

It is a complimentary review, of course, but the tasks the reviewer
outlines are absolutely right: you have to be prepared to research in
the field and in archives and in libraries and in photo archives and in
private collections: it all takes time! I do, though, have a valuable
resource in our students. As part of our forthcoming, and highly
innovative fourth-year, eight able students will be completing a
digital product (probably a set of web pages) considering the cultural
and environmental landscape of our area; this will generate further
material that will feed in, credited, to the new publication. I may also
use DVD, although it still seems that CD-ROM, which allows for
more interactivity, may be the best medium. I plan to use digital video
for filming; the quality is now acceptable compared to professional-
quality Betacam film as we used. As I said above, I will also use a
professional publisher; since our project started, several academic
publishers, like Routledge for instance, have initiated specialist digital
media lists.

There are, though, some things I would do the same. Most
importantly, I hope to work with people I trust intellectually; our team
dynamics worked very well. It is important that everyone involved
understands, and contributes to, the developing ethos of the project. I
would hope, too, to maintain the excitement and sense of fun in
making a miniature visitor attraction. It does allow users to meet
people travelling through the region who they might not normally
meet as tourists: from people in their homes, like Isobel Easton or the
Ballantyne family, to people as unusual and vibrant as the Black
Douglas brothers.

I think it is worthwhile to make a CD-ROM for the SW because of
the possibility of communicating the experience of meeting people
who know the region first hand, whether as tourists or at home. The
ability to give multi-media impressions of an area is useful as is the

way you can interlink diverse images, and experiences, to give a holistic impression of living within, and experiencing, the landscape within a specific area. I would, however, be interested in what the professionals working within this area think, before embarking on the proposed new project, particularly about the validity of such an approach within the context of tourism.

References

Bold, V and T. McKean (eds.) (1999), *Northern Folk: Living Traditions of North East Scotland*. Aberdeen: The Elphinstone Institute.
Bold, V. (2001), 'Digitising Scotland: From the North East to the South West', *Ethnologies*, 23: 2, 111-28.
Leask, A. and I. Yeoman (1999), *Heritage Visitor Attractions*, London: Cassell.
Milton, Colin (2001). Review article '*Northern Folk*', *Scottish Studies Review* 1: 1, 105-106.

Chapter 10

Responding to Market Downturn:
Private and public sector marketing partnerships
— The case of Glasgow's leading attractions

John Lennon

Introduction: the competitive environment

This paper calls for adequate planning and marketing to be in place for sectors when 'shocks' to the operating environment such as FMD or September 11, 2001 occur. A case analysis of the visitor attractions industry in Scotland is used to illustrate some useful lessons in Scottish tourism following the Foot and Mouth epidemic in the UK in 2001. The Foot and Mouth crisis of 2001 saw the tourism industry in Scotland lose substantial levels of business in many areas. This paper looks specifically at how the visitor attraction sector was affected and examines a key local city-based effort to provide assistance and development support to the tourism industry.

The year 2001 saw tourism in Scotland facing a number of major problems. In the late 1990s it became clearly apparent that the relatively high cost of sterling in comparison to the Euro-linked currencies was exerting a negative impact on perceptions of the destination in terms of 'value'. Currency movements in relation to the value of UK Sterling in respect of the US Dollar and the Euro for the period to July 2002 are detailed on graph 2.1 below.

Graph 2.1 US Dollar and the Euro Value in Sterling (January 2001 to July 2002)
Source: Bank of England (2002)

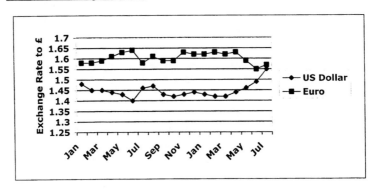

As a consequence there was within Europe a growing perception that the UK and Scotland were perceived as relatively poor value for money. Evidence of this view was detailed in the most recent major tourism visitor survey conducted on behalf of the national tourism organisation: VisitScotland (see NFO System 3, 2001).

Independent of currency, fuel prices (most notably petrol and diesel) have for some time been significantly more expensive than comparative prices in other European destinations. The price of fuel is a particularly significant cost in Scotland wherein the quality, extent and coverage of public transportation systems is limited. On top of such a context the advent of Foot and Mouth disease in early 2001 was a further blow to an industry already facing an extremely competitive world environment.

It was of course impossible to predict that September of 2001 would see the tragic attacks on the US followed by the protracted war in Afghanistan. The impact this has had on world tourism is now being reported and informed commentators now view the optimistic growth forecasts of the recent past more sceptically. From a Scottish viewpoint the impact was a further blow to the important international markets. The US market, which was approximately 25% of all overseas visitation collapsed and the downturn in general international traffic was considerable. Ironically the US dollar was the only major currency that has retained some medium term parity with the UK Sterling and had to some extent helped preserve a share of the international market.

The decline in the numbers of trips taken in the UK over 2001 as a result of these cumulative negative conditions is shown in table 2.2 below:

Country	No of holiday trips 2000 (millions)	No of holiday trips 2001 (millions)
England	82.7	80.1
Scotland	12.3	11.5
Wales	9.4	8.3
Northern Ireland	2.1	1.6

Table 2.2 Holiday Trips in the UK 2000-2001 (millions) Source: BMRB Research 2002

The Foot and Mouth epidemic was widely covered in world media and the imagery of burning carcasses were one of the enduring representations shown throughout tourism generating markets. What followed was significant misrepresentation and inaccurate reporting in the world press in relation to the extent of contamination in the UK food chain. The extent of reported cases are detailed in Appendix 1. While Scotland saw relatively limited out-breaks and some areas of the country remained untroubled, efforts to control the potential spread of the disease saw large parts of the countryside being closed to visitors in order to reduce the spread of the disease. The impact on tourism (and most particularly rural tourism) was mixed but in affected areas significant (see Hall 2001).

Government assistance following the out-break of FMD

Foot and Mouth of course affected farming significantly. In addition to the many millions of pounds spent on the slaughter of livestock in efforts to contain the disease some £600 million was distributed to the farming community in compensation. This was widely seen as a necessary response to an industry devastated by the outbreak and facing a long slow period of recovery.

The tourism industry was also affected, but received significantly lower levels of compensation. Agriculture in Scotland accounts for 1.5% of Gross Domestic Product (GDP) and with fishing accounts for some 4% of total employment. In comparison, tourism is responsible for 5% of GDP (or £4.5 billion) and some 8% of employment (NOMIS, 1999). However the Scottish tourism industry received less than £60 million in compensation and assistance following the FMD crisis. Tourism in Scotland is vital to the economy and employs more people than the oil, gas and whisky industries combined.

What became apparent during the crisis was the inability of the Scottish tourism industry to successfully lobby the Scottish Executive for realistic levels of financial assistance comparable to the significance of the industry and the problems it was facing in the short to medium term.

The geographical priority was the two identified Area Tourist Boards, Dumfries and Galloway and Scottish Borders, wherein the number of confirmed Foot and Mouth Disease cases was greatest. In Scotland these were the only two areas with confirmed infected premises (see table 3.1 below). This has to be seen against the much more significant levels of infection in England (see Appendix1)

Location	No of Infected Premises	% of Total Cases
England	1726	85.2
Wales	113	5.8
Scotland	187	9.2
Dumfries and Galloway	176	8.7
Scottish Borders	11	0.5
Total	2026	100

Table 3.1 Foot and Mouth Disease cases in the UK (DEFRA 2002)

The aid package for Scotland distributed from the Scottish Executive was concentrated in three areas - containing the disease, providing hardship relief and helping with long-term recovery. Tourism was one of the industries wherein the impact was felt most severely. It remains a hard industry to define with employment in a range of sectors. It is heavily dependent upon the countryside for part of its appeal, and the FMD outbreak illustrated the interdependence of different elements that constitute the rural economy. Tourism was affected not only by the closure of the countryside but also by the negative imagery (RSE, 2002). Following reopening of the countryside the public remained confused about warnings to avoid contact with animals and many public footpaths retained notices forbidding entry long after the original danger had passed.

The impact on tourism in Scotland was thus substantial. It was notable that between 2000-2001 spending by overseas visitors fell by £119 million (-3%). Although there was some increase in urban tourism over the period (possibly due to displacement) VisitScotland estimate a loss of £200-£250 million for Scotland in gross revenue terms. It is the consequent hardship relief and its utilisation that is of greatest interest for this paper. The Scottish Executive spent £30 million on FMD hardship relief (RSE, 2002) mainly distributed through VisitScotland, Local Enterprise Companies (LECs) and the local authorities. VisitScotland , the National Tourism organisation, channelled its relief predominantly into marketing (detailed below as table 3.2).

Activity	Expenditure
UK Marketing Campaigns	£4,950,000
International Marketing Campaigns	£1.850,000
Business Tourism	£210,000
Area Tourist Board Grants	£2,800,000
Dumfries and Galloway	£850,000
Scottish Borders	£240,000

Quality Assurance	£700,000
Dumfries and Galloway Environmental Campaign	£300,000
Total	£11,900,000

Table 3.2 VisitScotland Financial assistance allocation following Foot and Mouth
outbreak 2001 (data derived from VisitScotland internal documentation 2002)

The LECs in Dumfries and Galloway and Scottish Borders were able
to assist businesses directly and on top of the £30 million designated
these areas secured a further £ 5million and £2.5 million from
Scottish Enterprise budgets. This was utilised for: loans, interest relief
grants, community regeneration, specialist business advice, skill
training and a range of other uses divided between Tourism and
Agriculture. At the Local Authority level further funds were received
from the Scottish Executive for Business rates relief and to cover
costs associated with the disease. At best such support was reactive
and 'pilot' analysis suggests the clear need for government funding to
be co-ordinated by one agency. Analysis of the real 'effects' of FMD
was difficult to isolate and evidence requirements varied.

At individual level tourism businesses in the visitor attraction, food
and beverage and accommodations sectors were offered assistance
(short-term reductions) with non-domestic business rate payments.
This was provided in conjunction with Local Authorities for
businesses most affected by the foot and mouth outbreak for an initial
period of three months. This scheme only applied to certain local
authority areas, primarily, those with strong agricultural economies
who were experiencing greatest hardship. Application for this relief
was predicated on operators providing evidence of the hardship they
are suffering and demonstrating this through public auditable
documents (such as annual accounts). In addition, local authorities
were encouraged to defer rates payments in the medium to long term
for affected businesses. The programme for individual relief did
prove problematic and troublesome to administer and was perceived
as less than helpful by many in the tourism industry. Annual accounts
were rarely available for the period in question and other methods of
providing proof of hardship were difficult to validate. Assistance was
thus delayed and the process of verification of loss was slow for many
already experiencing a significant downturn in business levels.

Visitor attractions in Scotland and the impact of Foot and Mouth Disease

Specific questions were asked in the Visitor Attraction Monitor 2001 survey on the impact of FMD on attraction operations (Moffat Centre/ VisitScotland 2002). This event had both an immediate effect on attractions facing closure or restrictions on access. Knock-on impacts were also seen, with visitors choosing to avoid visiting certain areas of the countryside altogether, and going to city-located attractions instead. The Visitor Attraction Barometer, recording sample figures on a monthly basis during the main season is a representative survey produced by the Moffat Centre for VisitScotland (Moffat Centre / VisitScotland 2001). The sample of 330 attractions (of a total stock of approximately 1000), provides a useful barometer of visitation reported within 2-3 weeks of the end of each month. This survey showed the particular impact of FMD early on in the season. The chart reproduced below shows seasonality measured during the first 9 months of 2001. FMD had its greatest impact at the start of 2001 on specific attractions. The sample used in the Visitor Attraction Barometer charted this effect between January and October comparing the % change in visitor figures between 2000 and 2001 on a monthly basis.

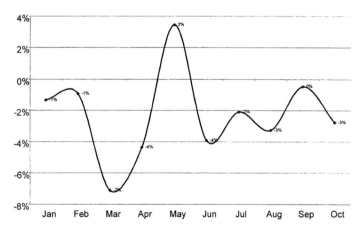

Chart 4.1 Percentage change in visitation of Scottish visitor attractions 2000-2001 (Moffat Centre/VisitScotland 2002)

In analysis of the impacts attraction closure due to FMD was examined. Table 4.1 shows the impact of the sample evaluated at the end of the period.

Affected by FMD	Sites	Average days closed
Yes	109	59
No	441	0
Sample: 550		

Table 4.1 Attraction sites effected by FMD 2001 (Moffat Centre/VisitScotland 2002)

Approximately 20% of those attractions responding were affected by FMD restrictions, causing the attraction to close for one or more days. The average number of days closed was around 60 days. Evidence emerged that geographical location was a key variable in impact. Accordingly this area was examined across the monthly survey producing the results detailed in the table below.

Location	Sites	Average days closed
Rural	79	61
Seaside	18	63
Urban	11	37
Sample: 108 + 1 farm attraction in City location		

Table 4.2 Attraction sites closed by location (Moffat Centre/ VisitScotland 2002)

Restrictions placed on tourists visiting certain geographic locations affected rural sites greatest. As a consequence such rural sites closed for two months or more on average. Urban attractions saw less restrictions, though those on the edge of towns which were in proximity to restricted countryside areas (e.g. Country Parks) did see access closed for around one month on average.

Location	Sites	Average visitors 2000	Average visitors 2001	% change
Rural	67	28,975	24,984	-14%
Seaside	15	15,309	14,328	-6%
Urban	11	135,121	119,911	-11%

Table 4.3 Movements in Visitation to Attractions by Geographical Location (Moffat Centre/ VisitScotland 2002)

The change seen in average number of visitors to attractions in specific locations shows more clearly the impact, which FMD had on the sector. Rural attractions saw the average number of visitors drop between 2000 and 2001 by -14%. The impact was much less severe in Seaside locations where alternative attractions are available in close proximity to those, which did suffer from restrictions on opening.

Category	Sites	Average visitors 2000	Average visitors 2001	% change
Castle/Fort	16	14075	11766	-16%
Distillery/Vineyard/Brewery	1	500	1500	200%
Museum/Art Gallery	5	3605	2681	-26%
Garden	11	10669	9796	-8%
Heritage/Visitor Centre	12	28190	22181	-21%
Historic House/Palace	6	12769	12001	-6%
Historic Monument/ Archaeological Site	10	11703	11613	-1%
Other Historic Property	1	1009	817	-19%
Safari Park/Zoo/Aquarium/ Aviary	3	43765	32020	-27%
Farm/Rare Breeds/Farm Animals	7	25421	14414	-43%
Nature Reserve/Wetlands/ Wildlife Trips	4	7393	9014	22%
Steam/Heritage Railways	1	2125	1435	-32%
Other Historic/Scenic Transport Operator	1	3000	3000	0%
Place of Worship	1	67750	66820	-1%
Industrial or Craft Workplace	2	27218	22043	-19%
Other	4	31524	26701	-15%
Country Park	9	252343	224082	-11%

Table 4.4 Analysis of sites which indicated they had been affected by FMD restrictions/closures during 2001(Moffat Centre / VisitScotland 2002).

Although the sample sizes are not wholly representative, an indication of the effects of FMD can be seen on attraction categories when broken down. The attractions analysed were those falling into areas that had restrictions placed on them, and so a clear impact on individual countryside locations can begin to be built up.

Responding to market downturn: case analysis

In the attempt to learn from the FMD crisis and consider the most appropriate utilisation of funds this section briefly analyses expenditure and impact of one approach that trades on the logic of businesses working together to improve performance in a beleaguered tourism sector.

Case Analysis: Glasgow's Leading Attractions – Marketing Consortia of Visitor Attractions

Examples of alliances of former competitors are now much more common amongst operators and examples exist in various service sectors from hospitals (Cardwell and Bolton 1996) to retailers and wholesalers (Hogarth Scott, 1999). Fundamentally a strategic alliance is defined as:

> Co-operation between two or more companies, whereby each partner seeks to add to its competencies by combining some resource with those of its partners. (Boer, 1992, pp. 13-14)

Such networking and joint development working across political or economic boundaries was seen as highly positive and favoured by senior politicians in Scotland at the time of the FMD outbreak (Alexander 2001). Such thinking fits with an established literature on strategic alliances in difficult environments (Porter 1995).

Glasgow's leading economic development agency, Scottish Enterprise Glasgow, was faced with an attraction industry request for assistance in developing a market network in the autumn of 2001. Despite some evidence of displacement to urban locations such as Glasgow the Enterprise Company was convinced by the business case and targeted an emergent network, Glasgow's Leading Attractions, for assistance (via its FMD intervention funds). Accordingly, around thirty city attractions were invited to join the network and initially some nineteen chose to do so. The local Area Tourist Board partnered them in this effort which brought the key City Centre Tourist Information Centre in as a partner.

The attraction offer was based around discount and value offers. In a city where many of the major attractions do not charge admission multi-entry tickets and city pass schemes were unsuitable. In such cases offers on retail or catering had to partner paid admission operations charges upon entry. The primary development was a brochure produced in striking colours that comprised a map with locations and tear off (perforated) discount vouchers.

Distribution and effective circulation of any brochure is key and this was the next major task. This was achieved via all members displaying the brochure and cross marketing colleagues but also via business-to-business marketing. Relationships with Glasgow Restaurateurs Association, Glasgow Hotelier's Association and Glasgow Retailer's Association saw brochures displayed in food operations, hotel bedrooms and retailers throughout the city. It is notable that within four months of launch a number of participating attractions were receiving up to 800 voucher returns per month. Whilst it is difficult to ascertain whether the discount reason is the only reason for visitation (without the development of a control group) some competing market indications are useful. Edinburgh City centre over the same period had not seen the buoyant attraction performance of Glasgow achieved in late 2001 and early 2002 (Moffat Centre / VisitScotland 2002).

As the season progressed a further five major paid admission attractions joined the group and further innovative marketing was undertaken. Distribution and partnership with Scotland's leading tabloid (high volume readership) newspapers was undertaken over a six-week period involving supermarket, newsstand, and newspaper shop promotion. An alliance with the City Convention Bureau ensured that GLA leaflets were present in all conference delegate packs for visitors coming to the city and the travel industry was targeted. A jointly hired exhibition stand at the leading Scottish International travel Fair, Expo 2002, was actioned. The cost (normally prohibitive) to one operator was now shared between the network. Good pre-show preparation and joint activity by all members resulted in the GLA stand receiving the greatest number of pre-scheduled meeting of the many stands at the exhibition. Travel companies and tour operators were very interested in being able to negotiate simultaneously with a network that represented over 80% of the attraction stock of a city.

Other innovative marketing campaigns have targeted local residents via retail crèche provision, treasure hunts for children, alumni networks of Universities and Colleges. The next stage of marketing features key calendar events: Half-term holidays, Halloween, Christmas, and e-marketing initiatives. Consequently the GLA network has become highly independent and under its own chairmanship is looking to reprint leaflets, develop web links and build strategic marketing for 2003. A value-added network has been declared in a highly competitive environment. The relative cost to the Local Enterprise Companies consisted of a 50% contribution to leaflet design and printing costs (the remainder being covered by the attractions themselves) and administrative and consultancy charges. Thus for a total contribution of £14,000 from Scottish Enterprise Glasgow, a significant impact was created at 24 visitor attractions that in major part will have contributed to the city's improved attraction visitation performance over the year 2001. Conservatively it is estimated that the GLA campaign has increased visitation at attractions by 30-35,000 visitors over the year 2001. This estimate is based on discount voucher redemption and attraction data from member surveys.

Lessons from the case analysis and the FMD intervention funding

It is difficult to draw major conclusions from what is basically a pilot evaluation of one approach to intervention and use of public sector funding following the FMD disease. However, what is clearly apparent is that the funds allocated by the Scottish Executive to a range of government organisations lacked co-ordination. A range and variety of intervention and assistance programmes were created often without cross- agency consultation. Furthermore, the lack of a rapid, co-ordinated and clearly led response was apparent in a sector that was bereft of any form of disaster or contingency plan. The exception at a local authority level was Dumfries and Galloway, which had a sophisticated plan and clear management system in place for agriculture and transport. This was a direct result of having faced the Lockerbie disaster some years previously. Calls for the need for contingency planning have also been made by other inquiries into the FMD crisis (see for example RSE, 2002).

The FMD outbreak demonstrated very clearly the interdependence of the different industries that constitute the rural economy and most particularly the significant relationship between agriculture and tourism. Furthermore impacts at a city level were evident and pointed to a level of unsystematic response. Emergency planning was not in place for the tourism sector. Clear leadership and co-ordinated responses were not always present. It is now vital that such disaster plans are put in place for the tourism sector to ensure that responses are rapid and cost effective as well as being user friendly.

Considerable pressure is now being brought to bear on the Scottish Executive to review all Scottish Councils emergency plans to ensure they adequately cover the action required in an FMD outbreak (RSE, 2002). Such plans must incorporate the tourism sector as an integral part of the rural economy. Furthermore, detailed project analysis on tourism assistance (as summarised in the pilot case related to visitor attractions reported above) is vital to ensure that decision-making and intervention is appropriate and cost-effective. Such detailed evaluation across all agencies is vital if an emergency plan for tourism in Scotland is to be effective and the lessons learned are to be replicated in other parts of the world.

References

Alexander W (2001)
    www.renfrewshirecvs.org/Documents/ENTERPRISE%20Stratedgy.htm
BMRB Research (2002) *The United Kingdom Tourism Survey UKTS 2001*,
    BMRB International.
Boer A (1992) 'The Banking Sector and Small Firms Failure in the UK Hotel and
    catering Industry' in *International Journal of Contemporary Hospitality
    Management*, Vol. 4 no 2 pp13-16
Cardwell R and Bolton D (1996) 'Strategic Alliances in Hospitals: a US
    perspective' in *Journal of Management in Medicine,* Vol. 10, no 9 pp40-46,
    MCB University Press
DEFRA website www.defra.gov.uk/footand mouth/newcounties/county.asp
Hall D (2001) FMD – view from Scotland. *Tourism – Journal of the Tourism
    Society*, Issue 110, p.6.
Hogarth Scott S (1999) 'Retail – supplier partnerships: hostages to fortune or the
    way forward for the Millennium' in *British Food Journal* Vol101 No 9 pp
    668-682, Emerald, London.
Moffat Centre / VisitScotland (2002) *The Scottish Visitor Attraction Monitor
    2001*, Glasgow.
Moffat Centre / VisitScotland (2001) *The Scottish Visitor Attraction Barometer
    2001* (April to October editions), Glasgow
NFO System 3 (2001) *Tourism Visitor Survey*
NOMIS (1999) *Census of Employment,* Office for National Statistics
Porter M (1990) *The Competitive Advantage of Nations*, Harvard Business Press,
    Harvard
Royal Society of Edinburgh (2002) *Inquiry into Foot and Mouth Disease in
    Scotland*, July, Edinburgh
Scottish Executive (2000) *A New Strategy for Scottish Tourism*, Scottish
    Executive, Edinburgh
Scottish Executive (2002) *Tourism Framework for Action 2002-2005*, Scottish
    Executive, Edinburgh
VisitScotland (2002) *Tourism in Scotland 2001*, Edinburgh, VisitScotland

The table below shows the number of confirmed foot and mouth disease cases in the UK as at 11 March 2002.

Name	Description	No. of Infected Premises
ENGLAND		**1726**
CTB		**893**
Cumbria County	County	893
EETB		**10**
Essex	County	9
Thurrock	Unitary authority	1
HETB		**216**
Derbyshire	County	8
Gloucestershire	County	72
Herefordshire	Unitary authority	44
Leicestershire	County	6
Northamptonshire	County	1
Shropshire	County	15
Staffordshire	County	45
Telford and Wrekin	Unitary authority	1
Worcestershire	County	22
Warwickshire	County	2
LTB		**1**
London	Greater London Authority	191
NTB		**8**
Darlington	Unitary authority	85
Durham	County	6
Newcastle Upon Tyne	Metropolitan District	
Northumberland	County	88
Stockton-on-Tees	Unitary authority	4

Name	Description	No. of Infected Premises
NWTB		**71**
Cheshire	County	16
Lancashire	County	53
Warrington	Unitary authority	1
Wigan	Metropolitan District	1
SEETB		**5**
Kent	County	3
Medway	Unitary authority	2
STB		**2**
Oxfordshire	County	2
SWT		**198**
City of Bristol	Unitary authority	1
Cornwall	County	4
Devon	County	173
Somerset	County	8
S. Gloucestershire	Unitary authority	3
Wiltshire	County	9
YTB		**139**
Bradford	Metropolitan District	5
Leeds	Metropolitan District	1
North Yorkshire	County	133

Name	Description	No. of Infected Premises
N. IRELAND		
SCOTLAND		**187**
Dumfries and Galloway	Unitary authority	176
Scottish Borders	Unitary authority	11
WALES		**113**
Caerphilly	Unitary authority	2
Newport	Unitary authority	3
Neath Port Talbot	Unitary authority	1
Powys – Powys	Unitary authority	70
Rhondda, Cynon, TAFF	Unitary authority	1
Monmouthshire	Unitary authority	23
Isle of Anglesey	Unitary authority	13

A Very Pleasant Melancholy in Paradise: Voyeurs, anthropologists and volcano tourism on Montserrat

Jonathan Skinner

> In the eighteenth century graveyards produced meditations on mortality, a pleasant melancholy in which regret for the anonymous departed was often accompanied by a secret satisfaction that one was not yet one of them. (Seaton 1996a: 241)

This chapter uses an anthropological perspective to look at tourism developments on Montserrat, a British colony in the Eastern Caribbean seeking to find her niche in the tourism economy. In the late-twentieth century and early twenty-first, Montserrat has marketed herself as 'The Way The Caribbean Used To Be' (Montserrat Dept. of Tourism 1993, 2001a), often referred to on-island and off-island as 'The Emerald Isle of the Caribbean' (Fergus 1992). These soubriquets represent the Montserrat Tourist Board's work to construct the island as a tourist destination, as an up-market 'colonial' residential tourist location that shuns backpackers and short-term visitors. This contentious and exclusive branding of the island - colonial niche tourism, one might say - has had a serious cultural effect upon the West Indian population whose identity has altered such that now many of them think of themselves, or are taught and socialised into thinking of themselves, as 'the Black Irish of the Caribbean'. In other words, establishing a tourist guest niche can entail disestablishing a local host identity.

Since 1995 the island has suffered an on-going volcanic eruption. Some have turned this natural disaster (that resulted in an initial voluntary tourist evacuation and local relocation to the north of the island) into a man-made venture (or rather, adventure) tourist attraction. This exemplifies a niche tourism transition, re-branding or re-focusing from a colonial tourism into a 'volcano tourism' or 'disaster tourism' niche: one that includes the existing colonial niche. To explore this new niche tourism on Montserrat fully, this chapter begins with a consideration of niche tourism in general. It then goes on to look at 'volcano tourism' on Montserrat as a weak variant of dark tourism. This second example of niche tourism on Montserrat is both contentious and 'edgy'.

Colonial niche and volcano tourism context

Essentially, volcano tourism is an example of niche tourism, just like 'the visit to the literary destination', or specific breaks such as 'walking and cycling weekends', 'garden tours' around Dumfries and Galloway for example, and 'culture and heritage' outings. According to Carlisle (2000), the word 'niche' refers, in the context of tourism, to the opposite of mass-market tourism. Thus, in his example of tourism to Palau, a tiny Pacific island country, the 'niche tourism' term is synonymous with small or low-key tourism. Carlisle gives us no threshold figure, however, for when a niche is no longer a niche. Hiller (1978: 14), for example, refers to all tourism in the Caribbean as 'sun lust tourism' which could be interpreted as a niche form of tourism for millions. The niche, then, is often used as a relative and evaluative term, generally referring to that which is not considered mass tourism. It can also refer to a 'tourism segment', to a special or distinctive form of tourism which has evolved or been constructed. Since 1961, 'book tourism' has been pioneered in Hay on Wye, a targeted niche form of tourism which has resulted in excess of 1 million book tourist visits per year (Seaton 1996b). Hedonism II is a tourist resort in Negril, Jamaica, which advertises Nude Week amongst other 'sex tourism' promotions (see also Pruitt 1995 on 'romance tourism' in the Caribbean). 'Solidarity tourism' (Beirman 2002: 175) is a less contrived form of niche tourism found in Israel as Jews return to the country during times of crisis which have discouraged general tourist visitors. Both Dominica and Montserrat in the Caribbean have been associated with 'alternative tourism' according to the geographer Weaver (1995) - using an expression often indicating 'ecotourism'. Cuba, by contrast, is becoming a specialist 'dance tourism' destination for salsa and modern jive (Danceholidays 2003: 24). Finally, Hirose (1982), presents an interesting case of the volcanic eruption of Mt Usu in Northern Japan covering traditional tourist destinations in ash, discouraging many tourists from these destinations but simultaneously attracting tourists to the volcano itself - tourists who are happy to visit the volcano by day so long as they can sleep the night away somewhere else (ibid: 90). This, I would describe as an example of 'volcano tourism'.

It is perhaps a little ironic that in this post-industrial and postmodern tourist age of play and pastiche, an increasingly safe 'risk society' but one prone to complex disasters - one of blurred boundaries and de-differentiation - we should, as tourists, turn to the tourist niche. In the Caribbean, to develop a regional example, niche tourism is alive and well even in the dissimilar marketing of each island: Antigua is marketed as 'the island with 365 beaches' - one for every day of the year; Guyana is the land of rivers and gold; Trinidad is the home of calypso and carnival; and St. Lucia is known for its volcanic Pitons which tower over the island and where tourists can be driven through some of the steaming volcanic craters. The island of Montserrat, referred to above by Weaver as a place of 'alternative tourism', is currently living up to his niche tourism label, but for very different reasons to those articulated in his 1995 publication as I will go on to show.

I was working as an anthropologist on Montserrat in 1995 when the island, island life and island tourism changed dramatically and forever. The island is a small British colony in the Eastern Caribbean close to Antigua - one of the Caribbean's mass tourism destinations. The island was approximately 40 square miles and had a population of 12,000, the majority of which were descendants of slaves who were bought and brought to the island as slaves from West Africa to work on sugar and cotton plantations. The island also had several hundred residential tourists - snowbirds - with exclusive villas set about the island in what some locals referred to as 'white ghettoes'. I was investigating Montserratian and British identity, the expressions (primarily through the performing arts such as poetry and calypso) and the clashes (trade union struggles, development morays, and the differences between the indigenous and expatriates).

The island was, for me, what Bourdieu (1984: 11) has described as 'a locus of struggle'. To give a tourism-related example of contest, whilst on Montserrat, the Montserrat Tourist Board was pursuing a long-term advertising campaign promoting the island as 'The Way The Caribbean Used To Be' (Montserrat Dept. of Tourism 1993). This label harped back to an era of tropical luxury and colonial service in the nostalgic imagination of the potential tourist, but it also called up an historical reality of brutal slave exploitation for many reluctant hosts. Professor Sir Howard Fergus, Montserratian Deputy Governor of the island when His Excellency The Governor was off-island, and University of the West Indies resident academic and 'barbarian poet', wrote the following warning to the expatriate residential tourists in his poem 'This Land Is Mine' (1978: 23, l.1-4):

Take it easy, stranger man
In your imperious drive
To build an ivory wall
In my black sand

Fergus was articulating a Montserratian - indigenous - 'black' reaction to the invasion of wealthy 'whites'. As Weaver (1995: 598-599) notes, and I paraphrase: the development of this 'residential tourism' on Montserrat has had profound social, economic and agrarian effects - the tourist industry developed on Montserrat in the 1960s from one hotel (founded in 1908) to 225 foreign-owned houses and two beach hotels by 1972. Throughout the 1960s the Montserrat Government subdivided and sold off a number of estates on the island to foreign controlled businesses. By the end of 1970, Weaver notes that 22.8% of the island was held by tourist companies - 0.8% of which was held by Montserratian-based companies. By the early 1980s tourism stay-overs had risen from several hundred (pre-1960) to 16,000/yr. Furthermore, the tourist sector had come to dominate the island economy, providing up to 25% of island employment, with visitor expenditure contributing up to 21% of the island's GDP. Related to this growth and reliance upon the tourism industry are the statistics for agriculture on Montserrat: in 1962 the GDP based on agriculture was 39%, a figure that had dropped to 4% by 1984. Clearly, the decades following the 1950s saw a significant shift in Montserrat's economic structure as the island was integrated into 'the pleasure periphery' (Turner & Ash 1975): leisure-supply regions such as the Caribbean, the Mediterranean and the South Pacific.

The alternative tourism Weaver describes attracts the 'allocentric' explorer type of tourist as opposed to the placid mass tourist. There is a similarity, then, between the tourist explorer and the colonial explorer. Structural similarities continue when we introduce Harrigan's (1974) observation that the tourist estates in the Caribbean are nostalgic echoes of the slave plantations, many built out of the existing ruins. In this sense, tourism in the Caribbean has become what Lowenthal (1972: 233) predicted of it from the 1970s - a new form of dependency which reinforces old colonial habits. It is 'informal empire' (Williams 1962: 47). Whilst Weaver makes comparisons with the new and the old cultural landscapes, he shies away from referring to tourism as a new kind of sugar. Weaver (1995: 595, 603) argues that such critical attitudes - small island syndromes - have done little for the locals other than to perpetuate their underdevelopment. His stance is more moderate than those of

Guyanese Black Power leader Evan Hyde (1970: 24) who believes that 'tourism is whorism'; and *The Guardian* journalist Polly Patullo (1996: 82) who believes that the Caribbean now represents Milton's Paradise Lost, a region of disenfranchised islanders ('Like an Alien In We Own Land' as St Lucian Rohan Seon's calypso runs) with deracinated cultures left to mimic the tourist - as chronicled in Naipaul's The Mimic Men: Antigua may have her 365 public beaches, but access to many of them is strictly controlled and policed by the foreign-owned resorts. For socio-cultural anthropologists such as Malcolm Crick (1989) and Davydd Greenwood (1977), tourist 'culture carriers' - carrion, even - are the sun-tanned destroyers of culture for whom local ways are commoditised, packaged and 'sold by the pound' with the result that their local authenticity and significance are lost.

When Mount Chance began to erupt in July 1995, it did so without warning, causing mass panic and a diversity of responses arising from coming to terms with 'living with the unexpected' (see Possekel 1999; Skinner 2000). One telling reaction was an immediate statement made by The Governor of Montserrat, Frank Savage, about how the new scenario could be a stimulus for a new type of tourism on Montserrat - 'volcano tourism' (personal fieldnotes 1995). This demonstrates how by 1995 tourism had completely seeped itself into the consciousness of senior members of the island community. When the pyroclastic mud flows swept through Plymouth, the island capital, two years later - the same year in which 19 Montserratians were killed by pyroclastic flow in a modern-day Pompeii - a similar tourism-tinted statement was made in the suggestion that a new capital be constructed in the north of the island of pastel-coloured tropical-styled buildings which could be called Port Diana in memory of the recently deceased Princess. The present-day scenario is one of disaster Diaspora and development: there are some 4,000 Montserratians remaining on the island alongside a dwindling number of expatriate snowbirds and British Government and development workers. The population is just above the viability threshold for the island, with large numbers of Montserratians currently residing on neighbouring islands, in the US and in the UK (some 3,500), resettled or awaiting a safe and stable environment to return to.

For several years now the island has been divided in half with an Exclusion Zone in place in the south, a Daytime Entry Zone in the mid-west which was once a densely populated region, and an apparently Safe Zone in the remaining north of the island. Tourist visitor figures have dropped drastically since the volcano crisis began:

1993 and 1994 had 20,994 and 21,285 tourist visits respectively, and
11,186 and 14,982 excursionist visits (Montserrat Dept. of Tourism
Statistics 2001b). These figures fell to 8,703 tourist visits and 8,604
excursionist visits in 1996, figures linked with an overall drop in all
arrivals from 46,812 in 1994 to 28,780 by 1996. What is interesting
about these figures, apart from the expected decline, is the parity of
excursionist visit figures with tourist visits in 1996. The large number
of excursionists could possibly be attributed to tourists who want to
view the volcano but do not want to remain on the island for long,
rather like the phenomenon noted by Hirose above. Certainly, the
Montserrat Volcano Observatory has had to construct new viewing
areas to cater for the influx of volcano tourists.

Dark semiotics and the dis-embedded tourist

In a recent description of the contemporary tourist-scape in India, Jo
Robertson (2002: 103) notes tourists' needs to confront and
contemplate their own mortality. They flirt with death, poverty and
the struggle for life in their Calcutta 'city of sorrow' tour of the
washing areas by the river and the open-air cremations. This is
described as though the First-World tourist finds him/herself through
visiting and returning from the Third World. Their sense of reality,
connectedness, meaning and embeddedness is realised away from
home. Tourism, to articulate Giddens (1991) and MacCannell (1989),
is the mechanism by which the modern individual searches for
authenticity. But that authenticity is constructed by the tourist
industry that shapes, advertises and institutionalises 'the tourist's
gaze' according to Urry (1990). Urry (cf. 100-102; see also Feifer
1985) points to the development of the 'post-tourist' who delights in
the inauthentic, who sees 'a spectacle' and 'a package' as just that,
and who is a far cry from the Victorian 'work tourist' who toured the
factories of Paris when on leave from their own work place.

Whether serious or playful, modern or post-modern, all tourists are
naturally pre-occupied with what they see, with the interpretation
done by themselves - or others - of the sights before them. In other
words, they are semiotic voyeurs, whether real or pretend. In India,
these tourists are titillated by fragility and the struggle to survive. On
Montserrat, the tourists come to see the island with the volcano: they
are less concerned with the people than they ever were pre-1995.
Before the volcano the people and its quietness were its assets. It was
in that pre-volcano period that Fortescue (undated: 16) described

Montserrat as one of the greenest places she had ever known, a verdant, emerald green island populated by a welcoming Black Irish population:

> Montserrat is known as "the Emerald Isle" for two reasons, one of which is immediately obvious. It is the greenest place I have ever seen. [...] The less tangible aspect - and perhaps one which contributes to the magic - is the strong affiliation with Ireland. [...] There is a charm about everybody you meet which is inborn and natural, to which is added humour, warmth and curiosity.

Montserrat, 'The Emerald Isle of the Caribbean', is forever to remain in inverted commas. Montserrat, a poor copy of Ireland, The [real] Emerald Isle, is where the 'natives of Montserrat and newcomers are forging a quietly enlightened society in the Renaissance tradition' (Lord 1981: 11). By 1995, The Montserrat National Trust had just begun to institute a policy of ecotourism, but it was still the whole island ambience that was the main attraction. Post-1995, the volcano has become the major tourist attraction, dwarfing the 'friendliness' of the people. The centre of the Holiday Montserrat brochure, for example, features an article on 'Nature Tourism on Montserrat' (Anon. 2001: 10-11). There, Chances Peak is billed as one of 15 potentially active volcanoes in the Caribbean, one which has recently grown in height by 500ft, and devastated much of the south of the island.

'The devastation of burned villages will astound you, and bear witness to the frailty and vulnerability of humans at the hands of such powerful natural forces' (Anon. 2001: 10). The balance between excitement and danger, curiosity and risk, is lost in this piece that mentions human frailty but shies away from referring to the deaths of Montserratians by the volcano - characterised as 'a wonder of nature to behold' (ibid.). The danger is there to see in front of your eyes, but not for you to experience personally. This is how it is sketched out near the end of the 'nature tourism' article:

> If you are lucky enough you may witness an ash cloud or small pyroclastic flow, and thus have *the unique opportunity to experience volcanic activity, from a safe distance, of course.* If not, then you can watch videos or see images of the volcano in action at the Montserrat Volcano Observatory

(MVO) and at the Montserrat Volcano Visitor's Centre. The
MVO houses the scientists who have been monitoring the
eruption since its inception, and have provided advice to the
authorities and population. You will have the chance to tour
the observatory with an expert, who will describe the
specialised science of volcano monitoring and the chronology
of events during the history of the eruption. *Before your very
eyes, you will see the pulse of the volcano being recorded* on
seismographs, which will show the small earthquakes that are
constantly occurring, even when the volcano is in a period of
quiescence. (ibid., my emphasis)

Powerful, raw, natural and dramatic the volcano might be, but from
your viewpoint on Garibaldi Hill, chance and fate play their hands
only to lift the clouds from the volcano so that you can see the
destroyed former capital. There, nature is scientifically framed from a
safe distance, enough to titillate but not to terrorise. The volcano is
even anthropomorphised into a living throbbing creature (amongst
some refugees it is known simply as 'The Beast'). The article
continues: 'Perhaps in future one will be able to drive through
deserted villages, evacuated in 1997 but now blanketed in grey ash, or
visit newly created beaches formed of volcanic sand' (ibid.). Indeed,
when visiting Montserrat during the Millennium celebrations, I found
that there is an illicit trade in guiding around the prohibited zones of
the capital the less risk-averse - the souvenir hunters and 'I was there'
photographers. It was also still possible to drive through some of the
Daytime Entry Zone which had an eerily deserted science-fiction
quality about it, more than 'abandoned and forlorn' (Anon. 2001: 11)
as the article declares. The last time I had been there, it had been
teeming with life and liquor.
    'Dark tourism' is how Lennon and Foley (2000) coin fatal
attractions, the modern pilgrimage sites in our de-sacralised world.
The dark aspects of human nature both repel and attract, resulting in
tourist destinations such as the Gestapo Museum in Berlin, Ground
Zero at Hiroshima (and New York), JFK's murder site, battlefields
and cemeteries. They include - in this quite literally 'questionable'
form of niche tourism - the demilitarised zone in Cyprus which has
become a tourist performance arena with 'dark edges' (Lennon &
Foley 2000: 129) to it, and Sarajevo where US tourists go for living
history tours of where 200,000 people lost their lives. We might refer
to the Montserrat case as one of a natural dark tourism. It is not

explicitly an example of 'thanotourism', 'travel to a location wholly, or partially motivated by the desire for actual or symbolic encounters with death' (Seaton 1996a: 240). Phenomenologically, the tourists and excursionists (not to mention those visiting Antigua who go on helicopter tours to see the volcano from the air or those on cruise ships who no longer berth at Montserrat but make sure to sail around the south of the island so that tourists can view the volcano at a remove) are attracted to volcano tourism for spiritual and earthly reasons. It is an opportunity to re-connect with life; it is escapism from a sense of alienation and from the suspicion of pseudo-events (cf. Boorstin 1964; Cohen 1979). For many, the nostalgia for a cultural landscape of a bygone plantation era has been superseded by a desire for the innocent beauty of a primitive geological landscape.

Marketing Montserrat and the missionary's position

Generally, nature's wilderness is a profane space, so tourism sociologist Erik Cohen (1978: 216) notes. It is the garden that is humanised and sacred, the constructed paradise. On Montserrat, a Caribbean and emerald paradise of gardens and tropical forests (and now tranches of devastation) all is made sacred by residential tourists, excursionists and locals. Amongst a devoutly religious population, Montserrat is still an island Eden, no less so for the American missionary turned 'videographer' David Lea. Mr. Lea and his family have been proselytizing on the island for the past twenty years. Their parish is Montserrat and the neighbouring islands which they can reach during their regular religious TV and radio programmes. When the volcano crisis began in July 1995, however, Mr Lea shifted his activities to become the island's self-appointed volcano videographer. He has turned his filming and broadcasting skills to documenting the volcano, and producing and selling educational videos. On his 'Price of Paradise' website, maintained by Living Letters Ministries, some seven videos are listed. The early editions chronicle the volcano and its devastation whilst the latter editions include histories of Montserrat, a field trip with the former head scientist of the Montserrat Volcano Observatory, and interviews with Montserratians. Volume Three, for example, has 'many interviews with the people of Montserrat you [sic] feel like you've really been there.' Volume Five is billed as follows:

It takes you on a drive from Salem Village, on the edge of the
unsafe zone, through the winding mountain roads into the busy
and beautiful North. Along the way, you will meet and hear
from the folks who've "stayed." Their positive attitudes and
resilient spirits create a montage of all that makes Montserrat
the special place that it shall always be.
(www.priceofparadise.com, 14/9/01)

Extracts from Volume One are particularly well known and have been
picked up on American (*National Geographic* and *Discovery*) and
British television. One of them shows Mr Lea in the Exclusion Zone,
at the top of Chances Peak, filming the crater of the volcano just as it
begins an eruption. Mr Lea then films himself running bare-chested
down the side of the mountain and, later, commenting upon the
"awesome" majesty of God's creation and powers, sitting in darkness
with a crucifix of light bulbs shining behind him. Later on there is
even footage of Mr Lea trying to drive his two children through a
manned Exclusion Zone barrier, giving the viewer the impression that
he believes in divine providence. Despite the warnings of the
scientists and the restrictions enforced by The Royal Montserrat
Police, Mr Lea appears to have devolved issues of risk and control to
his God.
    On Mr Lea's web-pages he advertises Bed & Breakfast at his
house, and a special 'Volcano Island' video which explores the
complex nature of Montserrat's Andesite (black volcanic rock)
volcano dome eruption. This is alongside a proposal for a 'Volcano
Hazards' video which will feature the volcano-related deaths on
Montserrat. In his own religious and risk-oriented words, Mr Lea
writes the following:

We also plan a Volcanic Hazards video, born out of the deaths
that occurred here in Montserrat on June 25, 1997. This was a
volcanic event in which I, myself, could have perished but for
the Grace of God and a basic understanding of the very real
dangers of this type of "grey" volcano. We trust that this
hazards video will be helpful in informing people living
around other Caribbean volcanoes what the dangers are, and
the risks involved in remaining in areas that are declared
unsafe due to volcanic activity. (http://www.volcano-
island.com/cruise/, 14/9/01)

This message is followed by a tourist advertisement for a 'Volcano Island Cruise' that Mr Lea organizes throughout the Caribbean, from St. Lucia to Guadeloupe, St. Vincent and Martinique to Montserrat. For US$200 per day, tourists can 'canyon' down waterfalls and streams that follow ancient lava flows, hike, and have 'incredible adventures' from their Tall Ship. Less tastefully, the advertisement ends with the following reference:

> One of the most memorable dives is on the wrecks of Saint Pierre, Martinique. As you may know, this is where 29,000 people were killed in just a few minutes on May 8th of 1902 by a monstrous pyroclastic flow that erupted from Mt. Pelee. The ships in the harbour all sunk and this makes for one of the most interesting dive sites in all the world.
> (http://www.volcano-island.com/cruise/, 14/9/01)

The excursionists to Montserrat looking at the volcano and the capital close-up, and the videographer and missionary Mr Lea and his fellow volcano adventure tourists, participate in 'edgework' (Lyng 1990: 855), voluntary risk-taking by restless sensation-seekers negotiating their own personal boundaries between chaos and order. Lyng coined this term whilst he was writing about his five-year ethnographic study of skydivers: an inquiry into socially contradictory behaviour, namely that in a society where the public agenda is to reduce the risk of injury, some people maintain a private agenda that increases such risk. Though the volcano sensation-seekers are not in the same league as the skydivers, they do exhibit similar behaviour patterns, motivations and 'findings' - a sense of exhilaration, omnipotence, focus and 'flow'. This 'hyper-reality' is linked with the sacred and liminal time of the tourist. These mild edgeworkers - 'impulse-anchored selves' (Turner 1976) - use these edgy experiences and their tourist time to throw off the constraints and artificiality they find in ordinary social settings.

On Montserrat, controlled anarchy and carefully delineated risk have been specifically packaged for volcano tourists. The living volcano, an example of extraordinary nature, is now also available as a new tourist excursion, a 'field trip' run in conjunction between the Montserrat Volcano Observatory (MVO) and the Montserrat Tourist Board (MTB) (www.mvo.ms/Field%20Trip.html). For two days, geologists, geographers and interested amateurs are invited to learn, examine and scrutinise the volcanic deposits, landforms and impact on the island. They will witness the volcano and take its pulse as professional insiders. Subject to volcanic activity, naturally, they will 'visit the observatory and receive first-hand accounts of the latest techniques used to monitor the world's active volcanoes'; view 'spectacular photographs and video footage' of the 1995-2001 eruption; learn first-hand about the science of volcanology and the problems of crisis management on a small island from members of the MVO staff; visit the old and the new volcano domes and deposits; and collect their own samples/souvenirs.

Lyng (1990: 882) concludes his article on edgework by describing an internal shift in some of the skydivers, a collapse of the distinction between 'self' and 'environmental other' as they become self-actualised. The result can be the development of a sense of oneness with the environment. This is what Mead (1950) refers to as a loss of 'Me': it is a supra-linguistic feeling; something beyond words; an experience which cannot be conveyed but can only be sensed; a union of natural (volcanic) and man-made (tourist) pulses in an increasingly synthetic world. Whereas thanotourism can no longer remain the overt motivation for travel that it used to be in the eighteenth and nineteenth centuries (Seaton 1996a: 243), dark tourism (a strong variation) and volcano tourism (a weak variation) are flourishing as new niches. Ironically, it is through the latter practice - 'workplace tourism' - at the MVO that tourists' and excursionists' 'alienated attention' (Csikszentmihalyi & Rochberg-Halton 1981) is obviated by an 'alienated leisure' (MacCannell 1989). This, I would suggest, is a natural response to *modern-day commodity fetishism* and *tourism's experience fetishism.*

Conclusion

Montserrat's volcano tourism developed in the 1990s, during the UN 'International Decade for Natural Disaster Reduction'. It is a form of niche tourism more linked with ecotourism (pollution viewing in Sydney, Nova Scotia, a coal/steel town gone to rust) and disaster tourism (twister watching in the mid-West US) than agri-tourism (mid-California tomato farming) or sports tourism (Manchester's hosting of the 2002 Commonwealth Games). Its development shows how deep-seated tourism is in the modern consciousness. And it represents a canny marketing of the island, a re-branding from low-key, up-market residential tourism to low-key, high risk, educational and experiential volcano tourism. The shift is still pitched under the slogan 'The Way The Caribbean Used To Be', though now the emphasis is upon nostalgia for nature rather than colonialism as tourists and excursionists look to the volcano as a link to the island's 2.5 million year history. Once again, the history of suffering on the island - to which we can include those who perished by natural disaster - is glossed over. The plight of modern-day Montserratians, and their slave ancestors continues to be marginalised in favour of representations of the discovery of the island and its flora and fauna.

Though Montserrat's political economy might be absent from the representations of the island, it is the political economy of the island that has led to its volcano marketing. Volcano tourism is viewed as one of the island's business strategies; a new Montserrat Volcano Observatory is now being planned as well as a new tourist facility overlooking the old capital, Plymouth. Through volcano tourism, Montserratians are coming to terms with living with the unexpected. The responses and reactions to the initial eruption of the volcano in 1995 - those of avoidance, denial and detachment (Skinner 2000) - have given way to tales of struggle, return and survival (Skinner 2003). Now, when I return to the island, instead of panicking and dreading the eruption as I once did, I too revisit the uninhabited Daytime Entry Zone with a video camera, and pay a visit to the MVO to see the working seismographs, the volcano posters, postcards and fossilised fruit and melted bottles on display.

If, as Butler (1980) declares, all tourist destinations have their evolutionary cycles and asymptotic curves of growth and stagnation, then volcano tourist destination Montserrat is on the rise. This means, however, that niche tourism ventures are inevitably time-limited and that Montserrat cannot come to rely upon her new tourism niche. The tourist industry remains highly flexible and adaptable. It is now starting to come to terms with a complex market and general issues of disaster management (cf. Faulkner 2001). It has to because tourist destinations are by their very nature particularly vulnerable to natural disasters. These exotic, high-risk locations are often prone to hurricane, avalanche, forest fire and volcano. They are also prone to rapid re-branding and recovery: Purchase's (1999) study of tourism following a landslide in New Hampshire shows how an event can turn even the scientists into 'speculators in scenery'; and Murphy and Bailey's (1989) investigation of the consequences of the 1980 Mt St Helens eruption chronicles the successful creation of an audiovisual centre and the establishment of a 110,000 acre geological reserve which received over half a million tourist visitors in its first year of opening. The latter study also drew comparison between natural disasters and tourism cycles because of their effects on the industry. For now, Montserrat has a tourist attraction which is desirable in an 'edgy' manner. In this uncertain and unexpected time for the islanders, volcano tourism offers the island temporary economic stability. It is the second example of niche tourism on Montserrat, and its projected influence upon the islanders is yet to be felt.

Acknowledgements
I am grateful to the staff of the Montserrat Tourist Board, the Montserrat National Trust, and to Dr Fergus for their time and assistance. Their views are not necessarily reflected in this chapter for which I alone am responsible.

References

Anon. (2001), 'Nature Tourism on Montserrat: The Soufriere Hills Volcano', in *Holiday Montserrat - The Way The Caribbean Used To Be: An Official Tourist Guide of the Montserrat Dept. of Tourism*, holiday brochure, St. John's, Antigua: West Indies Publishing Ltd., 10-11.
Beirman, D. (2002), 'Marketing of tourism destinations during a prolonged crisis: Israel and the Middle East', *Journal of Vacation Marketing*, 8:2, 167-176.
Boorstin, D. (1964), *The Image: A Guide to Pseudo-Events in America*, New York: Harper & Row.
Bourdieu, P. (1984), *Homo Academicus*, Stanford: Stanford University Press.
Butler, R. (1980), 'The Concept of a Tourist Area Cycle of Evolution: Implications for Management of Resources', *Canadian Geographer*, XXXIV: 1, 5-12.
Carlisle, L. (2000), 'Niche or Mass Market? The Regional Context of Tourism in Palau', *The Contemporary Pacific*, 12:2, 415-436.
Cohen, E. (1978), 'The Impact of Tourism on the Physical Environment', *Annals of Tourism Research*, 5, 215-237.
...   (1979), 'A Phenomenology of Tourist Experiences, *Sociology*, 13, 179-201.
Crick, M. (1989),'Representations of International Tourism in the Social Sciences: Sun, Sex, Sights, Savings, and Servility', *Annual Review of Anthropology*, 18, 307-344.
Czikszentmihalyi, M. & Rochberg-Halton, E. (1981), *The Meaning of Things*, Cambridge: Cambridge University Press.
Danceholidays (2003), *Dance Around the World*, holiday brochure, Sussex: Carefree Travel (International) Limited.
Faulkner, B. (2001), 'Towards a framework for Tourism disaster management', *Tourism Management*, 22, 135-147.
Feifer, M. (1985), *Going Places*, London: Macmillan.
Fergus, H. (1978), *Green Innocence*, St. Augustine, Trinidad: Multimedia Production Centre.
...   (1992), *Montserrat - Emerald Isle of the Caribbean*, London: Macmillan Caribbean Guides.
Fortescue, E. (undated), 'The Magic of Montserrat - Edna Fortescue explores the 'Emerald Isle', *BWIA SUNJET* (British West Indies Airlines) in-flight

magazine (probably), pp.16-17, no other references available.

Giddens, A. (1991), *Modernity and Self-Identity: Self and Society in the Late Modern Age*, Stanford: Stanford University Press.

Greenwood, D. (1977), 'Culture by the Pound: An Anthropological Perspective on Tourism as Cultural Commoditization', in *Hosts and Guests - The Anthropology of Tourism*, V. Smith (ed.), Philadelphia: University of Pennsylvania, 37-52.

Harrigan, N. (1974), 'The Legacy of Caribbean History and Tourism', *Annals of Tourism Research,* 2:1, 13-25.

Hiller, H. (1978), 'Sun Lust Tourism in the Caribbean', *Caribbean Review*, 7, 12-15.

Hirose, H. (1982), 'Volcanic eruption in Northern Japan', *Disasters*, 6:2, 89-91.

Hyde, E. (1970), 'Tourism Is Whorism', *Time*, 3 August, 24.

Lennon, J. & Foley, M. (2000), *Dark tourism: the attraction of death and disaster*, London: Continuum.

Lord, J. (1981), 'Antigua and Montserrat - Why Canadians are choosing the little Leewards as their home away from home', in-flight magazine, *Wardair World*, Spring, pp.8-11.

Lowenthal, D. (1972), *West Indian Societies*, Oxford: Oxford University Press.

Lyng, S. (1990), 'Edgework: A Social Psychological Analysis of Voluntary Risk Taking', *American Journal of Sociology*, 95:4, 851-886.

MacCannell, D. (1989), *The Tourist - A New Theory of the Leisure Class*, New York: Schocken Books Inc..

Mead, G. (1950), *Mind, Self, and Society*, edited by C. Morris, Chicago: University of Chicago Press.

Montserrat Dept. of Tourism (1993), *Holiday Montserrat - The Way The Caribbean Used To Be: An Official Tourist Guide of the Montserrat Dept. of Tourism 2001-2002*, holiday brochure, St. John's, Antigua: West Indies Publishing Ltd..

...   (2001a), *Holiday Montserrat - The Way The Caribbean Used To Be: An Official Tourist Guide of the Montserrat Dept. of Tourism 1993/94*, holiday brochure, St. John's, Antigua: West Indies Publishing Ltd..

...   (2001b), *Montserrat Tourism Statistics*, unpublished figures courtesy of Ms E. Cassell.

Murphy, P. & Bailey, R. (1989), 'Tourism and Disaster Planning', *Geographical Review*, 79:1, 36-46.

Patullo, P. (1996), *Last Resorts - The Cost of Tourism in the Caribbean*, London: Cassell.

Possekel, A. (1999), *Living with the Unexpected: Linking Disaster Recovery to Sustainable Development on Montserrat*, London: Springer-Verlag.

Pruitt, D. (1995), 'For Love and Money - Romance Tourism in Jamaica', *Annals of Tourism Research*, 22:2, 422-440.

Purchase, E. (1999), *Out of Nowhere: Disaster and Tourism in the White Mountains*, Baltimore: John Hopkins University Press.

Robertson, J. (2002), 'Anxieties of Imperial Decay: Three Journeys in India', in *In Transit: Travel, Text, Empire*, H. Gilbert & A. Johnston (eds), New York: Peter Lang Publishing Inc., 103-124.

Seaton, A. (1996a), 'Guided by the Dark: from thanatopsis to thanotourism', *International Journal of Heritage Studies*, 2:4, 234-244.

...   (1996b), 'Reports – Hay on Wye, the mouse that roared: book towns and rural tourism', *Tourism Management*, 17:5, 379-382.

Skinner, J. (2000), 'The eruption of Chances Peak, Montserrat, and the narrative containment of risk', in *Risk Revisited*, P. Caplan (ed.), London: Pluto Press, 156-183.

...   (2003), 'Anti-social "social development"? The DFID approach and the 'indigenous' of Montserrat', *Negotiated Development*, J. Pottier, A. Bicker and P. Sillitoe (eds.), London: Pluto Press (in press), 98-120.

Turner, L. & Ash, J. (1975), *The Golden Hordes: International Tourism and the Pleasure Periphery*, London: Constable and Company.

Turner, R. (1976), 'The Real Self: From Institution to Impulse', *American Journal of Sociology*, 81, 989-1016.

Urry, J. (1990), *The Tourist's Gaze - Leisure and Travel in Contemporary Societies*, London: Sage Publications.

Weaver, D. (1995), 'Alternative Tourism in Montserrat', *Tourism Management*, 16:8, 593-604.

Williams, W. (1962), *The Tragedy of American Diplomacy*, New York: Delhi Publishing Company.

PART III

TOURISM AND THE NATURAL ENVIRONMENT

Chapter 12

The Niche Pastiche
Or what rural tourism is *really* about

Lesley Roberts and Derek Hall

At the threshold of the 21st century, marketing theory faces a number of challenges. The marketing concept holds that the key to an organization's success is through determination of the needs of its target markets - and this must be done more effectively and efficiently than by its competitors (Blankson and Stokes, 2002). Beneath the apparent simplicity of this statement, however, lies considerable confusion and complexity. Changing behaviour patterns, lifestyles, demographic shifts, and increasing consumer choice are some of the supposed causes of a fragmentation that have rendered consumption patterns unpredictable (Thomas, 1996). Moreover, it is increasingly recognised that consumption is less about the product/service attributes that confer tangible benefits upon the buyer than the symbolic nature of consumption that defines images and demarcates social relationships (Featherstone, 1991: 16).

The shift of focus towards the importance of the subjective in consumption conflicts with the critical realist perspective of object signification that continues to influence many consumption studies (Holt, 1995). But if one accepts the postmodern shift of emphasis from the objective to the subjective then what counts as reality can never be viewed objectively, and one thereby accepts that the world is socially constructed (Thomas, 1996). Meanings attached to actions (consumption among them) are thus as much about the perceptions of consumers as they are about the objects being consumed. What is important, therefore, is neither commodity nor consumer: but the way the one is consumed by the other (Holt, 1995; Sharpley, 2000). But much marketing and marketing research are essentially modernist in nature (Thomas, 1996; Gómez Arias & Acebrón, 2001). They are rooted in a perspective that is based on sets of assumptions about behaviour – that it is rational, consistent, planned and organised. Indeed, the entire marketing concept – customer orientation - is based on modernist assumptions that the customer can be recognized, understood and served in a consistent manner.

In their expansion of the concept, Narver and Slater (1990) state that market orientation comprises three components:

- Customer orientation (a 'sufficient' understanding of target buyers)
- Competitor orientation (understanding strengths, weaknesses and capabilities of competitors), and
- Inter-functional co-ordination (the utilization of business resources in value-adding for customers).

This expanded version of the concept reveals the same assumptions, and is therefore largely influenced by the modernist structure of marketing precedent yet it still underpins much current practice.

Despite its contemporary practical appeal, however, the fundamental usefulness of the modernist, scientific approach to marketing is now falling into question (Brown, 1995: 143; Thomas, 1996; Holt, 1997; Gómez Arias and Acebrón, 2001). Conventional wisdoms are considered less useful in the postmodern context where demands change constantly and markets become more volatile as a result. Postmodernists argue that contemporary social characteristics such as fragmentation, de-differentiation, pastiche and hyper-reality render frameworks and typologies meaningless for the marketer who must, instead, treat each marketing situation as unique (Gummesson, 1987: 19). Indeed, the marketing concept itself is deemed inappropriate in a number of contexts (Brown, 1995: 44; Harris, 1998).

This paper argues that tourism in general, and rural tourism in particular, represent contexts that challenge the 'traditional' approach to marketing. It focuses on the increasingly cited practice of niche marketing, the popular profile of which is not reflected in the marketing literature, and it argues that a better understanding of niche marketing, and its re-labeling, are required if it is to be useful in the 'rural tourism' context. The paper has 4 main aims, which are to:

1. Establish the essential characteristics of so-called 'niche' tourism markets
2. Analyse the complex nature of tourism in rural areas with particular reference to changes in demand
3. Identify an homogenization of demand in postmodern markets for tourism in rural areas that reduces the likelihood of establishing niche markets, and

4. Highlight the potential dangers, for businesses and for the environment, of continuing to label tourism in rural areas as market niches.

What are niche markets?

A number of social influences have given rise to the niche market. Technological advances, new products and services, better marketing expertise, increasing consumer discernment and power, and, latterly, growing recognition of the importance of social expression and identification through consumption have all contributed to the perception of consumer markets as divisible, distinguishable and defensible in marketing terms. The principles of segmentation, based on such premises, dominate marketing practice, and (set as it is within a modernist framework) segmentation's efficacy too has been questioned (Rapp and Collins, 1990: 3; Piercy, 1991: 15, Brown, 1995: 43: Thomas, 1996). This is not merely an intellectual debate. Within the marketing industry, segmentation and profiling techniques have been described as "pseudo-science" and "over-engineered solutions based on simplistic premises of consumer behaviour" (Titford and Clouter, 1998).

A number of features that form the modern/postmodern dichotomy are identified as fundamental contributors to social changes that render profiling and segmentation less useful than they may have been in the past. Postmodern social influences are critical to, for example, a lack of behavioural consistency in consumers that resists structured and scientific methods of data collection and analysis (Thomas, 1996). The utility-maximising, a-social individual is unlikely to help form useful theories on the nature of contemporary consumption (Urry, 1995: 131).

The questioning of segmentation as a useful means of marketing may have ramifications for market niches that often appear to be based on the same principles. Does the fragmentation and dynamism of consumption render niches obsolete too, or is it the case that the increasing diversity of markets, advanced technologies enabling new marketing approaches, and the lessening usefulness of traditional marketing approaches, make niche marketing more appropriate (Dalgic and Leeuw, 1994)?

Two key characteristics of a niche market seem to emerge from the (relatively scant) literature on the subject. On the demand side, a niche market segments its consumers into identifiable groups for targeting purposes. On the supply side, it is able to differentiate products and services from those of competitors. Thus far, niches are indistinguishable from segments.

Dalgic and Leeuw (1994) describe niche markets as:

- Of sufficient size to be potentially profitable . . .
- With no real competitors
- Having growth potential, and
- Demonstrating sufficient purchasing ability . . .
- With a need for special treatment and
- The existence of customer goodwill
- Presenting opportunities for an entrance company to exercise its superior competence.

These characteristics also may be applied to market segments, blurring attempts to distinguish between the two.

According to Davidson (cited in Moutinho, 2000: 130) clarification of a niche's existence may be achieved by answers to three questions, the responses to which must be positive if a niche exists in terms of commercial reality:

- Is the niche recognized by consumers and distributors: or is it a figment of their imagination?
- Is the niche product distinctive, and does it appeal to identifiable groups of consumers?
- Is the product priced at a premium giving an above-average profit margin?

This is, perhaps, a more useful approach, and the criterion regarding price would seem to offer a distinguishing characteristic, at least from an operational point of view. A niche that offers a distinction both recognized and valued by consumers will command a higher price that may result in a higher profit margin.

From a theoretical perspective too, a distinction can be drawn between a market segment and a niche. Although many texts on the subject (and many practitioners) view a niche as a 'super-segment', and use niche and segment interchangeably, Shani and Chalasani (1992) point out that rather than being an extension of segmentation, niche marketing is an inversion of the practice. The distinction can be drawn by focusing not on the characteristics of each, but on the philosophies that underpin them both: whereas segmentation is a top-down approach to marketing that breaks mass markets into allegedly manageable portions, 'niching' involves a bottom-up approach whereby the marketer starts by identifying the needs of a few individuals and builds on this to satisfy the needs of a group with similar demands.

Have niche markets a place in the (rural) tourism context?

In many parts of the world, rural areas have long provided the setting for recreation and tourism activities that have not always been explicitly considered to be 'rural'. In recent decades, however, there has been a greater industry awareness of a requirement to segment and brand various aspects of tourism and recreation just at a time when the relationships between such activities and their rural contexts have been changing and becoming much more complex (Roberts and Hall, 2001: 4). Until a quarter of a century or so ago, most leisure activities in rural areas were closely related to the character of the setting (Butler, 1998, Butler *et al.,* 1998), and were clearly different from those activities enjoyed in urban areas. Such 'traditional' pursuits, such as walking, picnicking, and bird watching, for example, have been categorised as relaxing, relatively passive, often individual, and reflecting a need to escape from the pressures of urban living. They offer leisure in a place and setting where physical and human elements are thought to blend in a state of harmony. Whilst such activities are still practised, Roberts and Hall (2001) argue that, more recently, many other recreational activities in rural areas have emerged that may be characterised more accurately as physically active, competitive, and prestige or fashion-related. Activities such as off-road four-wheel vehicle driving, survival games, munro-bagging, ecotourism and leisure shopping more accurately reflect an imposition of urban values on rural space to the extent that the location is far less important than the activity and in some cases, almost irrelevant to it. Alongside such changes in the nature of countryside consumption, changes in volume are also evident. Much research identifies growth in tourism and recreation in rural areas (EuroBarometer, 1998; Countryside Agency, 2000; VisitScotland, 2001). Thus greater numbers of people now consume the countryside differently from the ways relatively smaller numbers did in the past.

Postmodernism's demands on theories of consumption are that they focus on the *culture* of consumption rather than the *process* that simply derives from production (Featherstone, 1991: 13). If the importance of the products we buy lies largely in their potential as social markers, tourism marketers must focus both on tourism's social signification and on meanings attached to spaces in which these occur. Explanations of tourism consumption cannot be derived in isolation from the social relations in which they are embedded (Urry, 1995: 129). New users of the countryside are redefining what constitutes 'rurality' (Blake, 1996: 211) and there is a need to take postmodernism and the construction of the rural much more seriously (Hopkins, 1998). Contemporary social construction often transcends the countryside's tangible characteristics and qualities of open space or fresh air by representing the setting for the achievement of a range of personal goals (Roberts and Hall, 2001: 38). The need for a wider sociological approach to tourism studies has been emphasized by Sharpley (1999: 173) who argues for the recognition of broader social and cultural influences that shape consumer behaviour as a whole and influence consumption patterns. In the interests of the rural environment, therefore, and of the (often small) businesses trying to meet the needs of emerging markets, it is necessary to look beyond classical marketing theory to gain a useful understanding of 'rural tourism' consumption.

The increasing need for analysts to focus on consumption as an improved means of understanding contemporary forms of (rural) tourism demand requires a dynamic framework within which the analysis can be conducted. One such framework is suggested here as an adjunct to Lane's (1994) analysis of the urban-rural nature of tourism activities. A continuum to measure the relative importance of the countryside to the consumption of tourism in rural areas is proposed to indicate the importance of the countryside to the purpose of the trip and to tourist satisfaction (Roberts and Hall, 2001: 184. See appendix 1). The significance of the model is in its recognition of the primacy of neither tourism nor tourist types: but the ways the one is consumed by the other. This focus on forms of consumption of the countryside for purposes of tourism and recreation makes it useful for the direction it can give to policy and management decision-making. Significantly in the context of this paper, the importance of the countryside model illustrates that the likelihood of identifying a true market niche within the broad church of what we might loosely term 'rural tourism' decreases as we move away from 'traditional pursuits' such as those described above.

Research suggests that there may be identifiable market niches and 'products' with which they may be targeted at the 'pure' end of the scale, for example, for hiking or climbing trips and for conservation holidays (Greffe, 1994: Clemenson and Lane, 1997; Herries, 1998).

However, where consumers' focus is placed on the satisfaction of a personal or social need, and this may be achieved in a number of different ways with little regard to (rural) context, it becomes increasingly difficult to identify a product or experience's core value and thereby to identify a niche it may serve.

Rural tourism: or tourism in rural areas?

While the need to identify a rural 'niche' is perhaps one means whereby the industry can escape from the perceived pejorative connotation of 'mass' tourism, the potential roles of recreation and tourism in rural areas remain poorly understood. One classic general tourism motivation - the pursuit of a personalised response to emotional and social needs - has been emphasized for the rural context by Grolleau (1994: 7), and it begs recognition of much recreational consumption of the countryside for what it is – another form of mass tourism. 'Pure' forms of rural tourism constitute a lesser part of the 'rural tourism phenomenon' than does 'tourism in rural areas', and both rural industries and the rural environment are served badly by the use of a lexical style that creates perceptual barriers to a recognition of this fact. And this is more than a mere question of semantics because the labels we use influence perceptions that shape the nature of policy issues and management practices. Use of the term 'niche' suggests the existence of qualities which may be more apparent than real. For example: "rural tourists are generally not mass tourists and this reduces pressures relating to carrying capacity; the natural environment can more easily sustain smaller visitor numbers." (Killion, 2001: 179). It is important to recognise that 'rural tourism' is *not* a small-scale, low-impact phenomenon (Roberts and Hall, 2001: 219) and that, in itself, it does *not* constitute a niche within tourism markets. Rather, its contemporary consumption patterns demand a high degree of place commodification for large numbers of visitors often motivated by factors other than an interest in the countryside. Views of markets as niches divert attention away from the critical issues of appropriate management of mass visiting to rural areas.

Niches and the small business

For rural tourism businesses there are hidden dangers in looking at what appear to be niche markets but may, in reality, be vulnerable parts of a mass market (Moutinho, 2000: 130). An attempt to price at a premium a product that is, in reality, exposed to the demands of an undifferentiated market will fail - a critical fact in an industry traditionally represented as offering low value-added products (AEIDL, 1994; 21; Wanhill, 1997; Roberts and Hall, 2001: 206). Additionally, a great deal of time may be wasted trying to communicate a distinctiveness that does not exist in consumers' minds. The emergence of a new consumerism, more closely related to social identity and status message, has complicated our understanding of both markets and products. The consumer search for experience, too, provides challenges. A tourist seeking thrill and excitement may find this both in white water rafting and in dune buggy racing thus rendering the two experiences interchangeable. In this way, products lose their former distinctions, acquire more substitutes, and demonstrate an homogeneity rather than the distinctiveness required for the establishment of a niche market. It would seem, therefore, that although some 'traditional' markets may still provide an operator with a true market niche, the essential characteristics of niche markets are met by few tourism offerings within the broader phenomenon of tourism in rural areas.

Additionally, even where it is appropriate, niche marketing is an expensive process requiring a level of marketing expertise often not possessed by small businesses in the tourism sector (Hjalager, 1996; McKercher and Robbins, 1998; Clarke, 1999). Niche markets are not easily identifiable in their infancy, moreover, (McKenna, 1998) making it even more difficult for small business operators to understand the markets within which they operate.

Traditional marketing is a deliberate and planned process that proceeds carefully from an identification of markets and market needs whereas small businesses often work informally and in unplanned ways that emanate from the intuition and energy often of one person. It is perhaps therefore unsurprising that owners of micro and small businesses generally appear to give marketing a low priority compared with other business functions regarding it as the preserve of larger concerns (Blankson and Stokes, 2002). In practice, therefore, if not in theory, many of the dimensions of a traditional marketing orientation may not be applicable in the small business sector (Harris, 1998).

Where this leaves tourism marketers and developers . . .

Despite the above observations, it is generally agreed that there is a positive correlation between a business's market orientation and its performance, and it is neither theoretically satisfactory nor commercially useful to suggest that, as postmodernism reflects only subjectivity and uncertainty, tourism marketing, especially for small rural businesses, need not be attempted. Better use of marketing can reduce the isolation of small rural businesses and enable them to use resources more effectively (Clarke, 1999: 210). Postmodernists argue that frameworks and typologies that have their roots in the theories of modernity offer nothing to today's tourism marketer.   But the apparently persuasive powers of the niche marketing concept make it difficult to argue its demise particularly where no clear alternative can be suggested. Marketing research is an ongoing operation, however, and it is therefore capable of looking and adapting to future needs. It is anticipated that more human-orientated research methodologies, such as ethnography, will be employed to understand emerging consumer issues, not as a replacement for traditional qualitative techniques, but as a supplement (Malhotra and Peterson, 2001). And whether merely recognition of post-modern influences or a denial of absolute truth, the postmodernist approach is likely to lead researchers to a re-examination of some of the main assumptions that underpin current research agendas (ibid).

Other writers offer new ways of looking at markets and marketing research.   Shani   and   Chalasani   (1992),   with   their   bottom-up perspective on niching, suggest that niche marketing and relationship marketing are promising strategies to deal with fragmented markets as alternatives to segmentation. They argue that the two strategies might complement each other in the creation of a marketing tool to deal with a turbulent business environment.

Currently, the consumption of tourism is an inchoate process (Urry, 1995: 131) because the products and services sold (the bed, the ticket or the meal) are often incidental to the tourist experience. Pine and Gilmore (1998, 1999) take us beyond the provision of goods and services however, towards recognising *experience* as a distinct economic offering. Their basic premise is that experiences represent an existing but previously unarticulated genre of economic output that have the potential to distinguish business offerings. As an economic offering, experiences can add value to a business's goods and services, and are distinct from both. The customer who buys a service buys a set of intangible activities carried out on her/his behalf. The purchase of an experience, on the other hand, buys time enjoying a series of memorable events that engage the consumer in a personal way (Pine and Gilmore, 1999: 30). The term *mass customisation* is well understood in goods markets where standard goods are produced that are later modified to meet the individual needs of a consumer. Standard services, too, can be customised to meet particular needs. But true customisation should provide more than consumer choice. It should be customer-specific, designed to meet specific needs, and singular in its purpose, ie be exactly what the customer wants (Pine and Gilmore, 1999: 70). There are, therefore, different ways of perceiving markets that permit and even encourage a sideways approach to the marketing of tourism experiences that may reveal new means by which rural visitors can be encouraged to engage with the natural environment.

It has been identified that visitor consumption of the countryside takes many forms but can be broadly divided into traditional rural tourism and contemporary tourism in rural areas. It may be generally assumed that rural tourism is concerned with what Urry (1991, 1995) refers to as the 'romantic' tourist gaze – something to be experienced in relative solitude, providing an authenticity for the visitor. Rural areas have less commonly been associated with Urry's 'collective gaze' (ibid), a gaze necessitating the presence of large numbers of people. But if we consider the bustling market town or farmers' market, agricultural shows or one of the increasing number of rural events such as the Dovedale Dash cross country event or spectating at the mountain stages of the Tour de France then we can see that the collective gaze has a relevance for rural visiting too. Although different in both nature and scale, both traditional and contemporary forms of consumption converge in the creation of a tourist region. A region needs to attract a sufficient number of visitors to provide markets for supporting goods and services, and it needs to provide signs to direct visitors to the different kinds of gaze and to a number of activities that, together, form the basis of a range of visitor experiences.

Small businesses in rural areas must work in collaboration with each other in the development of a critical mass of attractions and a 'tourism region' (Fagence, 1993). Niche marketing, with its emphasis on distinction for competitive advantage, may encourage local competition rather than collaboration, and its application within many rural contexts is likely to be inappropriate. Tourism businesses must view their operations as part of a coherent regional offering. Within such a marketing approach, formerly perceived competitors become collaborators.

In conclusion ...

Perhaps rather than an outright rejection of processes of niche marketing, a more nuanced understanding should be nurtured to support rural tourism businesses. If this is the case, improved understanding may be aided by a change in terminology that better distinguishes a bottom-up approach from the top-down one of super-segmentation. The linguistic sophistry inherent in the term 'niche' not only confuses marketing practice, it attempts to influence perceptions of rural tourism as small-scale and by association, low impact and thus more benign than its reality. To 'soft', 'green', and 'eco-' might now be added 'niche' thus simply increasing the lexicon of terms used to mask the more aggressive and impacting nature of much rural visiting in the 21st century. The wider rural environment also may therefore benefit from such a fresh labelling of the principles of bottom-up niche marketing.

It is something of a paradox that pastiche, one of the key characteristics of postmodernity, is so evident in the continued application of modern marketing technologies to postmodern, contemporary forms of tourism consumption, when its effect is to perpetuate the hegemony of traditional practice and deflect us from a search for new ways of managing tourism consumption. Tourism marketing need represent an imitation of neither product nor services marketing. In its focus on experience creation, it need not slavishly follow 'the rules' and can, instead, establish (even if it needs constantly to re-establish) its own marketing characteristics.

References

AEIDL (1994) *Marketing Quality Rural Tourism.* LEADER Co-ordinating Unit, Brussels. http://www.rural-europe.aeidl.be/rural-en/biblio/tourism/art07.html.

Blake, J. (1996) Resolving conflict? The rural white paper, sustainability and countryside policy. *Local Environment* 1 92), 211-218.

Blankson and Stokes (2002) Marketing Practices in the UK Small Business Sector. *Marketing Intelligence & Planning* 20 (1), 49-61.

Brown, S. (1995) *Postmodern Marketing.* Routledge, London.

Butler, R. (1998) Rural Recreation and Tourism. In Ilbery, B. (ed) *The Geography of Rural Change.* Addison Wesley Longman, Harlow, pp 211-232.

Butler, R., Hall, C. M. and Jenkins, J. (eds) (1998) *Tourism and Recreation in Rural Areas*. John Wiley & Sons, Chichester.

Clarke, J. (1999) Marketing structures for farm tourism; beyond the individual provider of rural tourism. *Journal of Sustainable Tourism* 7 (1), 26-47.

Clemenson, H. and Lane, B. (1997) Niche markets, niche marketing and rural employment. In Bollman, R. D. and Bryden, J. M. (eds) *Rural Employment: an international perspective.* CABI International, Wallingford, pp 410-426.

Countryside Agency, (2000) *English Countryside Day Visits.* Countryside Agency, Cheltenham.

Dalgic, T. and Leeuw, M. (1994) Niche Marketing Revisited: Concept, Applications and Some European Cases. *European Journal of Marketing* 28 (4), 39-55.

EuroBarometer (1998) *Facts and Figures on the Europeans' Holiday*. EuroBarometer for DG XXIII, Brussels.

Fagence, M. (1993) Regional Tourism Strategies: the 'critical mass' as an optimisation tool in rural areas. In Bruce, D. and Whitla, M. (eds) *Tourism Strategies for Rural Development*. Mount Allison University, New Brunswick, pp 1-15.

Featherstone, M. (1991) *Consumer Culture and Postmodernism*. Sage, London.

Gómez Arias, J. T. and Acebrón, L. B. (2001).Postmodern Approaches in Business-to- business Marketing and Marketing Research. *Journal of Business and Industrial Marketing* 16 (1), 7-20.

Greffe, X. (1994) Is rural tourism a lever for economic and social development? *Journal of Sustainable Tourism* 2 (1/2), 22-40.

Grolleau, H. (1994) Putting feelings first. In *Marketing Quality Rural Tourism.* LEADER Technical Dossier, LEADER Co-ordinating Group, Brussels, p7.

Gummesson, E. (1987) The New Marketing – developing long-term interactive relationships. *Long Range Planning* 20 (4), 10-20.

Harris, L. C. (1998) The Obstacles to Developing Market Orientation: a study of small hotels. *Proceedings of the Academy of Marketing Conference.* Sheffield Hallam University, Sheffield, 8-10 July, pp 612-3.

Herries, J. (1998) *Glen Shiel Hillwalking Survey 1996: report of findings.* Scottish Natural Heritage, Perth.

Hjalager, A-M. (1996) Agricultural Diversification into Tourism. *Tourism Management* 17 (2), 103-111.

Holt, D. (1995) How consumers consume: a typology of consumption practices. *Journal of Consumer Research* 22, 1-16.

Holt (1997) Poststructuralist Lifestyle Analysis: conceptualizing the social patterning of consumption in postmodernity. *Journal of Consumer Research* 23, 326-350.

Hopkins, J (1998) Signs of the Post-Rural: marketing Myths of a Symbolic Countryside. *Geografiska Annaler* 80 B (2), 65-81.

Killion, L. (2001) Rural Tourism. In *Special Interest Tourism* Douglas, N., Douglas, N. and Derrett, R. (eds), John Wiley & Sons, Brisbane, pp 165-184.

Lane, B. (1994) What is Rural Tourism? *Journal of Sustainable Tourism* 2 (1/2), 1-6.

Malhotra, N. K. and Peterson, M. (2001) Marketing research in the new millennium: emerging issues and trends, *Marketing Intelligence and*

Planning 19 (4), 216-235.

McKenna, R. (1988) Marketing in an age of diversity. *Harvard Business Review.* September-October, 1988.

McKercher, B.and Robbins, B. (1998) Business development issues affecting nature-based tourism operators in Australia. *Journal of Sustainable Tourism* 6 (2), 173-188.

Moutinho, L. (ed) (2000) *Strategic Management in Tourism.* CABI Publishing, Wallingford.

Narver, C. J. and Slater, F. S. (1990) The Effect of a Market Orientation on Business Profitability. *Journal of Marketing* 54, 20-35.

Piercy, N. (1991) *Market-led Strategic Change: Making Marketing Happen in your Organization.* Thorsons, London.

Pine, B. J. and Gilmore, J. H. (1998) Welcome to the Experience Economy. *Harvard Business Review,* July-August, 97-105.

Pine, B. J. and Gilmore, J. H. (1999) *The Experience Economy.* Harvard Business School Press, Boston, Massachusetts.

Rapp, S. and Collins, T. (1990) *The Great Marketing Turnaround: The Age of the Individual – and How to Profit.* Prentice Hall, Englewood Cliffs, New Jersey.

Roberts, L. and Hall, D. (2001) *Rural Tourism and Recreation: Principles to Practice.* CAB International, Wallingford.

Shani, D. and Chalasani, S. (1992) Exploiting Niches using Relationship Marketing. *Journal of Consumer Marketing* 9 (3), 33-42.

Sharpley, R. (1999) *Tourism, Tourists and Society.* 2nd edn. ELM, Huntingdon.

...   (2000) The consumption of tourism revisited. In Robinson, M., Long, P., Evans, N., Sharpley, R. and Swarbrooke, J. (eds) *Reflections on International Tourism, Motivations, Behaviour and Tourist Types.* Business Education Publishers, Sunderland, pp 381-391.

Thomas (1996).Consumer Market Research: Does it still have validity? Some postmodern thoughts. *Marketing Intelligence & Planning* 15 (2), 54-59

Titford, R. and Clouter, R. (1998) The case for mass marketing in an increasingly segmented world. *Admap* November 1998, 37-39.

Urry, J. (1991) *The Tourist Gaze.* Sage, London.

Urry, J. (1995) *Consuming Places.* Routledge, London.

VisitScotland, (2001) *Tourism in Scotland 2000.* Scottish Tourist Board, Edinburgh.

Wanhill, S. (1997) Small and Medium Tourism Enterprises. *Annals of Tourism Research* 3, 47-70.

Chapter 13

Sustainable Tourism in Scotland

Sandy Dear

The Tourism and Environment Forum aims to promote greater sustainability in Scottish tourism. With a range of partners - from enterprise companies to representatives of landowners both private and public - we are working to highlight and make the most of the link between tourism and the natural environment, to the advantage of both the natural environment itself and to the businesses and communities linked to it. That is my definition of Eco Tourism. It may not involve turtle surveys on a Costa Rican beach or species counts in Tanzania. But Scotland has plenty of natural wonders to offer the modern world traveller, if we can only understand what it is that they expect from Scotland and make sure that's what they experience. More importantly, TEF partners are closely involved in minimising the impacts that tourism can have on the Scottish environment. For more information see www.greentourism.org.uk

What do we want from tourism?

We are all affected in some way by tourism in Scotland. What do we want from tourism? We're the people who live here, what do we expect from tourism?

- Jobs?
- Income?
- A cosmopolitan buzz about the place?
- Better public transport?
- More wet weather things to do to keep the kids happy?

Tourism is not an end in itself; it is a means to achieving things like:

- Economic prosperity
- Thriving communities

- A better environment in which to live

We all know that these three aims are interdependent but we are not always very good at making the most of these interdependencies. In many countries environment and tourism are assumed to be mortal enemies, in Scotland the Tourism and Environment Forum is showing how they can be the best of friends.

Tourism is an increasingly competitive game

Never before has the visitor had such a range of holiday experiences to choose from. Flights are cheaper than ever before. And visitors, who now grow up with foreign travel, are increasingly discerning. Times are hard because tourism is changing; not just because of recent developments like Foot and Mouth Disease (FMD), international terrorism or the high value of the Pound Sterling, but because a whole range of economic and social factors are changing and these changes are affecting our current markets.

Greater competition

The boom in the range of holiday destinations open to travellers has meant that while in 1960 almost 75% of all international trips were to European destinations, by 2010 this will have fallen to around 50%, why?

- Cheap travel - Easyjet, Ryanair, GO

- New destinations: strongest tourism growth will be in South America and Africa. By 2010 they are expected to receive 23 million European visitors a year between them

- Internet: E-commerce transactions are estimated to represent 12% of world wide travel industry sales in 2003

- Older and more experienced visitors
  A fifth of the population of Europe being aged 65 or over in 2020. In the UK (the main market for visitors to Scotland) this means that over 65s will increase from 9m to 12m.

These over 65s will not be hanging around in their slippers reading the Sunday Post. They will be more active than previous over 65s and may well choose to continue working past traditional retirement age. They will not abandon leisure and health activities when they retire and they will expect the range of offers and level of service that a lifetime of consumerism has accustomed them to.

These visitors will be better travelled than previous generations and more willing to travel but they will also be more aware of our competition and may therefore be harder to attract. They will have the time to take holidays throughout the year, will be more 'experience' focused than destination focused and will demand high quality of product and service as standard. Their 'experience' focus may mean greater scope for specialist or niche markets like soft, accessible activities. These changes and efforts to respond to them are causing market fragmentation: growing specialist markets and more niche marketing. To stay ahead of the game we have to better understand what visitors want.

Why do people come to Scotland: culture, history, family ties?

The natural environment is central to the image visitors have of Scotland.

Visitor Survey 1999 - UK, US, Germany

Attributes that visitors associate with Scotland as a holiday destination

- Fresh Air   80%
- Peace and quite   84%
- Beautiful scenery 90% (of £2.5bn is £2.25bn)

2001 Visitor Survey - France, Italy and Spain

Scotland's biggest advantage

- Beautiful scenery 22%
- Wildlife and nature   19%
- Main reason we came to Scotland
- Landscape / scenery   47%

Why do visitors come to Scotland?

When presented with a list of Scotland's attributes and asked to rate them in order of importance, the top three attributes in the 2001 survey of French Italian and Spanish visitors were all related to the natural environment:

- Nature and wildlife
- Fresh/clean air
- Peace/quiet and wilderness

In all the countries surveyed (France, Italy, Spain, Germany, USA, Scotland and England) the landscape, countryside and scenery were by far the most important factors that influenced the decision to visit Scotland (mentioned by 39% of all visitors). The countries listed account for over 85% of tourism spend in Scotland. Scottish tourism thrives on a high quality natural environment. What are the implications of this?

- We need to make sure that visitors know what the wonderful environment has to offer. We need marketing that focuses on the natural environment.

- We must make sure that once they are here visitors can easily 'access' the environment that they have come for - not through a car window but in far more enjoyable interactive ways.

- Most important of all - we must make sure that we look after and sustain the environment that attracts visitors to Scotland.

It is essential that we fully recognise the importance of Scotland's environment to Scotland's largest industry. We must put environmental sustainability as well as economic sustainability at the heart of tourism strategies and plans at the national, regional and local levels. And we must minimise or reduce visitor impacts on our most important tourism asset.

How do we make sure that visitors know what the wonderful environment has to offer?

Marketing that focuses on the natural environment
In terms of brochures and campaigns we are doing reasonably well.
- VisitScotland (the Scottish Tourist Board) has identified wildlife tourism as an important niche for Scotland
- Shetland is using its clean green image to attract visitors
- And Perthshire's Big Tree Country campaign focuses visitor attention on the amazing trees in the area.

Internet
On the Internet a partnership of Area Tourist boards has developed Walking Wild, a campaign aimed at those interested in walking in Scotland. But we need much more on the Internet and we're working with SNH and VS to achieve this.

TICs
TICs are a vital interface with visitors: however, the level of information about the natural environment has traditionally been very 'patchy'. That's why we're working with HIE and SNH to integrate natural heritage information into TIC training.

We must also make sure that once they are here visitors can easily 'access' the environment that they have come for - not through a car window but in far more enjoyable interactive ways. We need to provide visitors with 'green' things to see and do.

Green activities and attractions
Wildlife friendly wildlife watching, interpretation, expert guides, wildlife experts in TICs. We also need information and interpretation at accommodation venues and at sites out in the countryside, including visitor attractions.

Imaginative environment based attractions and operators:
- The peatlands centre at Forsinard
- The Knockan Geological Centre
- The Hebridean Whale and Dolphin Trust (Thistle Award)
- Shetland Wildlife - killer whales
- Speyside Wildlife – otters, deer and midges!
- Sealife Surveys - part of research into whales and dolphins
- The Scottish Seabird Centre near Edinburgh (recently

nominated for a British Airways Tourism for a Tomorrow
award)
- Ospreys, Red Kite and Sea Eagle remote viewing sites
- Capercaillie watching at RSPB Loch Garten
- The otter hide at Kylerhea on Skye
- Whales and Dolphins trips from many sites around the coast

Now let us take a look at the environmental impacts that visitors have on Scotland

Visitor impacts derive principally from:

- How they travel: *Transport*
  The majority of our visitors come by car (well over 85% in
  some rural areas), this means roads and all their problems (run
  off, animals killed), fumes and congestion in some honey-pot
  areas.

- Where they stay: *Accommodation*
  The tourism industry is made up of 20,000 businesses - it
  provides 70 million bed nights each year. All accommodation
  businesses have some environmental impact, whether it is the
  fuel they use for heating, the waste they produce or the water
  they use.

- What they do: *Activities and Attractions*
  Activities like walking or skiing clearly have the potential to
  impact on the environment. But attractions too will have an
  impact that depends on how they are built and managed.

All of these impacts potentially reduce the quality of the environment
that we know visitors come to Scotland to experience.

To reduce these impacts we need

- Sustainable visitor transport initiatives like: Sustrans routes,
  Cycle Scotland strategy, the Trossachs Trundler, the Northern
  Explorer, a Scottish Public Transport Timetable.

- Green accommodation initiatives like; Green Tourism Business Scheme, Hospitable Climates, Natural Cooking of Scotland.

- Green things to do and see like; codes of conduct for wildlife operators, information and interpretation, managed walking routes.

Seasonal and geographical dispersal
We also need to try to minimise exceptionally high visitor pressures at certain times of year and at certain popular destinations, Not by restricting numbers but by showing visitors that there are other times of year and other places to visit.

Conclusions

As tourism becomes increasingly competitive the growing eco tourism market appears to offer business opportunities. But eco tourists (as with all other visitors) choose their holiday as much on destination as on activity. Attempting to compete in the eco tourism market with true eco tourism destinations does not make sense. But there are some key tourism trends that we can take advantage of if we bear in mind why visitors come to Scotland.

Chapter 14

Tourism and Sustainable Development
Green Wash or Natural Allies
A Case Study of Costa Rica

Philip J O'Brien

Tourism and sustainable development: the international context

*The Development of an International Discourse*In the ten years
between the1992 Rio Conference on Environment and Development
and the 2002 World Summit on Sustainable Development (WSSD) at
Johannesburg the issue of tourism and sustainable development has
come to the fore. In the preparations for the Rio Conference and at the
Conference itself the tourist industry and the issue of tourism was
more conspicuous for its absence than its presence. Agenda 21, the
document designed and agreed to guide the world community towards
sustainable development in the 21st century, did vaguely mention
tourism as potentially offering sustainable development paths to
communities living in fragile environments, and urged governments
to promote environmentally sound leisure and tourist activities - but
that was almost all.

But since 1992 the growth in books, articles, journals, documents,
conferences, codes of conduct, and indeed numbers of tourists
concerned with the role of travel and tourism in sustainable
development has been enormous. Much of the change has been due to
the tourist industry itself, especially the efforts of the main
international organisations concerned with tourism, the World Tourist
Organisation (WTO) and the World Travel and Tourist Organisation
(WTTC) both of whom have worked tirelessly to highlight the
importance of the tourist industry and the contribution that the tourist
industry can make to sustainable development. Based on the belief
that tourism would be counted more by policy and opinion makers if
it was counted, the World Travel and Tourism Council (WTTC) and
the WEFA Group Research produced a major and innovative
econometric study (Travel and Tourism Satellite Accounting (TSA)
which measured and compared the impact of travel and tourism
across sectors and between countries, looking at its flows through the

whole economy. The TSA system claimed that in the year 2000 travel and tourism generated, directly and indirectly, some 11.7% of GDP and some 200 million jobs in the world-wide economy, making it the largest industry and creator of jobs world-wide. The tourist market has been growing at roughly 5% per annum since 1970. Prior to September 11th tourist arrivals were predicted to grow by 4.3% a year over the next two decades, and receipts from international tourism by 6.7% a year. (WTO 1998). In 2000 according to the WTO there were 698 million international tourist arrivals, an increase of 7.3% over 1999, international tourist receipts were $478b with an additional $97b earned by international transport carriers outside the country of origin. Average receipts per arrival in 1999 were $700. There was a downturn of about 7.4% in 2001 and 2002, leading to a loss of some 10 million jobs, reflecting the uncertainties surrounding travel after September 11th, 2001. Thereafter both the WTO and the WTTC are confident that travel and tourism will stabilise, and then continue its upward growth path - but with the growing proviso that international tensions can negatively effect the industry very quickly. The terrorist bomb in Bali, aimed at tourists, will undoubtedly have a major negative impact on tourist arrivals to Indonesia, most Muslim countries, and even wider. Terrorism and tourism do not go together.

The above figures, and projected growth rates, show that travel and tourism is likely to be one of the three great drivers of the global service sector, together with telecommunications and information technology, in the 21st century.

In addition the Chair of the WTTC, proudly began to claim that: "travel and tourism will be the 21st century's catalyst for sustainable economic and environmental development." Four reasons have been widely quoted to support such claims: tourism and travel has less impact on natural resources and the environment than most other industries; it has a direct and powerful motive to protect the assets of local culture, built heritage and natural environment; it can increase consumer commitment to sustainable development principles through its consumer distribution channels and it can provide economic incentives to conserve natural environments and maintain bio-diversity which might otherwise be allocated to more environmentally damaging land uses.

The campaign by the tourist industry produced its successes. The United Nations General Assembly in its special session, Rio+5, evaluating the follow-up to Rio after 5 years, specifically asked the United Nations Commission on Sustainable Development (CSD-established in 1993) to examine the issue of sustainable tourism at its annual conference. In the high level segment on tourism at the 1999 CSD -7, there were multi-stakeholder background papers and dialogues from representatives of the tourist industry, workers and trade unions, local authorities and non-governmental organisations on four themes: industry initiatives for sustainable tourism; influencing consumer behaviour; promoting broad based sustainable development while safeguarding the integrity of local cultures and protecting the environment and the coastal impact of tourism.. And in recognition of the growing importance of travel and tourism, 2002, the 10th anniversary of the Rio Conference, was declared to be the UN Year of Eco-Tourism. The Conference on Eco-Tourism, although not without its critics, held in Quebec was well attended. The position paper agreed at Quebec was sent to the Johannesburg Conference for endorsement. And also the travel and tourism industry, among 22 other industry sectors, gave a report there on its progress towards sustainability. In the final Johannesburg Declaration, section 41 on tourism agreed to:

> Promote sustainable tourism development, including non-consumptive and eco-tourism, taking into account the spirit of the International Year of Eco-tourism 2002, the United Nations Year for Cultural Heritage in 2002, the World Eco-Tourism Summit 2002 and its Quebec Declaration, and the Global Code of Ethics for Tourism as adopted by the World Tourism Organisation in order to increase the benefits from tourism resources for the population in host communities while maintaining the cultural and environmental integrity of the host communities and enhancing the protection of ecologically sensitive areas and natural heritages. Promote sustainable tourism development and capacity building in order to contribute to the strengthening of rural and local communities. This would include actions at all levels to:
> a. Enhance international co-operation, foreign direct investment and partnerships with both private and public sectors, at all levels;
> b. Develop programmes, including education and training programmes, that encourage people to participate in eco-tourism, enable indigenous and local communities to develop and benefit from eco-tourism, and enhance stake-holder co-operation in tourism development and heritage preservation, in order to improve the protection of the environment, natural resources and cultural heritage;

c. Provide technical assistance to developing countries and countries with economies in transition to support sustainable tourism business development and investment and tourism awareness programmes, to improve domestic tourism, and to stimulate entrepreneurial development;

d. Assist host communities in managing visits to their tourism attractions for their maximum benefits, while ensuring the least negative impacts on and risks for their traditions, culture and environment, with the support of the World Tourism Organisation and other relevant organisations;

e. Promote the diversification of economic activities, including through the facilitation of access to markets and commercial information, and participation of emerging local enterprises, especially small and medium enterprises.

The above declaration highlights both the strengths and weaknesses of the United Nations and the tourist industry's approach to sustainable development, and the ability of the industry to have the United Nations adopt its approach. Critics now assert that the approach adopted towards sustainable development is nothing but "the globalisation of greenwash."

The Industry Approach to Sustainable Development
To what extent is the tourist industry guilty of "greenwash" in its claim to be a major contributor to sustainable development? The imagery put out by the travel and tourist industry, particularly in its advertisements, is classic "greenwash", using beautiful images of natural scenery accompanied by declarations of respect for the environment. But what lies behind the glossy images?

The travel and tourist industry has been something of a pioneer in promoting a series of measures that both improved its image in relation to sustainable development, and genuinely began to change practices towards a more sustainable pattern.

The tourist and travel industry provides a good example of an industry approach to sustainable development and the way in which that approach has dominated the discourse on sustainable development. In the run up to the Rio Conference the then UNCED Secretary- General, Maurice Strong, asked a leading businessman, Stephen Schmidheiny, to bring business on board for the Conference. Schmidheiny, along with other businessmen, formed the World Business Council for Sustainable Development, made up of many, but by no means all, leading multinational corporations. This Council together with the long established International Chamber of Commerce, had a major influence on both the agenda of the Rio conference (the role of multinational corporations in unsustainable environmental and developmental practices was kept off the agenda) and its outcomes (the approach to sustainable development was to be voluntary rather than binding regulations).

In the ten years since Rio the power and influence of big business has increased, particularly in international fora. At Rio there were a lot of confrontations between business and the powerful NGO lobbies. Although clearly an exaggeration to say that the NGOs had equal influence with that of business, they nevertheless had real influence on the final documents adopted, and gave the Rio documents a broad based global vision. In the ten years since Rio, the World Business Council for Sustainable Development has increased its influence at the United Nations whilst many NGOs have become increasingly bureaucratised and more interested in the corridors of power than mobilising their grassroots. Working closely with the Secretary General of the United Nations, Kofi Annan, the WBCSD, persuaded the Secretary General to enshrine the principle that "confrontation has been replaced by co-operation," in return for their agreeing to a Global Compact. In this Global Compact the Secretary General, Kofi Annan, asked business to agree to nine principles all of which are enshrined in key environmental, labour and human rights agreements.

On paper the Global Compact is an admirable document. The issues embraced by the Global Compact commit businesses to support the following principles; to support and respect the protection of internationally proclaimed human rights, and to make sure their businesses are not complicit in human rights abuses; to uphold the freedom of association and the right to collective bargaining, to eliminate all forms of forced and compulsory labour, to effectively abolish child labour, and to eliminate discrimination in respect of employment and occupation; to support a precautionary approach to environmental challenges, to undertake initiatives to promote greater environmental responsibility, and to encourage the development and diffusion of environmentally friendly technologies .But the Global Compact is like so much in the United Nations: it is entirely voluntary with no mechanisms for enforcing implementation or even of adequately monitoring progress or lack of progress. Indeed many of the MNCs who signed up to the Global Compact have been guilty of major infringements of the agreed environmental, labour and human rights principles. The Global Compact states that it favours openness and transparency; yet it is impossible to know which companies are even participating. The Global Compact is meant to be more than a Public Relations exercise, but already some companies are exploiting their membership to claim green credentials. Nevertheless in spite of these difficulties the Global Compact once agreed was presented as the most important corporate partnership at the United Nations, allowing business interests to dominate the proceedings at Johannesburg.

In many ways the travel and tourist industry were pioneers of the new Global Compact, beginning to implement many of the nine principles at an early date. In the 1970s and 1980s the tourist industry began to develop codes of conduct such as the WTTC Code for Environmentally Responsible Tourism Businesses. However these codes are purely voluntary, and the industry has neither any means to implement the codes nor even to put in place adequate monitoring mechanisms. In the 1980s the industry began to promote the idea of eco-efficiency, and began to publish manuals, and tool guides on how to achieve this. The International Ecotourism Society published a useful set of guidelines for both tourists and operators. Many of the manuals published in the 1980s were good, clear guidelines, using best practice to encourage change. However they tended to be very general, and thus not specific enough to deal with the complicated issues faced on the ground. The manuals often dated very fast. Only a very few manuals gave clear advice on how to monitor progress, quantify the impact of changes, and where best to concentrate resources.

In the 1980s the larger tourist businesses and those businesses specifically focused on eco -tourism began to develop award programmes and competitions such as the BA ETC Tourism for Tomorrow Awards. These awards became quite popular: they undoubtedly were useful public relations exercises for the successful award winners. However, though the awards and competitions increased awareness both among the industry and the tourists, it was never clear what were the criteria for winning. The awards focused almost exclusively on eco-tourism, only a tiny segment of the tourist market, and tended to be snap-shots of some shiny new project rather than steady progress over time. Awards and competitions still remain popular, but it is doubtful whether these change either the majority of tourists or the tourist businesses.

At the beginning of the 1990s, recognising the weaknesses of the awards and competitions approach, groups within the industry began to develop complicated certification programmes. Most of these are fairly recent, usually in the last decade. Initially a variety of indicators and benchmarks, measuring progress towards sustainable development, were developed to provide a quantifiable assessment of progress towards sustainable development in tourism by unit or destination. These include for example the WTO's indicators of sustainable tourism. More complicatedly, tourism destinations became the focus through life-cycle assessments, focusing on impacts of all tourism activity. These programmes vary enormously in their sophistication. Both indicators and benchmarks, and to a lesser extent life-cycle assessments indicators, were incorporated into certification programmes. Some countries have developed their own certification programme. One of the most advanced certification programmes is that of Costa Rica which has a very detailed set of sustainable development criteria, covering environmental, economic and social principles. Australia has a National EcoTourism Accreditation programme covering ecotourism holiday products, and the Nordic countries follow a Nordic Ecolabelling standard almost entirely based on the standards provided by ISO 14024 "Environmental Labels and Declarations - Guiding Principles." The ISO explicitly states that "the criteria should be objective, reasonable and verifiable: that interested parties should be given the opportunity to participate and that account should be taken of their comments."

Probably the most important attempt to create a global certification programme is that provided by Green Globe 21. Green Globe 21 operates a company programme and a destination programme. Guides are provided to help companies understand and implement the Green Globe 21, and consultants are provided at extra cost to help companies achieve those standards. The Green Globe 21 goes beyond the ISO 14001 international standard for environmental management systems, though it uses ISO 14001 as its core. To obtain the Green Globe 21 logo is expensive and not easy. Companies are given standard and sector specific standards, and are expected to begin an environmental management programme immediately. That programme is designed to ensure compliance with local, regional and national regulations; assess the environmental aspects of the company covering energy efficiency, conservation, management of fresh water, social and cultural issues, land use planning, air quality, noise control, waste water management, waste minimisation, refuse and recycling, storage and use of hazardous substances. And in addition to all this the company is expected to ensure consultation and feedback from key stakeholders. To obtain the logo the company is subjected to a third party audit of on average three days, and thereafter is subject to an annual pre- arranged check and occasional unannounced spot checks. It is not easy for a company to obtain the Green Globe 21 logo tick.

The Green Globe Logo also offers a sustainable tourism programme for a location. This is also a programme that is hard to achieve. Some 10 steps have to be gone through to obtain the Green Globe 21 Destination tick. A Destination Management Group carry out a baseline assessment through a Scoping Study, then carry out a Destination Visioning programme to determine the views of stakeholders, create an environmental policy for the destination and establish overall objectives and priority areas, assess the impacts on the environment through a Strategic Environmental Assessment, define an Environmental Action Plan with targets, timelines and responsibilities and minimising impacts. If awarded a Green Globe Destination logo then results are monitored and reviewed, stakeholders informed, improvement targets agreed, and re-assessments done annually.

Green Globe 21 is time consuming, expensive, and rigorous. Usually only the bigger, more successful companies apply for it, and only destinations whose customers are looking for the sort of criteria applied by Green Globe who apply. In other words the majority of tourist companies and tourist destinations do not apply. Nevertheless Green Globe 21 is a good example of how sophisticated, and rigorous certification has become. The main problem with all these programmes is that the emphasis is more on the environmental side of sustainable development than the social and economic side, partly because the environmental side is easier to quantify. But also because the tourist industry is reluctant to discuss the inequitable share out of the gains from tourism, with the bulk of the monetary gains going back to the rich countries. The industry is also reluctant to discuss the very unequal power relations between the poor host tourist destinations and the rich tourists. The participants in the programmes are either companies or destinations for whom the award of Green Globe 21 is useful as part of a marketing strategy. It is still a minority process. Nevertheless the tourist industry can rightly claim that substantial progress has been made in establishing fairly objective criteria for measuring the environmental impact of tourism in particular destinations and companies

Thus some changes in practice have been genuine and welcome. But it is very difficult to disentangle greenwash from genuine sustainable development practices. Confrontation has been replaced by co-operation. But too often co-operation means either co-opting critical and dissenting voices or effectively sidelining them. Thus some of the NGOs critical of many of the practices of the tourist and travel industry have largely been sidelined, and the voice of the smaller tourist operators has been incorporated within the general discourse favoured by the big players. The international organisations representing travel and tourism, mainly the WTO and the WTTC, represent broadly the larger stakeholders in the industry, and these two have effectively monopolised the creation of an international discourse on tourism. Much of this discourse is genuinely positive such as the publication in 1995 the World Tourism Organisation (WTO) and the World Travel and Tourism Council (WTTC) together with the Earth Council, of a guide to Agenda 21 for the travel and tourist industry (WTO, WTTC and Earth Council 1995). But the discourse is bland. There is no real criticism of the industry, and awkward issues are put to one side. Indeed efforts are made to suppress the airing of these awkward issues at their meetings and at international fora.

Clarifying the Terminology
Inevitably, as with the whole debate over sustainable development, there has been a proliferation of terminology and concepts. The industry itself began to talk about sustainable tourism, the sustainable development of tourism, then a niche within tourism, often called green tourism or ecotourism. Thus terms such as "ecotourism", "green tourism" or "sustainable tourism"[1] began to be freely, and often interchangeably used. Aid agencies began to see tourism as a good strategy for poor countries to obtain foreign exchange, assist poverty alleviation, and even be part of sustainable development. Both bilateral and multilateral aid agencies now actively fund green tourism as part of a sustainable development strategy.[2]   For a while the lack of agreement over definitions initially confused the debate. For example definitions of what counted as ecotourism varied considerably. Early definitions emphasised the demand side focusing on the tourists who travelled to relatively undisturbed or

---

[1] M. Mowforth and I. Munt (1998) cite the following new tourism terminology: academic tourism, adventure tourism, agro-tourism, alternative tourism, anthro-tourism, appropriate tourism, archaeo-tourism, contact tourism, cottage tourism, culture tourism, eco-tourism, ecological tourism, environmentally friendly tourism, ethnic tourism, green tourism, nature tourism, risk tourism, safari tourism, scientific tourism, soft tourism, sustainable tourism, trekking tourism, truck tourism, wilderness tourism, wildlife tourism.
[2] See for example the German Federal Ministry for Economic Cooperation and Development (1995), *Ecotourism as a Conservation Instrument*. (Bonn:BMZ.)

uncontaminated natural areas with the specific objective of studying, admiring and enjoying the scenery. Such definitions made no mention of the needs of developing countries, nor whether the tourist activity itself was ecologically sustainable. The Ecotourism Society, founded by a broad array of professionals to make ecotourism a genuine tool for conservation and sustainable development, offered an early definition of ecotourism: "Ecotourism is responsible travel to natural areas which conserves the environment and improves the welfare of local people."[3] In a similar vein, the IUCN, now World Conservation Union, in 1996 defined ecotourism as "environmentally responsible travel and visitation to relatively undisturbed natural areas, in order to enjoy and appreciate nature (and any accompanying cultural features - both past and present) that promotes conservation, has low negative visitor impact, and provides for beneficially active socioeconomic involvement of local populations." But usually, within the tourist industry itself, tourist agencies chose their own home-grown definition. And even international agencies create their own guidelines. Membership of green tourist organisations such as the Environmental Conservation Tourism Association, Partners in Responsible Tourism and the Ecotourism Society only require a membership fee.

This confusion over terminology was partially solved through the first World Ecotourism Summit held in Quebec. One of the advantages of the United Nations International Conferences is that they help to reach agreement on terminology, even if that terminology is often deliberately ambiguous. The International Conference in Quebec 2002 clarified some of the basic concepts employed around tourism and sustainable development. 18 preparatory meetings were held in 2001 and 2002, involving over 3,000 representatives from national, and local governments, from tourism businesses (especially private ecotourism businesses) and their trade associations, from NGOs working in tourism, from academics, consultants, indigenous and local communities, and from intergovernmental organisations, under the aegis of the United Nations Environment Programme (UNEP) and the World Tourism Organisation. In addition the Planeta.com website hosted a pioneering forum for stakeholders involved in ecotourism to exchange experiences and comments, including criticisms of the whole process. And finally over 1,100 participants from 132 countries, including 40 Ministers, attended the

---

[3] Quoted in D. Western, " Defining Ecotourism" in K. Lindberg and D. Hawkins (1993), *Ecotourism: A Guide for Planners and Mangers.* (North Bennington: The Ecotourism Society.)

World Ecotourism Summit, and agreed a final Declaration, the Quebec Declaration on EcoTourism. The conclusion of all these meetings, as stated by UNEP's Tourism Program Co-Ordinator, is "that ecotourism in practice can contribute to poverty alleviation and environmental protection."

The UNEP Manual for the International Year of Ecotourism usefully distinguished between ecotourism as a concept under a set of principles and as a specific market segment. The tourist market can be divided into segments roughly as follows: Cultural; Rural; Nature; Sun and Beach; Business; Fitness and Health. Eco-tourism covers the first three: cultural, rural and nature. Adventure tourism ciovers rural and nature.

Ecotourism as a market segment

As a concept ecotourism is primarily a sustainable version of nature tourism, including rural and cultural elements. The strong emphasis on sustainability, using principles, guidelines and certification based on sustainability standards, gives ecotourism, according to UNEP (1996), " a unique position in the tourism field". This unique position is because ecotourism is seen as having a set of general characteristics. UNEP and the WTO agreed that these characteristics are as follows:

1. All nature-based forms of tourism in which the main motivation of the tourists is the observation and appreciation of nature as well as the traditional cultures prevailing in natural areas.
2. It contains educational and interpretation features.
3. It is generally, but not exclusively organised for small groups by specialised and small, locally owned businesses. Foreign operators of varying sizes also organise, operate and/or market ecotourism tours, generally for small groups.
4. It minimises negative impacts on the natural and socio-cultural environment.
5. It supports the protection of natural areas by:
   - Generating economic benefits for host communities, organisations and authorities managing natural areas with conservation purposes.
   - Providing alternative employment and income opportunities for local communities

- Increasing awareness towards the conservation of natural and cultural assets, both among locals and tourists.

UNEP and the WTO went on to recognise that there are a number of important issues that arise from their approach to ecotourism. They argue that the main ones are the issue of land tenure and control of the process by host communities; efficiency and fairness in protected areas; the importance of precautions and monitoring in very sensitive areas; and indigenous and traditional rights in areas being developed for ecotourism.

However, there are a number of problems with the whole debate surrounding the World Summit on EcoTourism. The main one is that the Conference was analysing only a very small segment of the total tourist market, albeit a fast growing one, but fast growing mainly because it is starting from a low base. It is estimated that ecotourism grew at a rate of between 10% to15% in the mid-1990s, the fastest growing sub-sector of the tourist industry, bringing in about $12 billion a year to tropical countries, out of a total of about $60 billion a year spent in developing countries. (World Wide Fund for Nature, quoted in Karin Adelmann 1997). The bulk of this ecotourism income came from visits to tropical rainforests, and is roughly equal to what tropical countries received from exports of their tropical hardwoods. Nevertheless this is a small segment of the overall tourist market. The WTO researched existing market data on ecotourism. The data varied greatly, partly depending on the strictness of the definition of "ecotourist". The US Department of Commerce In -Flight Survey on US travellers to overseas destinations in 1996 and 1999 found that the market represents about 4% of US international travellers. This low figure partly reflects their definition of ecotourist as someone who had to have participated in ecological excursions. Whereas a Canadian survey, using the definition of ecotourism as "related to nature/adventure/culture" suggested a potential ecotourism market of 13.2 million in just seven of the major urban areas of North America. An additional problem as Costa Rican surveys show is that there is no static profile of an ecotourist who in Costa Rica for example just wanted a good time enjoying all aspects of Costa Rica - its beaches, its tropical forests, its indigenous areas, its night life.

Supporters argue that ecotourism can represent not only one of the most agreeable forms of environmental education but also an excellent economic tool that maintains the equilibrium between use and preservation of a country's natural resources at the same time that it contributes to sustainable development. (T. Budowski 1992).

However recently doubts have been expressed about the so-called sustainability of ecotourism as it may merely replicate all of the problems associated with conventional tourism, but this time within previously undeveloped areas with delicately balanced physical and cultural environments. (Pattullo 1996). And for Anita Pleumaron ecotourism is fraught with images and myths, many of which bear little relation to what happens to the local people in practice (Pleumaron 1995). In an article in The Nation she went so far as to ask the question "Eco-tourism: A Cover for Eco-Terrorism?"[4]

The problem with the debate over ecotourism is that there are sufficient good case studies of how ecotourism has contributed to sustainable development and poverty alleviation, and some bad examples of how it has done the opposite. Given the nature of ecotourism and the specific market niche it is trying to fill one would expect good examples to outnumber bad. And this seems to be the case: but what about the rest of tourism? The tourist industry is making a general claim that tourism is a natural ally of sustainable development, and not just a small branch, namely ecotourism. The emphasis on ecotourism has been misplaced. It is the wider picture that matters, the sustainability of tourism in general. The WTO offered an early definition of sustainable tourism: "Sustainable tourism development meets the needs of the present tourists and host nations while protecting and enhancing the opportunity for the future. It is envisaged as leading to management of all resources in such a way that economic, social and aesthetic needs can be fulfilled, while maintaining cultural integrity, essential ecological processes, biological diversity and life support systems." UNEP went even further in emphasising the three key aspects of sustainability: socio-cultural; economic and environmental: "Sustainability implies permanence, so sustainable tourism includes optimum use of resources, including biological diversity; minimisation of ecological cultural and social impacts; and maximisation of benefits to conservation and local communities. It also refers to the management structures that are needed to achieve the above." This definition is an advantage over the WTOs as socio-cultural and economic aspects are given as much prominence as the environmental, particularly in relation to host communities. UNEP went on to claim that: "for tourism to be sustainable it needs to be integrated into all aspects of

---

[4] "Eco-Tourism: A Cover for Eco-Terrorism?" The Nation: 12.11. 1994.

development." And in a rare admission - one that the tourist industry has never admitted - UNEP pointed out that "some aspects of tourism such as long-haul travel, may simply not be sustainable with current technologies and best practices."

Contradictions in the Industry Approach
Neither the WTO nor the WTTC nor any other group in the tourist industry have been willing to face up to the major contradictions within tourism in respect of sustainable development. One major contradiction, particularly in the poorer host countries and communities, is that the distribution of benefits is very uneven. A variety of micro-studies show that the leakage from tourist revenues, including ecotourism, in poor countries is large.[5] Furthermore tourism, including ecotourism, can disrupt the lives and livelihoods of the local populations living near the tourist area. This is true of both ecotourism as well as conventional mass tourism. All too often locals feel alienated and hostile towards the tourist development, particularly as they are often not consulted about the developments nor any attempt made to explain the purpose behind the developments nor are they given a fair share of any benefits. In some cases local people have even been evicted from their homelands to develop ecotourism.

The tourist industry has developed the language of participation, but in practice participation is limited and often ritualistic whilst decision -making remains hierarchical and controlled by the tourist operators. So far poverty alleviation is hardly on the agenda of the tourist industry. But the very uneven power relations that lie behind the host communities and the foreign tourists threaten any possibility of sustainable development. The tourist industry is just not disposed to face up to the enormous inequalities in the distribution of the costs and benefits of tourism. And so far there are few indications that it is willing to do so. Thus leakages, the distribution of costs and benefits are still not yet on the tourist industry agenda. Related to this is the issue of the working conditions within the industry. Locals tend to do

---

[5] For example Spinrad's study of St. Lucia found that about 45% of tourist receipts flowed out of the country as first round leakages (Spinrad 1982); Patullo gives a figure of a leakage of 70% for most of the Caribbean (Patullo 1996); Madeley quotes a figure of 77% leakage for charter operations to the Gambia and also quotes an 1978 estimate by the Economic and Social Commission for Asia and the Pacific that when the airline and the hotel were both owned by a foreign company the leakage was between 75% to 78%, and when the hotel was locally owned between 55% to 60%   (Madeley 1996); and Stecker found that about two thirds of the revenues went to the foreign airline and tour operators, and of the remaining one third the bulk went to the local capital city tour operators (Stecker 1996).

the more menial tasks, and these are poorly paid, sometimes below minimum wage regulations. At the bottom end of the industry it is a low wage industry with long hours, poor health and safety regulations, an anti trade union attitude and practice. Again the industry fails to examine these aspects in any real detail. Tourism has a voracious appetite for the basic resources of land and water and energy. Although the public relations language may emphasise the land and water rights of local peoples, in practice many tourist companies try to undermine these rights, and monopolise the land and water. Golf tourism, a highly profitable segment of the tourist industry, is notorious for its unsustainable use of water and land, in some countries ignoring traditional rights to land and water.

The above are all real and pressing problems. But the major contradiction involves air travel. As prices drop and demand grows, air travel is the fastest growing source of CO_2 emissions in the world. Airplanes, by flying in the sensitive upper atmosphere, cause 2 to 4 times the amount of global warming than CO_2 alone. Each person on a long haul flight is responsible for the equivalent of 124 kg of CO_2 per hour of their journey. Each passenger on a flight from Delhi to London contributes as much to climate change as the average Indian citizen does in two years. There are various proposals to lessen the impact of air travel, ranging from a tax on air travel to at least slow down its rate of growth to voluntary contributions to such organisations as Climate Care who will calculate your CO_2 travel emissions and their off-setting costs in planting trees. Again the tourist industry vehemently opposes any air fuel tax or even the end to subsidies on air fuel. It has done nothing to promote schemes such as Climate Care. Travel and CO_2 emissions have been a taboo subject.

Behind all these contradictions lies the weakness of an industry led approach to sustainable development. Tourism and travel, as with all the other industries believes in an approach to sustainable development which is market led, based on voluntary codes of practice, relies on self regulation with the minimum of state regulation. It has no enforceable mechanisms for dealing with non-sustainable development practices, and is opposed to implementing any penalties, and indeed has no penalties. It favours increasing privatisation of e.g. airlines and airports. It favours limited and controlled participation, and wants stakeholders to emphasise the positive. It does not favour local control and ownership where this is seen as restricting the industry's access to resources. It dislikes what it calls 'excessive planning regulations', is opposed to ecological or tourist or aviation taxes, and is sceptical about enforced carrying capacity regulations. It wants to expand the size and number of airports. As the WTTC President openly said "we strongly believe that the environmental policy agenda should focus on the industry's self-improvement, incentives and a light handed regulation." And by and large the industry tries to ignore the socio-cultural and economic aspects of sustainable development. It is of course not just the industry's fault. Many of the problems stem for the customer, the tourist. As one exasperated tourist operator commented on a Christian Aid leaflet on tourism:

> With the exception of a handful of niche players, environmental awareness among operators does not result from pressure from clients but from our wish to educate them. Customers simply want a comfortable holiday in a 5 star hotel on an unspoilt beach, and they do not care how this is achieved. I almost forgot - they also want it cheap and to hell with who or what is exploited to get the price down.

It is thus doubtful whether the Global Compact will achieve the objective of moving the world closer to a sustainable development path. The travel and tourist industry is perhaps one of the better industries. But until it faces up to the contradictions in its approach to sustainable development then its many claims about being a natural ally of sustainable development will have to be seen as greenwash.

But if the government and the host community are willing to act then tourism can make a significant contribution to a more sustainable development path in the host country. The country that has most successfully projected itself as being a model for tourism and sustainable development is Costa Rica, the most stable, peaceful and socially cohesive country in Latin America. Much has been done but even in Costa Rica the reality has failed to live up to the rhetoric.

The conflict between ecology and development in Costa Rica
Lying at the junction of North and South America, and with both Caribbean and Pacific coastlines, Costa Rica is an ecologically rich, but also ecologically fragile, country. Within its 20,000 square miles, Costa Rica has 12 different ecological zones, ranging from tropical forests, sub-alpine dwarfed vegetation, tropical beaches, corals, mangroves and swamps. Packed into this tiny country is an immense wealth of species, including 10% of the world's butterfly and bird species.

Politically Costa Rica is peaceful and stable, particularly in comparison with its neighbours in Central America. The armed forces were abolished following a brief civil war in 1948. The reforms enacted thereafter have allowed the country to avoid extremes of poverty and wealth as well as cycles of violence and repression (Edelman and Kenen 1989). The combination of political and social stability, good communications, and a sophisticated and well-educated elite able to attract numerous United Nation and other international and regional organisations as well as attract funds for Costa Rica's pioneering initiatives in such things as debt-for -nature swaps, protected areas, bio-diversity prospecting[6], and carbon dioxide tradeable emissions permits[7] has enabled Costa Rica to be the leader of sustainable development in the region. It is also often cited more generally as the model for tourism and sustainable development.

Ecologically however its record in the past was bad.[8] The development process in the last 50 years in Costa Rica put a great strain on its fragile ecological systems, particularly as Costa Rica's population increased from 862,000 in 1950 to 2 million in 1975 and 3 million in 1980. For a period Costa Rica had the fastest rate of deforestation in the world. In 1950 72% of Costa Rica was covered in forest; in 1985 26% (Carriere 1991). The extraordinarily rapid depletion of its forests led to a number of ecological crises: serious erosion on the Pacific coast, watershed deterioration, silting of reservoirs, and loss of soil. Lack of planning and land use legislation, inadequate legislation and lack of implementation of existing legislation, contamination and inefficient disposal of wastes caused further widespread environmental damage. After pressure from Costa Rica's growing environmental movement and its internationally respected scientific community, the government began to establish a number of national parks and protected areas (Ranis Wallace 1992). At the beginning a purely conservationist approach was adopted towards the creation of the protected areas which sometimes led to conflicts with the local communities. But with the development of a more socially sensitive approach, the parks became popular with and

---

[6] Costa Rica's National Institute for Biodiversity, INBIO, became a model for such prospecting, signing a deal with Merck in 1991, and other pharmaceutical companies, whereby Costa Ricans collect and classify specimens and send them to the multinationals for testing and potential development in return for royalties.

[7] Already Costa Rica has 9 Joint Implementation Agreements worth some $140 million with Norway and USA companies.

[8] Even now Costa Rica's reputation for ecological sustainability is much exaggerated. There is rapid deforestation of old forest; indiscriminate and dangerous use of pesticides, uncontrolled dumping of wastes into its rivers, soil erosion, and air, noise and traffic pollution in San Jose is on a par with much of Latin America.

respected by the local people.

By 1990 some 26% of Costa Rica's territory was protected. In 2002 a new national park, Costa Rica's 28th, was created. The finance for some of the protected areas came from an aggressive debt- for-nature swap. Then with one of the highest per capita debts in the world, Costa Rica was particularly hit by the debt crisis in the 1980s (O'Brien 1993). Structural adjustment forced the privatisation of many State institutions, and led to cuts in social services and the discontinuation of government subsidies (Hansen-Kuhn 1993). As in the rest of Latin America, structural adjustment meant the dismantling of much of the state creating problems regulating the rapidly growing tourist industry.

Tourism and sustainable development: a disputed arena

In world ranking, Costa Rica is not a major tourist country: in 1995 for example it received just 0.14% of world tourists and 0.18% of tourist receipts – making Costa Rica 54[th]out of a total of 186 states. (WTO 1997). However, in terms of importance to Costa Rica, tourism is now the key economic activity. In 1955 only 21,637 tourists visited Costa Rica bringing in $3.37m. In 1960 the numbers doubled to 42,073 bringing in $6.55m; and in 1966 the numbers were 98,907 bringing in $15.39m   (ICT Memorias y Anuarios Estadisticos). Thereafter numbers increased rapidly to 340,442 in 1978. Then from 1979 to 1982 tourist arrivals increased at an average annual rate of 7.2%, and in 1982 foreign exchange receipts from tourism were six times those in 1970. From 1982 to 1988 tourist entries fell slightly initially, and then stabilised. Foreign exchange receipts ranked third, after the traditional exports of coffee and bananas. Then from 1988 onwards there was a veritable boom in tourism, thanks in part to the marketing of Costa Rica as an "ecotourist haven". Tourists, particularly from the USA and Canada were looking for something exotic and different but safe, and Costa Rica is undoubtedly exotic, different and safe. Costa Rica became extraordinarily well –covered by Guide Books in English, French, German, and Spanish. [9]

---

[9] In addition to the Best Guidebook Award winning 750-page Baker C. (1996), *Costa Rica Handbook*. (Chico: Moon Publications Inc), a small sample of English publications would have to include Blake B. and A. Becher (1993), *The New Key to Costa Rica*. (Berkeley: Ulysses Press) – contains sustainability stars for selected hotels; Franke J. (1993), *Costa Rica's National Parks and Preserves: A Visitors Guide*. (Seattle: The Mountaineers); Haber H. (1992), *Insight Guide to Costa Rica*.(Hong Kong: APA Publications); Itiel J. (1993), *Pura Vida! A Travel Guide to Gay and Lesbian Costa Rica*. (San Francisco: Orchid House); Meza Ocampo T. and R. Mesa Peralta (1992), *Discover Costa Rica: A Historical Cultural Guide*. (San Jose: Universal); Pariser H.

Tourism began to boom. In 1990 tourist receipts reached $275million. Between 1990 and 1993 tourist entries grew by just under 20% a year, and by 1993 tourism had overtaken coffee as Costa Rica's main foreign exchange earner. Then inexplicably the bubble first slowed down in 1993 and 1994 and then the rate of growth fell dramatically in 1995, and was negative in 1996.The main reason for the decline was the drop in numbers from Europe, particularly Germany. Thereafter tourism began to increase again: in 2000 1,088,075 tourists visited Costa Rica, and in 2001, in spite of the crisis engendered by September 11th, tourist arrivals increased to 1,131,598. Numbers from the USA and Europe did decline dramatically after September 11th, but Costa Rica managed to lure Latin Americans and by an advertising campaign and discounts for nationals the country managed to increase local tourism substantially. A massive marketing campaign (costing almost $10m), particularly in the USA, aimed at the medium to high-income travellers paid dividends. The marketing campaign concentrated on simple but powerful photographs highlighting Costa Rica's biological diversity, natural beauty, comfort and tranquillity. Through this Costa Rica seems to have avoided a major downturn in the tourist market.

In a questionnaire of 3,000 airline passengers arriving in Costa Rica conducted by the Institute of Costa Rican Tourism during both the high and low season of 1996, 70.6% of those arriving for pleasure or to visit families, cited sun and beaches as the main reason for the visit. Thereafter natural history (52.7%), adventure sports (49.1% - canoeing etc), and bird watching (38.3%) scored highly (ICT 1996). It is clear from the figures that most people visiting Costa Rica for a holiday went there for both "sun and beaches" and green tourism: Costa Rica being of a size where it is possible to do both easily. Its comparative advantage in tourism clearly lies in the ability to satisfy in the one holiday a mixture of green tourism and sun and beaches.

The very rapid growth of tourism in Costa Rica quickly revealed

---

(1994) *The Adventure Guide to Costa Rica.* (Edison NJ: Hunter Publishing); Price C. (ed) (1993) *Fodor's Costa Rica, Belize and Guatemala.*(New York: Fodor's Travel Publications); Rachowiecki R. (1994), *Costa Rica- A Travel Survival Kit.* (Berkeley: Lonely Planet); Samson K. (1993), *Frommer's Costa Rica, Guatemala and Belize on $35 a day.* (New York: Frommer Books); Sheck R. (1994), *Costa Rica: A Natural Destination.* (John Muir Publications: Santa Fe NM); Tucker A. (ed) (1994), *The Berlitz Traveler's Guide to Costa Rica* (New York: Berlitz Publishing); Tico Times(1993), *Exploring Costa Rica: The Tico Times Guide.* (San Jose: Tico Times); Tattersall Ryan J. (1993), *Simple Pleasures: A Guide to the Bed and Breakfasts and Special Hotels of Costa Rica.* (San Jose); Wood M., *Charlie's Charts of Costa Rica.*(Surrey .B.C. : Charlie's Charts). In addition there are guides to Retirement and Living in Costa Rica; dozens of tourist videos, and a variety of English Language Newsletters and Newspapers. For a country of its size Costa Rica must be one of the most "guided" places in the world!

both the strengths and weaknesses of Costa Rica's attempt to use tourism as its main strategy for sustainable development. The main problems stemmed from the politics of tourism, particularly the lack or ineffectiveness of government regulations, the inappropriate legislative framework, the unwillingness of both the tourists and the tourist industry to contribute adequately to conserve Costa Rica's unique environment and maintain local sustainable livelihoods, and the desire for some to make a quick buck. Other problems came from the "carrying capacity" of fragile ecological systems and inadequate participation from local communities. Another problem was the rapid entry of foreign, multinational capital, and probably the use of drug money for property construction and speculation, leading to accusations of bribery and corruption.

The politics of tourism in Costa Rica stems from weakness of the state to either help finance or regulate a new industry such as tourism. For a long time Costa Rica depended on foreign debt for nature swaps, donations and assistance to maintain much of the National Parks infrastructure. Constant pressure by the IMF and others to expand export earnings and to continue to pay back interest on the debt encouraged the Costa Rican government to cut corners, particularly if benefits seemed to be now and costs in the future. The weaknesses of legislation governing tourism soon became apparent. Initially there were very few plans for tourist development, and Costa Rica just responded to the characteristics and requirements of demand. At the height of the tourist boom, Costa Rica had no national plan for tourism, and the 40-year old law that created the Costa Rican Tourism Institute (ICT) had not given the Institute powers to protect natural resources. There was no legislation to make those who benefited from tourism contribute to its long-term promotion. The ICT did its best to encourage green tourism, but in the end could only study the problem. Carrying capacity soon became a problem. There were no adequate controls over which areas could be developed and to what extent. Indeed 17% of Costa Rica's National Parks still belong to private landlords although most do preserve the agreement to conserve the national parks. But not unsurprisingly some parks, such as Manuel Antonio National Park which is still only half paid for, became over-saturated with visitors causing major problems of pollution and disappearance of wild animals. In 1992 it was finally decided to restrict entry to the Park – although there is still a problem of heart attacks among the monkeys due to eating tourist snacks. Private reserves such as Monteverde did control admissions and charge for entry. But at the same time there was an enormous uncontrolled expansion of hotels outside the reserve, radically altering the nature of the local community. Admission prices to Costa Rica's priceless natural parks became a major bone of contention. Historically, even though charging more to tourists than locals, admission prices to the parks were always low, and nowhere near covered the costs of maintenance. With half a million tourists a year, the National Parks' guards running the parks remain ill-equipped. But when in 1994 the government did decide to unilaterally impose a $15 entrance fee (a ten fold increase) to the national parks, there was an outcry both from the tourists and from the Costa Rican tourist industry. Between 1994 and 1996 entrances to the national parks fell by over a quarter (though there is no evidence this was solely caused by the fee increase), and in 1996 the entry fee was lowered to $6. Part of the problem was that few people trusted the government to use the extra revenues for the national parks. Even before the increase, revenues from the parks just went to finance the government's overall expenditures. But the outcry did reveal a lack of willingness, on the part of both tourists and the Costa Rican tourist industry, to shoulder part of the burden of maintenance and conservation of the ecological systems on which both depend.Nevertheless, despite the failure of the government to act, sectors of the Costa Rican tourist industry did respond positively to conservation and maintenance needs.. The examples cover a wide-range of green initiatives. To take just one typology drawn from personal experience in the fairly remote region of Sarapaqui, the range of "ecotouristic" experiences is vast.[10] Examples range from the small peasant co-operative which seemed to get most things right. The co-operative had built a number of rustic lodges on their remote farmland for small groups of tourists, including school children, offering the tourist direct experience of their farm work, agro-forestry, fishing, herb growing, bird and mammal (the area is rich in monkey species) watching. Apart from that, the local – co-operative controls the tourist trade itself, which according to them brings not only welcome additional income and resources, but also entertainment and encouragement towards ecologically sound farming and conservation. Another example is the small peasant building tourist cabins next to a scenic attraction such as a waterfall, maintaining the area, building paths and charging for admission to the waterfall. Another is the Green Macaw conservation activist who built an addition to his house for tourists who could then accompany him on his work expeditions. Again tourism contributes

---

[10] Much of the following is based on personal interviews.

to a sustainable livelihood and the conservation of an area of beauty, and the fight to save an endangered species.

Frequently one comes across, "the Gringos' dream": a small-scale, often undercapitalised, cottage hotel run by foreigners with a romantic, often mystical view, of nature who convert themselves into local experts on the local ecology. An example of this is a small kayaking, primary forest trekking, and stained glass tourist operation, Rancho Leona, established in 1983. La Selva, the biological research centre and the Arenal Observatory, the volcano research centre, are examples of serious scientific enterprises that use tourism to supplement their income for their scientific and conservation work. More tokenistic is the big business, often foreign owned, "nature tourism" such as La Selva Verde which caters primarily for the over-60s offering them guided tours and talks on their own nature reserve to which they had introduced a non-native frog species to make it more interesting, causing problems for the less beautiful local frogs. The final example is a form of "Green Disneyland", the Aerial Tram, built at great expense by a foreign consortium, to provide a luxurious and risk free ride over the forest canopy as a side- trip to Caribbean cruises. Unlike in La Selva the experience is completely passive and not very educative, although most of the guides are from local areas. The café relies upon imported, portion- controlled foods, and nearly everything is run from the capital, San Jose. The Tram company projects a very "green" image, offering for example free trips for the best school conservation projects, but underlying the hype is a highly efficient profit making machine most of which ends up outside Costa Rica.

Outside of Sarapaqui other examples of green initiatives abound. Adventours, a San Jose based tourist company, for example, began to voluntarily pay a percentage of their profits into environmental protection programmes, and to draw up environmental codes of conduct.

A number of groups and people also set out to show that ecotourism can be a means to altering the view that the forests are an obstacle to development by offering viable, alternative livelihoods. For example the 1,300 hectare Rara Avis reserve, co-owned by a tourist company, research project and conservation groups, not only has eco-tourists but also has facilities for biological research and studies of how to make money out of the rain forest without destroying it. The founder of the reserve, Amos Bien calculated that cattle raising which small to medium size farm landowners turn to after they have cut down the rainforest produces an income of about

$20 per hectare. He showed that ecotourism combined with speciality plant and animal trade can add more to the economic livelihoods of the local community. He argued that to prevent forest being cut down outside the national parks, the forests have to be made economically useful. Together with others, Bien went on to establish a National Association of Private Nature Preserves of which there are a growing number in Costa Rica. All over Costa Rica small groups sprang up to earn an income from green tourism by genuinely offering ecologically friendly holidays. The Talamanca Association for Ecotourism and Conservation offers a variety of experiences including visiting Indian homes deep in the reserve. And an entrepreneurial local Indian constructed thatch huts in the style of the Bribri and Cabecar Indian tribes. Not unsurprisingly Costa Rica has attracted a large number of small, and not so small, foreign owned green hotels and tourist projects. Costa Rica has always attracted foreigners in pursuit of their "dream". All over Costa Rica there are now a number of luxury "dreams", inspired by Costa Rica's natural beauty. One such is an American film producer's "barefoot luxury villa hotel development", "Si Como No", in Manuel Antonio, which uses the best available environmental technologies. An increasing proportion of tourist establishments are explicitly environmentally aware. Even in downtown San Jose, the casino hotel specialising in American fishermen and gamblers, and where local prostitutes are welcome, consciously parades its green credentials, inviting guests to make their contribution to the environment by having their bed linen changed only every other day.

Attempts have been made to monitor some of the green tourist establishments. The Audubon Society in Costa Rica issues "green seals" of approval to environmentally sound tourist operators. Participating companies agree to adhere to a "Code of Environmental Ethics" and to allow Audubon to monitor their activities. Audubon together with the author of one of Costa Rica's most popular guide books, has compiled a list of eco-friendly hotels, based on replies to a questionnaire, rating them by three categories: ecologically sound practices; cultural ecology (awareness of impact on local culture and measures to preserve it); and economic contribution to the local economy. Many of the small tourist operators in Costa Rica are native born, and have a strong interest in avoiding the money from tourism concentrating in one place and in one group. Costa Rica's very diversity meant that there are small hotels all over the country with tourists travelling and exploring the whole country. A wide variety of people could thus benefit: rent- a- car companies, small hotels, small stores, gas stations, local guides, local artisans etc. In addition most of these small establishments buy local produce – foodstuffs, coffee, soft drinks, soap and often pride themselves on using local wood and craftsmen for furniture and design features. There is thus a demand to "democratise" tourism, and keep it that way. The small operators are sensitive to local people, recognising the need to ensure that benefits from tourism do go back to the local community if local communities are to protect the parks.

But tourism cannot ease all the conflicts between social needs and conservation. Disagreements over forests in particular are rife. In 1997 problems arose again over the new forestry laws that made it easier to obtain permits to cut down trees. Environmentalists complained bitterly that there was a huge increase in illegal logging, eventually forcing the government to suspend logging. Local small farmers then complained equally bitterly that they had to sell a little wood to survive.

Also the rapid increase in tourism means that without adequate legislation which is actually implemented, the boom in hotel building has already violated many of the country's coastal laws, and too many hotels are being built too close to national parks. In 1998 for example both the ICT and the local municipality gave permission to an Italian owned firm to construct condominiums and shops only 250 metres from Manuel Antonio Park gates. In this case the local tourist operators are protesting vigorously.With the government desperate for foreign exchange, licenses are being readily given to the large foreign operators. The case for the international hotel chains, the USA Marriott group, Jacktar Village Resort, the Spanish Barcelo group and Sol Melia to name just some, is usually presented as improving hotel standards. The Spanish group, Grupo Barcelo, was allowed to build a 400-room hotel in the Pacific coastal area of Tambor. To do this it is accused of filling in a swamp, dredging a river, building too close to the coastline and even bringing in white sand to replace the black sand and despite protests it was backed by the Government. Other examples followed. The most notorious example was the so-called "Papagayo Ecodevelopment", a massive development project designed to build 1,144 homes, 6,544 hotel rooms, 6,270 condo-hotel units, shopping centres and golf courses on the Pacific coast. The project was finally partially postponed by the previous government after many protests only for the new government to re-open the possibility of the project going ahead. As so often in the Third World large sums of money carried more sway with the Government than the wishes of the local people and environmentalists. These developments brought home to Costa Ricans that, in spite of all the hype, too often eco-tourism hype was little more than green-wash.The main problem lies with the Costa Rican government. On the one hand, it wants to publicise Costa Rica as a "laboratory for sustainable development", and is willing to create the image of small-scale tourism to attract green tourists. On the other hand it is attracted to the large mega-projects, believing that these will dramatically increase its revenues from tourism.

In addition, the place where most Costa Ricans live, the capital city, San Jose, is becoming increasingly unsustainable as traffic grinds to a halt, air pollution worsens, waste management is in crisis, the city infrastructure collapses, and poverty is increasingly visible. There is also a notable Americanisation of Costa Rican life. Tourism, if it is to contribute to sustainable development, must also contribute to the quality of life in places like San Jose. Much of the money from tourism does come back to the capital, but not to the poorer areas. For these areas tourism has brought mainly the negative aspects: an increase in drugs, prostitution, crime and youth delinquency.

Conclusions

Costa Rica is at a crossroads as regards tourism. The rapid growth in tourism took the government by surprise. They were happy to help market Costa Rica as a "natural holiday" and as an "eco-tourist haven". But as the numbers of tourists grew, it became clear that without regulations and controls the very basis of the "eco-tourist haven" could become threatened. And the financial crisis of the state, with the often externally imposed pressure to privatise and cut budgets, soon overshadowed the Government's plans for sustainable development.With the failure of government action, sectors of the tourist industry launched a number of their own initiatives in an effort to keep tourism "democratic" i.e. numerous and diverse, small-scale local operators, including local community involvement – and "ecotourism Costa Rican style" as it was called (Budowski T. 1992). But inevitably the more tourist numbers increased, the more interested were the multinationals to enter the market with "mega tourist" projects. And the more strapped the government was for cash, the more attractive some of these offers became. What the growth in tourism quickly revealed is the lack of local government planning and local participation. Local Agenda 21 is conspicuous by its absence in Costa Rica. Instead both the government and the NGOs went for an extraordinarily complicated participative structure for a National Programme for Sustainable Development. The establishment of such structures was very time consuming, and in the end achieved remarkably little. The government wanted to turn the national meetings into a public relations exercise for itself in which the President of the Republic delivers a lot of rhetoric and promises, but allows no debate and critical comment.(O'Brien 1997) The financial crisis of the state also showed up the inability of the government both to monitor what is happening and to implement even existing legislation.

Without any architectural heritage, historical ruins or strong indigenous cultures Costa Rica is completely dependent on its natural environment to attract tourists. This is a strong attraction- a "Jewel of Nature" as one guidebook puts it. But the Jewel has to be protected. And without an effective tourist strategy and plan, then there is a danger that tourism will eventually have a negative impact on Costa Rica's environment. At the moment tourism has overall had a positive impact, particularly when compared with Costa Rica's other main alternatives, coffee, bananas, and cattle. Ordinary Costa Ricans increasingly appreciate that the parks and wildlife are a reliable generator of attractive and sustainable livelihoods. It can provide attractive local employment and small business opportunities throughout the country, including remote rural areas. And tourist revenues have contributed to paying for state services and infrastructure that is vital to Costa Rica's social stability.

But local entrepreneurs and local finance are scarce, and Costa Rica's famous "democratisation" of tourism is coming under strain. Small-scale foreign hotel owners and tour operators, who usually settle in Costa Rica, have helped Costa Rica go up market through the building of "boutique" hotels and the marketing of "adventure tours" etc. All of these tend to maximise local linkages and multipliers. But without low cost finance and support to local entrepreneurs, including communities, for eco-tourism, there is an increasing danger of multinational tourist firms, using the rhetoric of eco-tourism, taking over more and more, and building bigger and bigger establishments with a loss of local linkages and local multipliers. It may be these large-scale developments can be confined to just a part of Guanacaste, the main sun and beach area, as well-managed, carefully supervised and carefully sited "honeypots", but so far government controls are inadequate, and it is unlikely that the multinationals would want to be so confined.

Costa Rica still has to fully develop its clusters of competitive advantage in tourism. Its training, art, craft and design schools, and its local design talent, is not adequate to take advantage of the tourists' demands. Local plans and local participation on tourist developments are woefully inadequate.

The state, both national and local, has to carefully monitor, regulate and control the expansion of tourism. Unfortunately the ideology of free markets strongly influenced the last Costa Rican government. This Government went down the road of free markets, and put further strains on Costa Rica's fragile environment.

The new Government (that of the Christian Social Unity Party under President Abel Pacheco) recognised the need for greater regulation. The Minister of the Environment and Energy almost immediately refused to allow a US-based oil company to drill for oil along Costa Rica's Caribbean coast, citing over 50 legal and environmental problems. Then on World Environment Day, the President announced new logging regulations which restricted the transportation of logs and made tagging of logs compulsory, in an effort to stop illegal logging which accounts for some 34% of commercial logging. In addition he proclaimed a moratorium on new open pit gold mines. And then in a bold move the President proposed to include environmental guarantees in the Costa Rican Constitution. If passed the amended Constitution, Article 76, would read.

> The State guarantees, defends, preserves and maintains a public interest on air, water, subsoil, biological diversity and its components; as well as hydrocarbons, minerals and energy, coastal resources, patrimonial sea, economic exclusive zone and protected areas within the nation.

Article 76 also proposes that the state will regulate the public and private use and exploitation of these resources, so that it is done according to the rules of science and in the public interest. And the proposed article 78 categorically states that: "any public or private activity affecting the biochemical and genetic heritage of the country will be obliged to deal with the law to guarantee a sustainable and ecological development." This is a crucial change. The major weakness in Costa Rica's tourist strategy has been the inability to use the law to enforce regulations. The proposed new law will give the public a right of recourse to the law to defend the new constitutional guarantees. In spite of all the rhetoric, and in some cases good examples of practice, Costa Rica's attempt to achieve sustainable development had been floundering because of its inability to enforce its regulations. As the President said, the 'deterioration of the ecosystems, the lack of policies and legal instruments able to protect the environment, and the non existence of environmental planning, needs a change to the Constitution'. If the proposed changes go through, and there are strong vested interests opposed to the changes, then there is a good chance that Costa Rica can be a model for sustainable development to its neighbours and show that tourism and sustainable development can be natural allies.

The days of the "Jewel of Nature" are under threat but may not yet be numbered.

References

Budowski T. (1992) "Ecotourism Costa Rican Style" in: V. Barzetti and Y. Rovinski(eds), *Towards a Green Central America*. Connecticut: Kumarian Press.

Carriere J. [1991] "The Crisis in Costa Rica: an ecological perspective" in: D. Goodman and M. Redclift (eds), *Environment and Development in Latin America: the Politics of Sustainability*. Manchester: Manchester University Press.

Centro Latinoamericano para la Competitividad y el Desarrollo Sostenible (1996), Turismo en Costa Rica: El reto de la competitividad. San Jose: INCAE.Edelman J. and J. Kenen (eds). (1989) *The Costa Rica Reader*. New York: Grove Weidenfield.

Hansen-Kuhn (1993), *Structural Adjustment in Central America: the Case of Costa Rica*, Washington D.C.: The Development Group for Alternative Policy.

Lindberg K. and D. Hawkins (eds.) (1993), *Ecotourism: A Guide for Planners and Managers*. North Bennington: The Ecotourism Society.

Mowforth M. and I. Munt (1998), *Tourism and Sustainability – new tourism in the Third World*. London: Routledge.

O'Brien P. [1993], "The Latin American Debt Crisis" in S. Riley (ed.) *The Politics of Global Debt*. London and New York: St Martin's Press, and McMillan Press.

O'Brien P. (1997), "Global Processes and the Politics of Sustainable Development in Colombia and Costa Rica." in Auty R. and K. Brown, *Approaches to Sustainable Development*. London: Pinter.

Patullo P. (1996), *Last Resorts: The Cost of Tourism in the Caribbean*. London: LAB.

Pleumaron A. (1996) "Eco-tourism: A New "Green Revolution" in the Third World" in Kohler G. and C. Gore, U. Reich, and T. Ziesemer (eds.), *Questioning Development*. Marburg: Metropolis-Verlag.

Rains Wallace D. (1992), *The Quetzal and the Macaw: The Story of Costa Rica's National Parks*. San Francisco: Sierra Club Books.

Sittenfield A.[1994] "Bio-diversity Prospecting Frameworks: the INBIO Experience in Costa Rica". Paper presented to *Biological Diversity:*

Exploring the Complexities. University of Arizonia, Tucson.

Spinrad B. (1982) "St. Lucia" in Seward S. and B.Spinrad , *Tourism in the Caribbean: the Economic Impact.* Ottawa: IDRC.

The United Nations Environment Programme. (1999) *Our Planet. Tourism.* Volume 10. Number 1.

World Tourism Organisation (1991), *What is WTO?* Madrid: WTO.

World Tourism Organisation(1997) (1998), *Yearbook of Tourism Statistics.* Madrid: WTO.

Chapter 15

Tourism and Ecotourism Development in Malaysia
An Overview

Rosazman Hussin

Introduction

As predicted by Kajiwara, tourism is the largest industrial sector in
the world and it is expected to maintain that distinction until the
middle of the 21st century (Kajiwara, 1997:164). The development of
tourism in Malaysia has received serious attention from development
planners and policymakers in the country as a tool of development
from the 1970s. Estimates show that Malaya received some 25,000
tourists in 1959, growing to 36,000 in 1963. In 1972 the government
established the Tourism Development Corporation of Malaysia
(TDCM) so tourism products could be developed and promoted
systematically. By 1974, tourist arrivals to Malaysia increased at a
growth rate of 6.5% from 2.3 million in 1980, to 3.1 million in 1985
(Hamzah, 1986:2). As mentioned by Yahya Ibrahim (2002), the
reasons why the tourism sector became more important to Malaysia
in those decades are:

- The price of most major commodity exports such as rubber, tin
  and rainforest timber is not stable on the international market.
  This situation can be a harmful element for Malaysia's
  economic progress and development.
- In 1972, Malaysia conducted the 21st Pacific Asia Tourism
  Association Conference (PATA) in Kuala Lumpur. As a result,
  Malaysia was appointed as a Chair of the PATA Committee for
  three years (1972-1975). This task to promote the ASEAN
  region as a tourist destination through various marketing
  mechanisms and strategies, gave Malaysia the knowledge and
  skills to develop its own tourism industry.
- In 1986 Malaysia was chosen to host the 35th PATA
  Conference. As a consequence, it attained huge international
  media coverage, especially for its tourism products and
  developments. On 19th May 1987, the government introduced

the "1st Malaysian Fest" with its major aim to promote Malaysian cultural activities, recreation and sports events, marketing local arts and handicrafts and so on.

At that time, the strategies employed were for mass tourism developments in Malaysia. The tourist growth rate expanded to double figures until it reached its height in 1990 with an average arrival growth of 55.5 per cent bringing in RM4, 473.00 million in total tourism revenues (see table 1). As a newcomer to tourism most of the policy makers argued that the growth signalled the potential for a remarkable tourist development.

In the1990s, however, the tourism policy makers in Malaysia began to realise that "mass tourism" could have some problems in maintaining the tourist arrival growth rates because of regional competition from ASEAN country neighbours, the emergence of international tourism related-security issues such as terrorism and so forth. The main concern of the Malaysian government towards tourism, nowadays, is with *"sustainable tourism development"* rather than just to achieve high growth rates in tourist arrivals. Thus, this essay intends to explore why this notion has occurred and how the government plans to achieve its tourism "niche market" in the future.

The decline in tourist arrivals in Malaysia

In 1991 the government introduced what has been called "the National Tourism Policy" (NTP). The NTP was enforced by government as an action plan and framework for tourism development in the 1990s. The general objectives of the NTP in 1991 are:

i.   To increase foreign currency exchange.
ii.   To stimulate rural economic development.
iii. To increase new opportunities in domestic trade and businesses.
iv.   To ensure every ethnic group of Malaysia's population participates in the tourism industry.
v.   To promote positive images of the state at the international level.

In relation to the emergence of NTP, the government has taken various actions and measurements in order to implement it. These include:

i.   The formation of the Cabinet Committee on Tourism under the chairmanship of the Prime Minister, to formulate and review policies affecting tourism development.

ii.   An introduction of tax incentives for tourism projects both for accommodation and non-accommodation projects invested by tour operators especially by local investors.

iii.   The reduction of the government Service Tax from 10% to 5% to ensure lower costs in terms of room and restaurant charges.

iv.   Reduction of electricity tariff rates for the hotel industry to facilitate the hotels in Malaysia to become more price competitive with other regional ASEAN destinations.

v.   The establishment of the New Investment Fund (NIF). Its major aim is to provide financial assistance such as extended loans on approved tourism projects (Hamzah, 1986: 3).

As a result, a big jump occurred in 1990 when tourist arrivals increased dramatically by 55.5 per cent. However, after the Visit Malaysia Year promotion in 1990, it seems that Malaysian tourism has undergone a period of stagnation from 1995-1998. For instance, earlier than 1991 the statistics show a decline in growth rates of tourist arrivals in Malaysia to –21.7 per cent, then it declined again to –4.4 per cents in 1996, to –13.0 per cent in 1997, to –10.6 per cent in 1997 (see table 1). In 1999 the tourist arrival growth rates in Malaysia returned to positive track with an increase of 42.9% but it then declined to 28.9% in 2000 with a further decline to 25.0% in 2001 (Tourism Malaysia, 2001).

Table 1: Total Tourist Arrival and Total Tourism Revenue in Malaysia (1980-1999)

Year	Total Tourist Arrival	Average Growth Arrival (%)	Tourism Revenue (RM million)	Average Growth Revenue (%)
1980	2,067,020	1.4	618.9	25.0
1981	2,344,933	13.5	867.3	40.3
1982	2,588,772	10.4	1,019.0	17.5
1983	2,750,397	6.2	1,329.0	19.2
1984	2,779,081	1.0	1,426.0	7.4
1985	2,933,271	5.6	1,543.0	8.2
1986	3,217,462	9.7	1,669.0	8.3
1987	3,358,983	4.4	1,795.0	7.7
1988	3,623,636	7.9	2,012.0	11.3
1989	4,553,392	25.7	2,803.0	39.3
1990	7,079,107	55.5	4,473.0	59.6
1991	5,543,376	-21.7	4,282.6	-43
1992	5,687,247	2.6	4,419.6	3.2
1993	5,503,860	8.1	5,066.0	10.2
1994	7,197,229	10.7	8,298.0	63.8
1995	7,468,749	3.8	9,174.9	10.6
1996	7,138,452	-4.4	1,0354.1	12.9
1997	6,210,921	-13.0	9,699.6	-6.3
1998	5,550,748	-10.6	8,580.4	-11.5
1999	7,931,149	42.9	12,321.3	43.6
2000*	10,221,582	28.9		
2001*	12,75,073	25.0		

Source: Adapted from Malaysia Tourism Promotion Board (MTPB) various years.
* Data gathered from Tourism Malaysia, 2000 and 2001[a]
http://www.tourismmalaysia.gov.my

There are a number of reasons why these declines in tourist arrivals took place in Malaysia:

i.   In the early phase of tourist development in Malaysia, the Ministry of Culture, Arts and Tourism of Malaysia (established by the government in 1989) commissioned a national tourism policy and study. Thus, the management and coordination of tourism policies within the government bodies and private sector became more effective. For some tourist analysts such as Kadir Din (1997), the establishment of the Ministry in fact was very useful and good for tourism development in Malaysia. But, the way the tourism official thinks and works is still restricted: they regularly took for granted that the cultural elements of a plural society are attractive to foreign tourists; in fact they do not conceptualise that a national culture is an attractive tourism product. This is because they saw their role to be to simply serve tourism promotion and the compilation of tourist statistics rather than give full attention to the potential of Malaysia's culture as a unique tourism product in terms of a holistic approach (Kadir Din, 1997:111). The main concern within both public and private sectors in this early phase of tourism development was almost exclusively with promotional issues such as how best to promote Malaysia as a tourist destination in Southeast Asia in the sense of "a mass tourism marketing strategy". As a result the tourist arrival rates could grow from year to year but it cannot grow in terms of sustainability.

ii.   Malaysia is lacking an image and identity to promote tourism as compared with Thailand or Singapore. It does not have the brash, racy image of Thailand's night life, or the modern urban image of Singapore (Yamashita, 2001). In this manner it is hard for Malaysia to compete in tourism with its neighbours.

iii.   The Malaysian Government has introduced the programme "1st Visit Malaysia Year" in 1990. Then the same programme called "2nd Visit Malaysia Year" followed in 1995. The growth of tourist arrivals in Malaysia, however, is still in a downward trend. The government explains this negative trend of tourism development as being due to smoke problems from forest burning in the Southeast Asia region (Khan, Toh and Fathima, 2001:225), the spread of Coxsackie's syndromes and Japanese encephalitis virus in Malaysia. Political economy analysts argue that the negative trends actually related more to the Asian economic crisis. This was followed by Malaysia's domestic political crisis when the fight between political leaders such as Anwar Ibrahim's camp and Dr Mahathir received international mass media attention in 1997-1998. All these events have given a negative image to Malaysia's tourism industry.

iv.   There is disparity in term of tourist arrivals distribution rate for a major destination in Malaysia (see table 2) within

1998-1999. For instance, peninsular Malaysia has received 94.4% of the tourist arrivals, while only 3.3% visited Sarawak, and 1.8% visited Sabah respectively. The main reason usually given by the tourism official is that Sabah and Sarawak are located on Borneo Island, far from the mainland capital, and Malaysian airfare is expensive (Yamashita, 2001: 2). As a consequence Sabah and Sarawak have been backward in term of mass tourism development in Malaysia.

v.   In 1999, the Ministry of Culture, Art and Tourism introduced a new promotion theme of tourism in Malaysia called *"Malaysia Truly Asia"*. What the theme means is that, if international tourists visit Malaysia they will find that it is not a single culture but the tourist will experience the variety of Asia's cultures (Abd Jalil Ali & Ahmad Yani, 2000). In other words the Ministry is now more concerned about the diversity of Malaysia's culture as a new product. In the short term this strategy seems successful because the growth rate of international tourist arrivals to Malaysia was 8.1 million, compared to only 5.5 million tourists in 1998. But the step taken by the Ministry was already quite late because the culture's product did not receive special attention before the year 2000. At the same time this strategy does not reflect an effective "image" of Malaysia's traditional culture in the way that it should be, but it emphasises more a "mix dance culture" of the society. In this manner, we can say that Malaysia's tourism niche product is still not clear.

Table 2: The Distribution of Tourist Arrivals in the Main Domestic Area/Region in Malaysia (1998-1999)

Main Domestic Tourist Destination	1999	Tourist Arrival Growth Average (%)	1998	Changes (%)
Peninsular	7,483,823	94.4	5,203,355	+43.8
Malaysia	7,931,149	100	5,550,748	+ 42.9
Sarawak	264,285	3.3	195,051	+ 35.5
Sabah	142,982	1.8	106,494	+ 34.3
Labuan	40,054	0.5	45,848	- 12.6

Source: Adapted from Malaysia, 1998 and 1999

vi.   Although there is a positive impact from the tourism industry in Malaysia, for instance, to support the preservation of the traditional cultures such as stage performances and handicraft productions, in general the tourism industry has been criticised because of its negative impact on the socio-culture of Malaysia society (Bird 1989, Kadir Din 1997). It is claimed that the tourism industry has inevitably led to a more materialistic lifestyle, which is readily imitated by local populations (Kadir Din, 1997:112). Accordingly, it is regularly cited that tourism is involved with prostitution, alcoholic consumption, drugs, voyeurism, gambling, and indulgence in recreational clubs and hotel culture, which all encourage a permissive lifestyle, which is in conflict with the traditional values of a large section of the Malaysian society. At one stage all these issues became political: a dispute between the coalition National Front (Barisan Nasional) and the alternative opposition coalition which is lead by PAS (Malaysia Islamic Party). PAS argued that the tourism industry does not make positive social benefits, especially to the younger generation of Malaysian society: instead it creates social problems.

These criticisms, the negative impacts of the tourism industry in Malaysia, and the realisation that the tourism industry regularly faces uneven tourist arrivals because of competition in the regional tourism market, has forced tourism policy makers to search for a new icon tourism product for Malaysia. Finally, in the Eight Malaysia Plan, 2001-2005 (RMK 8) the government has announced their future tourism to be a "niche" market plan: "ecotourism" development in Malaysia.

Ecotourism development in Malaysia

For the first time in this decade of the new millennium there was a joint conference organised by the Malaysia Tourism Co-operation (MTC), the State Government of Selangor and Triways Holding (M) Sdn Bhd: *"Sustainable Ecotourism Development: Concept and Approach"* on 29th to 31st October 2001. This initiative should have be taken by the MTC earlier because the country has plenty of attractive natural sites such as the tropical rain forests, beaches, rivers, mountains, limestone caves, waterfalls, islands, marine life, wildlife, flora and fauna. These natural assets were not seriously developed as a tourism "niche" product for Malaysia after the 1970s, rather they were developed as protected areas *per se.*

To avoid all criticisms and negative factors that affected the tourism industry in Malaysia, its tourist officials began to promote the "National Parks of Malaysia" in year 2000 as a new tourism product. The tourist brochure guides produced by Tourism Malaysia; Ministry of Culture, Arts & Tourism promoted products such as:

> Malaysia's *forests* are indisputably the *oldest* in the world and its National Parks are *showcases* of its *rich natural* heritage.

> There's the chance to see and do something different – something beyond the normal tourist sights and pursuits. Experience the tranquillity of being one with nature in all its glory, in our National Parks. Here, within the awesome splendour of our virgin rainforests, beneath the cool shady canopy of trees hundreds of years old, one comes to realise that "conservation" is not a mere concept but a way of life – that "bio-diversity" is here to stay! (Tourism Malaysia, 2000: 3-4).

In brief, the "National Parks" brochure will provide tourist-related-information such as the general description of the parks, the specific location of the parks, *how to get there,* the tourist-related-activities, the accommodation facilities, park regulations and guidelines for visitors and so forth (see Appendix).

Earlier in 1995, Malaysia's Ecotourism Master Plan was formulated by the Ministry of Culture, Arts & Tourism and accepted by the government in 1996 (Shahril Saat, 2001:1). The main objective of the Ecotourism Master Plan is to assist both the Federal and State Governments in Malaysia to develop ecotourism potential. The plan is also intended to serve both as an appropriate instrument for the overall sustainable development of Malaysia's economy, and as an effective tool for conservation of the natural and cultural heritage of the country. To achieve this aim, Malaysia has adopted *the official definition of ecotourism* produced by the International Union for Conservation of Nature (IUCN) of which Malaysia is a member:

> Environmentally responsible travel and visitation to relatively undisturbed natural areas, in order to enjoy and appreciate nature (and any accompanying cultural features, both past and

present), that promotes conservation, has low visitor impact, and provides for beneficially active socio-economic involvement of local populations. (Ceballos-Luscurain, 1996 – *Consultant, Malaysia National Ecotourism Plan*)

In brief, the Malaysia Ecotourism Master Plan is divided into six major parts.

i.   Proceeds from policy matters to the identification of broad strategies, which should be utilised in developing ecotourism (Shahril Saat, 2001:12-14). The Ministry of Culture, Arts and Tourism is a lead player and co-ordinator, but the 21 Action Plans should be taken together with other related government agencies, private sectors, NGOs, local population etc.

ii.   A list of existing and potential ecotourism areas in each State throughout Malaysia with details of access, facilities, attraction and activities of each one. It has been said that ecotourism development must be accompanied by reservation of land to conserve the natural assets.

iii. About ecotourism practices and guidelines for planners, area managers, private sector and ecotourists.

iv.   Describes some of the perceptions and attitudes of foreign and domestic tour operators, ecotourists and local communities especially on the current sites of ecotourism in Malaysia.

v.   Describes the tourism and ecotourism situation in countries of the Asia Pacific region, and places Malaysia within this context.

vi.   Databases information regarding ecotourism related material such as bibliography, a list of training institutions and contacts, a list of nature-based tour operators in Malaysia and other countries.

Ideally, the Malaysia Ecotourism Master Plan will create awareness at all level of Malaysian society, and will promote the idea of sustainable development. In reality, there are still some critically negative impacts on everyday life of local communities in an area that is implementing an ecotourism project. Although the Ministry realised that socio-economic participation by local communities in ecotourism sites can enhance sustainable development, in reality the promotion of ecotourism is more intimately linked to the conservation of biodiversity, especially in the form of national parks and wildlife sanctuaries, and it is lacking in promotion of "a sustainable local community participation" in ecotourism. In order to elaborate on this situation, the following part of this essay will discuss the case of ecotourism development and local community participation.

Ecotourism development and local community participation in Sukau Village Kinabatangan, Sabah.

Throughout the previous decade Sabah's economy was strongly dependent on its primary exports from the agricultural and forestry sectors. However, in 1980 Sabah's commercial forest (available for logging) was reduced to about 2 million hectares, against 5.219 million hectares in 1972 (Ti Teow Chuan and Arroyo 1988, Yamashita, 2001:3). In 1985, the Forest Department estimated the remaining virgin forest to be 1.5 million hectares. This means the reduction of commercial forest from 1972 to 1985 was 3.319 million hectares, which gives an average logging rate of 286,000 hectares per year. As a consequence, the forestry sector is playing a smaller role because Sabah's state government has recognised since the mid-1980s that "nature-based tourism" should become a means of regional economic development. Thus, the future government policy toward the forestry sector is to ensure a more sustainable management of natural resources (State Government of Sabah, 1996:12). As Tan Sri Bernard Dompok, former Minister of Tourism Development, Environment, Science and Technology, Sabah states:

> ...tourism is now second only to the manufacturing sector in foreign exchange earnings and its economic importance has led to tourism being given greater emphasis; the country intends to make it an industry contributing to the new sources of growth required for socio-economic development. (New Sabah Times, May 21, 1998).

The Chief Minister of Sabah wants the local tour operators to step up efforts to increase international tourists coming to Sabah. He said 775,000 people visited Sabah in 2000, compared with only 483,991 in 1999 (Borneo Mail, April 9th, 2001). Sabah is well known as the *Land Below the Wind,* had abundant natural attractions like mountain Kinabalu, hills, rain forests, rivers, beaches, and islands that are important assets and heritage for developing nature-based tourism.

There are more than 30 ethnic groups living in Sabah, potentially a resource for developing "cultural tourism" (Pugh-Kitingan, 2000:2). It is also considered as the most attractive and unique nature and adventure destination in Malaysia. The major market for nature-based tourism are tourists from Asian Countries (Taiwan, Hong Kong, Japan), the European countries (United Kingdom, Ireland, Germany, Denmark), North America, Australia and New Zealand.

The Sabah State Ministry of Tourism Development, Environment, Science and Technology adopted the ecotourism definition by the IUCN. Ecotourism development and plans by several stakeholders such as the local lodges investors, Sabah's Wildlife Department, the World Wildlife Fund for Malaysia (WWF), the local community and the tourists, must follow the Malaysia National Ecotourism, Guidelines for Sabah, 1999, and a *Sabah Tourism Master Plan, 1996* (State Government of Sabah, 1996). For the Sabah Government, they hope that ecotourism in this sense is based not only on an interest in nature but also concerns for the conservation of nature. Thus, in the Visit Sabah Year 2000 campaign, the project promotes ecotourism with the theme, *"Malaysia's Nature Adventure Destination in the New Millennium"* or *"Sabah Natur(e)ally"* (Yamashita, 2001:7). Although ecotourism development and projects has become a popular subject for the tourism policy makers and the local investors in Sabah, the implementation of ecotourism projects in certain areas has created critical problems for those stakeholders involved. One such case is in Sukau Village, Kinabatangan, Sabah. There are several controversial issues regarding the ecotourism project in this area.

First: the shrinking of the forest area by agricultural and logging activities. Ecotourism regularly attempts to link the needs of tourists (visits to natural attractions), the need for conservation (protected biodiversity) and the needs of local communities: for instance, improving standards of living (Schulze and Suratman, 1999:5-6). Sukau village, located in the lower Kinabatangan River, has been a major ecotourism destination for Sabah since 1991. However, with the rapid pace of development in Sabah, the growth of the timber industry and the expansion of agriculture, the landscape in this area has been dramatically transformed. In consequence, the forested areas are shrinking and many have declined in quality. With the loss of vital habitat has come the loss of wildlife. Vaz and Pyne have indicated that the Sumatran rhino, elephants and "orang utan" have become endangered as a result of shrinking forest area (Vaz and Pyne, 1997:5).

Second: the conflict of interest between local community and other stakeholders. The local people in this area generally known as "orang sungai" or "people of the river" have lived in the Kinabatangan for centuries. Many older riverine settlements have a fascinating history, engaging in the early trade of forest products, such as edible bird nests, rattan, beeswax, camphorwood, hornbill ivory and rhinoceros horn (Vaz and Pyne, 1997: 9). The local community obtains a livelihood by a variety of means: some harvest freshwater prawns and fish, while others are involved in timber cutting, agriculture, or work in local government agencies. Thus the establishment of a Wildlife Sanctuary in the lower Kinabatangan affects the livelihood of local people. Policy makers in Sabah recognised that ecotourism might be a better solution for conservation and development. Its success, however, depends on the ability and willingness of local peoples to adopt forms of resource use that are more compatible with the maintenance of habitat for wildlife conservation.

If the local community in Sukau Village does not recognise the importance of protected areas and the benefits of ecotourism industry, it is likely that illegal activities such as poaching and logging will occur. When the state government placed the lower Kinabatangan as a Wildlife Sanctuary under the New Wildlife Conservation Enactment (1997), the major aim was to protect endangered species such as proboscis monkeys, elephants and birds. Within this forest reserve, commercial logging, taking of timber for domestic purposes and unauthorised hunting are prohibited by law. Conservation of forest will also help to protect the quality of water taken from the Kinabatangan River to supply both urban and rural areas in the Sandakan district (Vaz and Pyne, 1997: 8). Furthermore, the Kinabatangan area (including Sukau village) could be sustained as a major ecotourist destination in Sabah.

Third: the rigid interpretation and implementation of protected area procedures by the Sabah Forestry Department. As Schulze and Suratman (1999) claim, the implemention of Kinabatangan Wildlife Sanctuary programme has much benefited the town-based tour operators. But the costs of establishing the protected area are borne by the villagers. The villagers, however, are prevented and excluded from access (or at least "legal" access) to the natural resources of that area. A villager expresses a strong protest against the newly protected area:

Why should the tour operators make money at our expense? If

we cannot benefit from tourism we will shoot the last proboscis monkey so that the tour operators will have nothing to show their tourists! (quoted in Schulze and Suratman,1999:5)

In this manner, it is important to the Sabah State Government to implement the Nature Conservation Policy in the Wildlife Sanctuary Area of Sukau Village without the emergence of conflicting interests between area managers (the Sabah's Wildlife Department enforcement unit) and the villagers. A fairer approach towards the distribution of costs and benefits is needed. Although the ecotourism industry in Sukau Village has a negative impact, it could provide possible solutions through local community participation and the sharing of benefits from the development. This is because ecotourism involves:

...travel to natural attractions that contributes to their conservation, (and has) a minimum impact on soil, water, air, flora, fauna, and biophysical processes; use little energy; cause little pollution; educate the tourist; and contribute to the welfare of local and indigenous population" (Marsh, 1995)

Therefore, to ensure that ecotourism develops successfully in term of *"sustainable development"*, the level of local community participation in ecotourism has to be evaluated. As the World Tourism Organisation (WTO) states, sustainable tourism can be rigorously implemented through a system of effective planning and operating controls, all these studies and regulations will constitute the cornerstones of long term, local management strategies and plans.

[In the same time] it also requires acceptance of the concepts of validity and co-operation in its implementation from the tourism private sector, as well as the participation of local communities and tourists themselves. (WTO, 1990:47)

According to O'Brien, the Brundtland report 1987 has brought together human activity and the environment in a single concept, that of sustainable development: then it has brought together the ideas of environmental management and participation (O'Brien, 1997: 171). Thus a new spirit of co-operation between the state, private enterprise, NGOs and local community was considered essential for sustainable development in the Third World countries such as in Sukau Village,

Kinabatangan, Sabah.

Fourth: the definition of an ecotourist is not clear to those ecotourism stakeholders in Sukau Village. This is because a definitive understanding of the term ecotourists is not internationally agreed, it is important for the Sabah government to categorise the term into two mutual categories such as "hard ecotourists" and "soft ecotourists" (Deng, King and Bauer, 2002: 425-426). The candidates for the hard ecotourists include ornithologists, botanists and geologists. Whereas sightseers, photographers and those who undertake an ecotourist activity on at least one day during their trip away from home commonly fall under the category of "soft ecotourists". Both of these ecotourists exist in ecotourism related activities in Sukau Village.

In this manner, according to Deng, King and Bauer (2002), all mass tourism is potentially nature-based and may be categorised as such when spending a period as short as a day or even a few hours in an ecotourism area. This categorising could help protected area's managers ensure that implementation of nature conservation programmes can avoid conflicts of interest with ecotourists and other stakeholders.

Fifth: a concept of "local community participation" is not well defined by the Sabah government and policy makers. According to Stiefel and Wolfe (1994), the concept of participation has several meanings in rural area development processes, especially in Third World Countries. The United Nations Research Institute for Social Development (UNRISD) has identified six dimensions of participation. For the purpose of implementing the ecotourism project in Sukau Village, the Sabah government suggested the definition of participation with reference to two main dimensions:

i.   Participation as a "biography" or the individual participatory experience. It's important to examine the life experience of the individual and their perception of the nature conservation programme in Sukau Village. The reason is that "individual consciousness is the crucible in which social forces are translated into human action" (ibid: 7). Whether they intend to participate in sustainable ecotourism development through a direct or indirect manner, or if they are reluctant to participate at all, is based much on individual levels of consciousness.

ii.   Participation as a "programme" or "project" proposed by a
       government agency and non-government organisation.

This type of participation is referred to as significant of what is really
happening. This is because the nature conservation programme and
ecotourism development in Sukau Village "could be expected to
generate major changes for the better in the livelihood of the poor"
(ibid). Thus in this evaluation research the following questions have
to be asked: how is ecotourism development through nature
conservation programmes related to wider national policy and its
social and ideological context? Is the programme initiated in a
community characterised by gross inequalities of power and wealth?
How is this reflected in participatory programmes, its staffing and its
aims? Has the implementation of the programme or the legal
enforcement been undertaken in a "rigid" or "flexible" way?
Furthermore, questions should take into consideration what levels of
participation local communities have achieved. To what extent does
the promotion of participation lead to democratic involvement in the
decision making process? Does the local community gain a real voice
in the control of resources and regulative institutions? All these
questions will be applied in order to measure the definition of
participation.

    Therefore, we would say that the term "local participation" can be
generally defined as "the ability of local communities to influence the
outcome of development projects, such as ecotourism, that have an
impact on them (Drake, 1991:132): an example being the "orang
sungai" in case of Sukau Village. It is impossible to maintain
ecotourism without the commitment of the local population.
Therefore, it is important to the Sabah State Government and related
agencies to review the implementation methods in conservation
policy in Sabah. The enforcement's method and the programme
interpretation of the Wildlife Sanctuary area in Sukau Village need to
be reviewed and adjusted. Ecotourism and conservation programmes
in Sukau should not inflate the conflicting interests between the
protected area managers (the Sabah's Wildlife Department) and the
villagers.

    Finally, the emergence of tourism carrying capacity management
related problems in both contexts, either from an environmental based
or a community based perspective. From the environmental based
perspective, the concepts refer to maximum number of tourists or
ecotourists that can be accommodated within a specific geographic

destination (O'Reilly, 1986; Mathieson and Wall, 1982). This is related to the issue of a specified "limit", "ceiling" or "threshold" which ecotourism development should not exceed. A community-based perspective claims that the carrying capacity should be related to a destination area's capability to absorb tourism before the local community feels negative effects (Williams and Gill, 1994). This approach requires considerable consensus building among community stakeholders such as the villagers, developers, tour operators and government to determine the desired conditions for the destination area, and how tourism is to be managed most effectively toward that end. In Sukau Village for instance, there is a tendency for the growing number of visitors to seriously disturb the evening roosting rituals of troops of the proboscis monkey (Sale and Mahedi, 1994). For the Sabah Wildlife officer in Sukau it is time to consider dispersing the observing activity to other areas, rather than it being concentrated on the Menanggul River.

Conclusion

The above discussion has shown how tourism and ecotourism development has taken place in Malaysia's socio-economic development agenda from 1970s to date. The Malaysian government has been criticised because they were not serious in forming the right "image" for the tourism industry in Malaysia compared to her ASEAN neighbours. At the same time, they were also criticised for not taking action on the negative impacts the tourism industry has on culture and society. However, as with the other Lesser Developed Countries such as Costa Rica, Mexico, Brazil, and Tanzania, Malaysia has plenty of natural areas or "National Parks". This "natural capital" can be developed as an "ecotourist industry". Therefore, in order to avoid all the criticism, and to improve the tourism industry in Malaysia, the government has introduced a new policy and strategy toward ecotourism development and sustainability: ecotourism became a "niche" market for Malaysia's tourism industry only recently.

However, the ecotourism project proposed by the Malaysian government can also be questioned. For instance, in Sabah, the state government has developed a site for ecotourism activities in Sukau Village, Kinabatangan since 1990 in order to determine the implementation of the nature conservation and wildlife sanctuary programme. It is obvious that conflicting interests have emerged between the enforcement unit, the local community and the local lodge owners on the interpretation of procedures of the conservation programme (Schulze and Suratman, 1999). Thus, ecotourism development based on the conservation of natural resources in Sukau Village needs to be considered and reviewed in order to evaluate and adjust the current policy implementation. The success of the ecotourism development in Sukau depends much on the participation of the local community in the programme. Therefore, the Malaysian government must ensure that the implementation of the ecotourism programme can benefit the local community and the other stakeholders in a "sustainable" manner in the near future.

APPENDIX

Table 3: The National Parks of Malaysia.

Name of the Parks	Location and width (sq km/hectares)	Tourism Related Activities
1.Taman Negara	Kuala Tahan, Pahang (434,340 sq hectares)	Jungle Tracking, Wildlife Observing, Bird-watching, river canoeing etc.
2.Kenong Rimba Park	Kenong Valley, Pahang (121 sq km)	Mountain climbing, Cave-exploring, jungle trekking
3.Endau Rompin National Park	Johor-Pahang (488 sq km)	Jungle tracking, Bird-watching, Camping, Nature Study
4.Tunku Abdul Rahman Park (the Marines Park-a group of 5 Islands)	Kota Kinabalu, Sabah (4,929 sq hectares)	Beaches, trekking, crystal clear water ideal for diving, snorkelling, swimming
5. Crocker Range National Park	Between Beufort and Tenom, Sabah (139,919 sq km)	Mountains, rainforests, home to primates such as *orang utan* and gibbons, and *rafflesia pricie*
6. Pulau Tiga Park (a group of 3 Islands)	Kimanis Bay, Kuala Penyu, Sabah (15,257 sq hectares	White beaches, *volcanoes,* bird-watching, snake island
7. Kinabalu Park	Kundasang, Ranau Sabah (754 sq km)	Climbing Mt Kinabalu, hot springs spa, jungle trekking
8. Turtle Islands Park	Pulau Selingan, Sandakan, Sabah (1,740 sq hectares)	The marine park, the sea and surrounding coral reef, green turtles nesting and hatching
9. Tawau Hill Parks	Tawau, Sabah (27,972 sq hectares)	Hot springs spa, jungle trekking, hill climbing
10. Danum Valley	Lahad Datu, Sabah (438 sq km)	A virgin lowland rainforest, rainforest and ecological research, wildlife observing
11. Kinabatangan Floodplain*	Sandakan, Sabah (27,000 sq heactares)	River boating, wildlife viewing, photography or observational study and research related primates such as proboscis monkeys, orang utans, snakes, lizards, hornbills, elephants, crocodiles etc.
12. Gunung Mulu National Park	Miri and Limbang Division, Sarawak (52,866 sq hectares)	The major sites for caves exploring, river boat trips, jungle trekking
13. Niah National Park	Miri, Sarawak (3,140 sq hectares)	The cave exploring-40, 000 years Southeast Asia human pre-historic site, archaeological site, visit to Iban Long house

14. Bako National Park	Kuching, Sarawak (2,728 sq km)	Bird-watching, primates such as proboscis monkeys, jungle trekking and camping
15. Similaju National Park	Bintulu Division, Sarawak (7,067 sq hectares)	Cool jungle streams and pools, primates observing, beaches, camping, angling
16. Kubah National Park	Batu Kawah, Sarawak (2,230 sq hectares)	Visiting Wildlife Centre, jungle trekking and waterfall picnics
17. Lambir Hills National Park	Miri, Sarawak (6,952 sq hectares)	Bird-watching, jungle trekking, waterfall
18. Gunung Gading National Park	Lundu, Sarawak (4,106 sq hectares)	The *refflesia* site, waterfall, jungle trekking
19. Batang Ai National Park	Lubok Antu, Sarawak (24,040 hectares)	Home to orang utan, jungle trekking, river boating
20. Tanjung Datu National Park	Sematan, Sarawak (1,379 sq hectares)	Marine park, beaches and diverse marine life
21. Loagan Bunut National Park	Miri Division, Sarawak (10,736 hectares)	The largest natural lake in Sarawak, various bird population such as darters, bitterns, egrets, herons, hornbills and kites, primates such as gibbons, participate in the traditional "Selambau" method of fishing

Source: adapted from Tourism Malaysia, 2000. National Parks Brochure
*It was officially declared a permanent Wildlife Sanctuary on 16 January 2002. WWF, Malaysia, 2002. http://www.partnersforwetlands.org/malaysia.html

References

Abd Jalil Ali and Ahmad Yani. (2000) "Malaysia Wajah Sebenar Asia: Dato' Abdul Kadir Sheikh Fadzir". Dewan Masyarakat, Ogos: 23-25.

Bird, B.D.M. (1989) *Langkawi-From Mahsuri to Mahathir: Tourism For Whom?* Kuala Lumpur: Insan.

Ceballos-Luscurain, H. (1996) *Tourism, Ecotourism and Protected Areas.* Cambridge: IUCN-The World Conversation Union.

Deng, J. King, B. Bauer, T. (2002) "Evaluating Natural Attractions For Tourism". *Annals of Tourism Research*, 29(2): 422-438.

Drake, P.S. (1991) "Local Participation in Ecotourism Projects". In, W. Tensie (ed), *Nature Tourism: Managing For the Environment.* Washington, DC: Island Press.

Hamzah Abd Majid. (1986) "Policy Directions and Programmes on Tourism in Malaysia – With Special Reference To Sabah". In, Conference Proceedings on Tourism Potential in Sabah (Land Below the Wind) held at Kota Kinabalu on October 24th-25th, 1986. Kota Kinabalu: Sabah Development Bank Berhad, Sabah Tourism Promotion Corporation (STPC), & Institute For Development Studies-IDS (Sabah).

Kadir H. Din. (1997) "Tourism and Cultural Development in Malaysia: Issues
    For a New Agenda".pp, 104-107. In, S. Yamashita, Kadir H. Din, J.S.Eades
    (eds). *Tourism and Cultural Development in Asia and Occenia.* Bangi:
    Universiti Kebangsaan Malaysia.
Kajiwara, K. (1997) "Inward-bound, Outward-bound: Japanese Tourism
    Reconsidered". pp, 164-177. In, S. Yamashita, Kadir H. Din, J.S. Eades
    (eds). *Tourism and Cultural Development in Asia and Oceania.* Bangi:
    Universiti Kebangsaan Malaysia.
Khan, H. Toh, S.R. Fathima, K. (2001) "Asian Contagion: Impact on Singapore
    Tourism". *Annals of Tourism Research*, 28(1): 224-226.
Malaysia, (1989) "Laporan Ekonomi 1989/1990". Kuala Lumpur: Jabatan
    Percetakan Negara.
Malaysia, (1999) "Kajian Separuh Penggal Rancangan Malaysia Ketujuh, 1996-
    2000". Kuala Lumpur: Jabatan Percetakan Negara.
Marsh, J. (1995) "Ecotourism". In, R. Paehlke (ed), *Conservation and
    Environmentalism: An Encyclopaedia.* London and Chicago: Fitroy
    Dearbon Publishers.
Mathieson, A.W and Wall, G. (1982) *Tourism: Economic, Physical and Social
    Impacts.* Harlow, England: Longman Group.
Ministry of Tourism Development, Environment, Science and Technology,
    Sabah. (1999) "The Malaysian National Ecotourism Plan: Guidelines For
    Sabah". Kota Kinabalu.
O'Brien, P.J. (1997) "Global Processes and the Politics of Sustainable
    Development in Colombia and Costa Rica". In, R.M.Auty and K. Brown
    (eds), *Approaches to Sustainable Development.* London and Washington:
    Pinter.
O'Reilly, A.M. (1986) "Tourism Carrying Capacity". *Tourism Management,*
    7(4): 254-258.
Pugh-Kitingan, J. (2000) "Cultural Tourism in Sabah". Paper for ATI Tourism
    Symposium held at Kota Kinabalu on October 17th –18th , 2000. Kota
    Kinabalu: Asian Tourism Institute (ATI).
Sale, B.J and Mahedi @ Andau, P. (1994) "Wildlife as a Tourist Attraction in
    Sabah". In, Ti Tiew Chuan (ed), *Issues and Challenges in Developing
    Nature Tourism in Sabah".* Kota Kinabalu: Institute for Development
    Studies-IDS (Sabah)
Schulze, H and Suratman, S. (1999) *Villagers in Transition: Case Studies From
    Sabah.* Kota Kinabalu: Universiti Malaysia Sabah.
Shahril Saat. (2001) "Malaysia Ecotourism Master Plan: The Malaysia
    Experience". Seminar's Paper on Sustainable Tourism Development:
    Concept and Approach, held at Shah Alam, Selangor on October 29th – 31st,
    2001. Shah Alam: Malaysia Tourism Co-operation, The State Government
    of Selangor & Triways Holding Sdn Bhd.
State Government of Sabah, (1996) "Sabah Tourism Master Plan". Kota
    Kinabalu: Ministry of Tourism Development Development, Science and
    Technology, Sabah.
Stiefel, M and Wolfe, M. (1994) *A Voice for the Excluded, Popular Participation
    in Development: Utopia or Necessity.* London and New Jersey: Zed Book
    Ltd.

Ti Tiew Chuan and Arroyo, C, (1998) "Toward Perpetuating Sabah's Forest Resources". Berita IDS, 3(4): 2-4.

Tourism Malaysia. (2000a). "Malaysia Tourist Arrivals, 2000". http://www.tourismmalaysia.gov.my/tourism_bak/report/20001a.html. (access on 20.2.2002).

Tourism Malaysia. (2000b). *National Parks*. Brochure. Kuala Lumpur: Ministry of Culture, Arts & Tourism, Malaysia.

Tourism Malaysia. (2001) "Malaysia Tourist Arrival, 2001". http://www.tourismmalaysia.gov.my/tourism_bak/report/2001b.html. (access on 20.2.2002).

Vaz, J and Pyne, J, (1997) *The Kinabatangan Floodplain: An Introduction*. Kota Kinabalu: WWF Malaysia.

WWF (World Wildlife Fund, Malaysia). (2002) "Kinabatangan Wildlife Sanctuary Gazzetted". http://www.partnerforwetlands.org/malaysia.html (access on 2.4.2002.

Williams, P.W and Gill, A. (1994) "Tourism Carrying Capacity Management Issues." In, W. Theobold (ed), *Global Tourism: The Next Decade*. Oxford: Butterworth

Yahya Ibrahim. (2002) "Pembangunan Sektor Pelancongan Dan Perubahan Komuniti Di Pulau Redang." PhD Tesis. Institut Pengajian Siswazah dan Penyelidikan. Kuala Lumpur:University Malaya.

Yamashita, S. (2001) "Tourism Development in Sabah, Malaysia: A Remark on Ecotorism". Workshop's Paper on Social Cultural Processes of Development: Sabah and BIMP-EAGA held at Kota Kinabalu on August 28th, 2001, Kota Kinabalu: Research Institute for Languages and Cultures of Asia and Africa, Tokyo University of Foreign Studies & Institute for Development Studies (Sabah).

Chapter 16

Niche Tourism Markets in Scottish Tourism: An Investigation of Niche Markets reliant on the Natural Environment

Rory MacLellan

Introduction

The focus of this paper is the relationship between niche tourism markets and natural environmental attractions in Scotland. This relationship operates on a number of levels. The natural environment acts as the primary attraction and as the backdrop to a variety of tourist activities. Tourism activities impact, in a physical sense, on the natural environment and require an investment in infrastructure on the one hand, yet provide the incentive and economic means to conserve and enhance the environment on the other. This complex set of relationships raise a number of issues regarding the management of these key Scottish assets and the development of niche products. For example, VisitScotland promotes niche opportunities for tourism businesses in Scotland, many of which depend on public goods of the countryside. The care and protection of these resources lie in the hands of other agencies or private landowners. Estimates of the relative economic values of these niche markets are unclear due to imprecision in measurement techniques and definitional confusion in terminology involving leisure, outdoor recreation and tourism data. The policy and management implications of encouraging business investment in these niche products are explored in terms of costs and benefits.

The chapter includes a brief examination of walking as a niche market. Walking has been identified as the activity with both the greatest value to the rural economy of Scotland and with excellent prospects for growth. However, recent surveys indicate that walkers are not a homogenous group; rather they include a diverse range of sub-segments, each with specific characteristics and resource requirements. The operators and managers involved in providing resources for walking are equally diverse in nature and purpose. These range from private tour operators specialising in walking holidays to public agencies charged with providing and maintaining paths to satisfy wider, often local objectives such as social and health benefits. Implications are discussed in terms of current management and future policy making.

Niche markets and niche products

Niches are a part of market segmentation that can take many forms. Early studies tended to focus on specific demographic or sociological attributes such as age, gender, income and family lifecycle. Segmentation studies based on geographic origin are also common. Later, more sophisticated segmentation studies focused on purpose of trip, behavioural factors and psychographic characteristics. Product related segmentation studies are less common and relate to product related benefits sought such as a recreational activity that relies on specific products and services (Mill and Morrison, 2002; 175). Kotler, (2000: 257) provides a classic definition of a niche market:

> A niche is a more narrowly defined group, typically a small market whose needs are not well served. Marketers usually identify niches by dividing a segment into sub-segments or by defining a group seeking a distinctive mix of benefits.

He goes on to explain that whereas segments are fairly large and normally attract several competitors, niches are fairly small and normally attract only one or two. Some larger companies have therefore turned to niche marketing, which has required more decentralisation and some changes in the way they do business. Niche marketers should understand their customers' needs so well that the customers willingly pay a premium. An attractive niche is thus characterised as where the customers have a distinct set of needs, will pay a premium to the firm that best satisfies their needs and the niche is unlikely to attract other competitors. The 'nicher' gains certain economies through specialisation and the niche should have size, profit, and growth potential. Companies that wish to survive, grow and be profitable, or presumably countries through National Tourism Organisations, should find markets which have: sufficient size to be potentially profitable; no real competitors, or markets that have been ignored by other companies; growth potential; sufficient purchasing ability; a need for special treatment; customer goodwill; and opportunities for an entrance company to exercise its superior competence (Dalgic and Leeuw, 1994: 39- 40). The official VisitScotland definition seems to take a more product-based perspective and the scale of niches identified indicate the potential market is much greater than accepted for a niche in marketing literature.

> A niche market is a specific segment of the market with a particular interest such as golf. Niches have well-defined markets where the tourism product and marketing can be tailored to meet the interest of the visitor. (Scottish Tourist Board 2000b).

Much of the confusion derives from work done by the Scottish Tourist Board 'Tourism Futures' Department in 2000. Their work on niche products seems to have been based on consultation with the tourism trade in Scotland and formed the basis of later strategies for Scottish tourism with a strong emphasis on marketing some niche products at a national level, namely golf, culture and genealogy (Scottish Executive, 2000). The divergence from marketing theory, which clearly requires a niche to be a small, well-defined market, is illustrated by the original 15 'niche products' identified by the STB. Far from being based on market research, the niche tourism products seem to be derived from an industry brainstorming session. The development of detailed market profiles had to be pulled together after the 'niche' had been identified. This explains the diversity of niches and the variation in quality of market data (STB, 2000c).

This raises some interesting questions relating to the product or market focus in niching. A product focus can result in development of products catering for the mass market or at least to a wide range of market segments, as is the case of walking. The chicken or egg question is whether to design products for specific markets or find markets for existing products. Do we identify the niche market or the niche product first? It seems the product has come first in Scotland. This leads to problems regarding the geographical basis of the marketing effort. Should 'niche marketing' be on a national scale, led by a National Tourist Organisation such as VisitScotland or would it be more appropriate to leave it to regional organisations or individual companies? Which level should lead in the identification of niche markets? Is it appropriate to talk of niche markets for a whole country and its products (Scotland) or parts of Scotland or specific aspects of Scotland, for example golf, fishing or walking? They may seem to appeal to some niche markets but are equally attractive to large numbers of the mass market. For example, walking is largely a mass activity although specific walking niche markets exist. This muddle seems to be at the root of the difficulty in understanding niche tourism in Scotland.

Natural environment based niche tourism in Scotland

There are no clear figures from Scotland-wide surveys on how much income from tourism is attributable to the natural environment, how much is spent directly on/in natural environmental attractions and how much goes back into the conservation and enhancement of the natural environment. The broad indications do, on the other hand, assist in the identification of growth markets and niche opportunities. The STB have identified a number of niche areas with prospects for further development (STB, 2000b).

Table 1 Niche opportunities for tourism businesses in Scotland

Excellent Prospects:
<ul><li>City breaks - £820m; expected growth of 20%</li><li>Golf - £100m of expenditure; unique competitive advantage/new strategy</li><li>Walking - £438 of expenditure; likely to remain strong in future</li></ul>
Very Good Prospects:
<ul><li>Culture - £36m of expenditure; growing interest</li><li>Wildlife - £57m of expenditure; moderate growth predicted</li><li>Cycling - £73m of expenditure; strong growth</li><li>Genealogy – 28m Scots around world; growing interest/ unique advantage</li><li>Food and Drink - £417m of tourism spending; growing interest</li></ul>
Good Prospects:
<ul><li>Field Sports - £53m of expenditure; moderate growth, fishing on decline</li><li>Gardens – 2.2 m visits; growing interest</li><li>English as a Foreign Language - £55m of expenditure; static market</li><li>Sailing - (yacht/dinghy etc.)- £10m of expenditure; growth moderate</li><li>Cruising – (boat/liner) £12m of expenditure; moderate growth but over-capacity risk</li><li>Skiing - £18m of expenditure; uncertain prospects</li><li>Archaeology - no accurate figures but relatively small; strong regional niche</li></ul>

Source: STB, 2000b

Leaving aside the questionable methods on which these are based, the prominence given to growth areas that rely on the quality or unique characteristics of the Scottish natural environment is noteworthy. It indicates the value of these assets to the future development of tourism in Scotland but also the potential for management problems in future. Half of the top categories, 'excellent' and 'very good prospects' (Golf, walking, wildlife, cycling) fundamentally rely on natural environmental resources. Their growth must be managed with the protection of these resources as a top priority. Estimates of visitor numbers and the concomitant visitor management issues are compounded by the grey area between tourism and recreation. What proportion of the market are tourists, leisure day visitors or local users?

The relationship between tourism and the natural environment

Tourism requires three levels of resources: unique attractions and events for tourists including natural, cultural and purpose built; an infrastructure and superstructure to support tourist activities; and the social and cultural setting, including the hospitality of the community. Successful transformation of these into an effective tourism product requires the efforts of travel companies and tourist organisations to package and promote the destination. All components are interrelated with the attraction at the core. The landscape and natural heritage of Scotland has long formed the basis for attracting particular types of visitors that could be considered niches: from the Romantic Movement of the early nineteenth century to the sporting estates later in that century (Smout, 1993; Lister-Kaye, 1994; Hunter, 1995). The core attraction, then as now, is scenery and landscape, perceived to be wild and natural. There is some debate over how 'natural' the landscape is in reality (Hunter, 1995, p150; Fraser Darling and Boyd, 1964) but it remains natural and attractive in the minds of the majority of tourists. In terms of tourism demand this means that the romantic vista is of greater importance than the ecological quality of the natural environment. Bryden (1999) provides a fuller discussion of landscape and sustainable tourism in Scotland.

If Scotland is to optimise the mix of tourism resources in order to improve the economic performance of the tourism industry without undermining the natural or man-made resources on which the industry depends, it must plan tourism carefully to preserve and enhance these special features. There is very little evidence of this being done in a systematic, integrated way in the promotion of niche products. The involvement of conservation organisations in collaboration with tourist agencies is required to raise industry and visitor awareness of Scotland's ecology and find more sustainable practices.

There are four important ways in which tourism and the environment interact:

1. **Primary attraction** - the environment as the key attraction for tourism activities; to gaze, to hunt, to study, to do sport;
2. **A backdrop** - the environment as the backdrop/scenery for relaxing holidays (Romantic Movement, cultural landscapes);
3. **Environmental costs** - the impact of (or the environmental costs of) tourism development (infrastructure and facilities) and direct tourist activities on the environment;
4. **Contribution to conservation** - the influence of tourism on environmental protection and positive conservation, where tourism provides the economic value justifying preservation of the environment. (MacLellan, 2001)

Tourism researchers tend to focus on category three; the tourism industry tends to concentrate on one and two; and conservation organisations try to raise awareness of the possibilities of four. However it is rare for research to take a holistic perspective that includes all four categories.

The relationship is further complicated by wide variations in the extent to which tourism markets rely on the natural environment. Some rely directly on natural environmental assets such as field sports or wildlife watching, other activities require particular physical landscapes such as recreation on hills and lochs, whilst tourist facilities and amenities often rely on attractive natural settings: 'you pay for the view'. Establishing a clear model of direct and indirect relationships would require a level of complexity that current data is unable to support. Suffice it to say that all tourism relies on the natural environment to some extent, but for some niche activities, in certain locations, the connections are much more direct. This is true of the tourist motivation for visiting and the impacts of tourism on the area, both positive and negative.

From an economic perspective, the relationship seems clear, at least on first examination. Holden (2000) maintains there is a clear link between economic benefits, environmental quality and satisfying tourist needs: economic success depends on satisfying tourist needs and environmental quality is the key to satisfying tourist needs.

(Holden 2000: 97).

However there is a difficulty in separating environmental based tourism income from all tourism income. There has been no comprehensive research making this distinction on a Scotland wide basis. Mackay Consultants' (1997) as cited in Masters et al. (1998) provide one approximation although this uses a very broad interpretation of terms: that total wildlife and environmental tourism expenditure in Scotland was £105 million, or 3% of the total tourism revenue. There have been a number of more rigorous studies looking at the economic impact of various tourist activities that rely on the natural environment that have more moderate estimates (Table 2).

Other indicators of economic value of the natural heritage through tourism are more indirect but nevertheless important. One example is the planning inquiry into the wind farms proposal in Helmsdale (Hutchinson 1997; p147) where the proposal was refused on the basis of 'very clear risks to the local tourist industry'. The report notes 'tourism is of fundamental importance to the local economy' and the local tourism industry has several distinguishing characteristics including: 'A heavy reliance on natural assets; freedom to appreciate these assets in tranquil conditions, and, reliance on field sports'. The importance of unspoilt landscapes and traditional tourism activities, such as the well-defined niche of field sports, should not be underestimated. Their value lies in their ability to displace relatively small numbers of high spending tourists into remote rural parts of Scotland and thereby underpin otherwise fragile economies.

To assist in understanding the economic impacts of these activities, it is worth considering some of the characteristics of rural economies in Scotland. The levels of leakage from rural economies seem much more rapid than industrial or urban areas. Surrey Research Group (1993) found that the rates of leakage are greater from rural areas and that greater tourist spending is required to produce an FTE job in large hotels compared to bed and breakfasts. Variations in multiplier values (depending on rural accommodation types) are confirmed in a study of alternative rural accommodation: Slee, Farr and Snowdon (1997). These studies reveal that there are marked differences within regions with respect to the effects of visitor spending. Slee (1998: 105) points to the proliferation of studies looking at economic impact of various tourist and recreational activities in rural Scotland: sports shooting (McGilvray, 1990); salmon fishing (Mackay Consultants, 1989); hill-walking (Highlands and Islands Enterprise, 1996), and general access-related recreation (Crabtree et al 1992). Many of these relate to niche products such as wildlife tourism, which gained international recognition as a growth activity in the 1990s. The links between the value of nature conservation and economic benefits are demonstrated in studies looking at the bird watching niche at Natura 2000 sites and RSPB reserves (Broom *et al* 1999; Rayment 1995). Although the estimates are for all jobs generated through activities related to the protection of the environment, this includes those related to nature-based tourism.

Table 2 Economic impact studies of wildlife tourism

Study	Key findings
Morrison (1995)	Wildlife watching boat trips in The Minch generated direct income of £445,000 in 1994, supporting 29 full-time and 17 part-time jobs.
Arnold (1997)	In 1993, the potential revenue from dolphin adoptee holidaymakers in the Moray Firth was calculated at £1.4m (n.b. this scheme has increased to £7.4m as more people have joined the scheme).
Crabtree *et al* (1994)	Site-based wildlife tourism revenue in Wester Ross, Orkney and Highland Perthshire was estimated at £5.15m in 1993, supporting 351 full-time equivalent (FTE) jobs
Rayment (1995)	26% of the total tourism expenditure in the Shetland Isles in 1994 came from birdwatchers (£1.07m), supporting 43 FTE jobs
Mackay Consultants (1989)	Tourists 'with an interest in wildlife' generated £3.1m expenditure on Islay and Jura in 1989, supporting 152 FTE jobs.
Surrey Research Group (1993)	Tourism multipliers vary considerably in Scotland, ranging from one FTE per £19,000 visitor spend to one FTE per £28,000.
A&M Training and Development (1997)	In terms of income generation wildlife tourism in Scotland is worth £11m (STB) and supports 1,500 FTE jobs.

Source: adapted from Masters et al., 1998

Estimations of the economic value of a wider range of activities are provided by VisitScotland in their website *scotexchange.net*. Market information is given for industry benchmarking and for potential investors. These may be valuations on new niche growth markets or for established markets. However, there is no uniform basis for collecting data. The estimates are derived from a variety of sources based on surveys using differing methodologies over different time periods. This makes direct comparisons difficult. Some have figures for trips, bed nights or number of visitors only. Others have estimates of expenditure and the number of jobs supported.

The figures do, however, provide a clear indication of the importance of certain broad categories of activities that are based on the natural environment, in particular to the economy of more northerly, rural parts of Scotland. For instance, the study of the economic impact of hill walking and mountaineering in the Highlands and Islands (HIE, 1996) estimated that 767,000 hill walkers visited the topographical highlands over a twelve-month period, incurring direct expenditure totalling £157.9m. This level of expenditure was estimated to generate an income of £53m for the area and support approximately 6,100 full-time equivalent jobs (HIE, 1996).

Table 3 Economic impact of selected activities

Activity	Economic Impact
Golf	Golf is estimated to be worth almost £100m to the Scottish economy, £70m of expenditure from UK visitors and £28m from overseas golfers.
Walking	In 1998 walking was estimated to generate 1.1m trips to Scotland, during which visitors stayed for 9.6m nights and spent over £438m.
Garden Tourism	The 59 garden attractions in Scotland attract around 2.2m visits a year.
Field Sports	110,000 visitors fish in Scotland every year, generating just under £30m worth of spending. Around 100,000 trips to Scotland are made each year to shoot and spending totals £23m. Angling holidays generate £12m expenditure and 400,000 bed nights annually for the Tayside area alone.
Skiing	Specific skiing holidays generate 100,000 trips to Scotland, 300,000 bed nights and around £15m expenditure. An additional £18m is generated by 100,000 trips by people on general holidays that spend 400,000 bed nights of their time at a ski area.
Cycling	Cycling holidays by UK residents accounted for 750,000 trips to Scotland in 1998. Cycling tourism in Scotland has grown by almost 50% since 1994. They stay an average of 7 nights and spend £48m in Scotland each year.

Source: adapted from STB, 2000b.

Visitor perceptions of the Scottish natural environment

A more rational and useful means of defining niches would take a market perspective but the complexity of motivations for nature tourism makes identification of precise niche markets difficult. For example, the interaction between consumer and environment can be distant for 'gazers,' or up close for walkers. The motivation may be to conquer for adventure tourists or to commune with nature for ecotourists: specialisms exist with quite different sets of values and expectations. Visitors often combine a mix of motivations such as to escape from the city, view a romantic landscape or have an adventure in a wilderness area with attractive wildlife. Thus, the promotion of the natural environment as a 'tourist attraction' must combine a variety of messages to target specific niches. Some examples are shown in table 4.

Table 4 Promotion of the natural environment

Visitor Motivation	Promotional messages
Romantic	Landscape/nostalgia/harmony
Power of nature	Wonder/risk/adventure
Setting for activities	Hunting/walking/sailing/skiing
Exotic	Exclusive/inaccessible
Escape	Remote/back to nature
Rest	Peace and tranquillity
Wellbeing	Safe/clean/healthy

The Tourism Attitudes Survey 1999, (System Three, 2000a) illustrates the diversity and complexity of customer expectations. Based on face-to-face interviews with visitors during their holidays at sites throughout Scotland, the four main visitor origins are sampled: England (47%); Scotland (20%); USA (18%); and Germany (12%).

Pre-visit, the main attraction of Scotland for holiday visitors, irrespective of origin or lifestyle, is the *landscape, countryside and scenery*: three out of ten mentioned this as the main attraction which influenced their decision to holiday in Scotland during 1999. Reinforcing the importance of the Scottish natural environment as a draw to visitors, other specific aspects of the countryside were mentioned as having influenced the visit: *mountains and hills* (10%); *lochs and rivers* (4%); *nature and wildlife* (3%); *the coast and seaside* (2%). In terms of specific associations with Scotland prior to the visit the vast majority (90%) had associated '*beautiful scenery*' with Scotland. Two other phrases had strong pre-visit associations: '*interesting history and culture*' (65%) and '*friendly people*' (63%). Three others were mentioned by forty to fifty percent: '*plenty to see and do*' (46%), '*good place to relax and get away from it all*' (43%) and '*a good hiking and walking destination*' (40%).

In terms of activities undertaken whilst in Scotland on holiday, the most popular was *shopping* (71%) followed by *visiting built heritage* (69%) and *short walks (under 2 miles)* (69%). *Wildlife watching* scored relatively highly (39%) and *hill walking*, whilst undertaken by only 14% of all visitors, had a significantly higher level for German visitors (31%). More active pursuits in natural environmental settings, such as *swimming outdoors* (6%), *cycling/mountain biking* (6%), *mountaineering/rock climbing* (3%) and *sailing* (3%) were significantly less popular. Other more traditional sports also had relatively low participation rates: *fishing* (5%), *golf* (4%), *horse riding* (1%).

Respondents were asked to indicate the 'main' activity undertaken. Experiencing Scotland's history was by far the most popular with slightly under 30% *visiting castles, historic houses, stately homes and gardens*. The second most popular main activity was *relaxing/doing nothing* (17%) followed by *low-level rambling/walking* (13%). Other activities associated with the natural environment had small but significant scores: *hill walking* (4%), *watching for wildlife* (3%), *cycling/mountain biking* (2%). The mix of motivations and expectations suggest that the majority of visitors do not fall within a specialist niche with a single primary motivation. If popularity of activities were the key indicator of niche importance then shopping would take number one slot.

In terms of visitor types who would enjoy a holiday in Scotland, the vast majority of respondents thought Scotland would *appeal 'a lot' to 'those who enjoy outdoor activities'* (95%), *middle aged people* (93%), *those interested in history and heritage* (92%) and *'those who prefer peace and quiet holidays'* (92%). The most frequently mentioned advantages Scotland was perceived to hold over similar destinations included *the beautiful scenery'* (27%), *the friendly people* (19%) and the fact that the country was *not too far from home or was easy to get to* (18%). Other advantages cited were: *peace and quiet* (11%); *history* (11%); *variety of activities* (8%); *wildlife/wilderness* (4%); *hills and mountains* (3%).

Although these findings indicate that the natural environment is an extremely important consideration for visitors to Scotland they do not identify individual niches. Rather, the mass market value and wish to experience the natural environment, albeit in a variety of forms. For the majority the environment is important as a backdrop rather than something to engage with close up. Having said this, there may be small but important niche markets where natural environmental assets are the primary reason for their visit.

Aggregate figures on participation rates in activities are often misleading as there are large variations depending on visitor markets. For example, Table 5 illustrates differences in activities undertaken between overseas and British tourists and distinguishes between cerebral and physical activities. Overseas tourists seem more likely to undertake activities than British tourists in Scotland. Both overseas and British tourists are more likely to visit built heritage attractions than take part in physical or sporting activities, yet this does not seem to have been recognised in the identification of growth niche markets.

Table 5 Activities and sports undertaken by overseas and British tourists in Scotland

Activities	Overseas Tourists 1996 % Holiday Trips (1.19m)	British Tourists 1999 % Holiday Trips (6.1m)
Visiting Castles, Monuments, Churches, etc.	83	26
Visiting Museums, Art Galleries, Heritage Centres, etc.	58	14
Watching Performing Arts (Theatre, Concert, Opera, Ballet)	16	8
Field/Nature Study	9	5
Sport		
Hiking/Walking/Rambling/ Orienteering	39	23
Swimming	5	16
Golf	2	3
Watching any Sport	2	5
Fishing	1	5
Any 'Activity' undertaken	85	61

Source: STB 2000a

The figures suggest that visitors are attracted by images of the Scottish countryside but are not necessarily interested in specific outdoor activities. This is supported by a study of the perceptions of the Scottish countryside by visitors from mainland Europe (Macpherson Research, 1996). This study confirmed that the main attraction was the *vast stretches of wild, open scenery* and *rugged landscapes* but noted that, although most were active in the outdoors, only 6.5% claimed outdoor activities was the main purpose of visiting. As the report states:

> This would suggest that most visitors come with broad holiday intentions and get drawn into using the countryside as a natural consequence of being here rather than as the prime reason for coming. (Macpherson Research, 1996: 50).

On the other hand, this does not diminish the importance of having opportunities for outdoor activities and the right facilities. The most common activity of the Europeans sampled was *walking* (86%) followed by *climbing a hill or mountain* (40%), *wildlife watching* (38%) and *cycling* (18%).

The artificial distinction between leisure and recreation

The figures quoted so far have concentrated on tourists rather than all users of the natural heritage. Broader leisure and recreation studies include day visitors and local users in addition to tourists. Although their per-capita economic impact is less significant they would still have a physical impact that requires management. Hunt (2000), in a review of informal outdoor recreation in the Scottish countryside, notes that tourists make up only a small (albeit significant) component of participants in outdoor activities in Scotland. He estimates that activity holidays represent only 5% of all countryside participation. Day visits to the countryside by Scots represents the highest number, with most Scots taking 3.5 day visits a month, half of which are to the seaside/countryside.

There is a danger of devoting national resources to tourism promotion of niches where the majority of the market are local or day visitors. Outdoor activity participation rates are increasing by 3-4% per year, although the proportion going to the countryside is rising only slowly. Walking is the most popular outdoor activity (24%) and the fastest growing, with the widest appeal across Scottish society (Scottish Sports Council, 1998: 6). Other, more active pursuits have a small but secure niche, and appeal to younger and higher income groups. Those who do go to the countryside are mostly satisfied with the provision. The requirement for specific infrastructure to support outdoor activities very much depends on the user group. For example, in a survey of walkers in Scotland (System Three, 1998) casual, low-level walkers, prefer to have more paths, signs and trails, whereas mountaineers and hill walkers felt non-natural infrastructure is inappropriate.

The supply side – management and protection

Tourism impacts arise through the construction and operation of tourist facilities or services and from the activities of tourists themselves. They can be short-term or long-term, localised or national, positive or negative, direct, indirect or induced. They are often divided into economic, socio-cultural and ecological impacts with the first usually categorised under benefits, the second and third as costs. The complexity and diversity in range and type of impact reflects the characteristics of tourism and makes accurate evaluation of impacts problematic. There is a tendency to examine impacts separately. Tourist authorities tend to focus on economic impacts through visitor expenditure, usually at national scale. Countryside conservation authorities and land managers tend to focus on physical environmental impacts in terms of damage and disturbance. However they cannot distinguish local users from day trip, recreational users or staying tourists from day visitors. Each may have the same level of physical impact on a footpath but would have widely differing effects on the local economy. An additional complication is the difficulty in establishing where to draw the boundary in tourism impact studies. The destination may be a village, a loch or a hillside but the total impact of a tourist, in terms of economic impacts (spending en-route) and environmental impacts (transport pollution) should include the journey to the destination. This element is seldom included in tourism impact analysis.

Although a number of detailed case studies have investigated the impacts of tourism in Scotland, they tend to focus on a particular sector (e.g. wildlife tourism), activity (e.g. hill walking) or location (e.g. The Trossachs) and seldom take a holistic view of impacts. Development agencies concentrate on measuring economic impacts, conservation agencies on ecological impacts. One of the few attempts at a holistic review of the interaction between tourism and the environment in Scotland was carried out through consultation with experts 'in the field' (PIEDA, 1991; STCG, 1992). Their tourism/environment balance sheet summarised the benefits of tourism in Scotland. Economic benefits were measured in expenditure (overseas/other UK); contribution to GDP broken down by region (rural/urban); employment; supporting local services and infrastructure; revival of declining economies; generation of inward investment. Environmental benefits were listed under environmental improvements; reuse of redundant buildings for visitors; provision of new, improved leisure facilities; restoration and preservation of historic buildings; improved transport (access) infrastructure; encouragement of good design in development; growth in appreciation of the environment. However, little attempt has been made to quantify non-economic benefits in detail.

A full examination of the costs of tourism in Scotland would require inclusion of data on all facilities and infrastructure used by tourists, in particular transport and accommodation, in terms of energy consumption, waste management and pollution of air, water and soil. Macro-scale data at national level, separating tourism impacts from other variables, are not currently available. However a recent review of transport, tourism and the environment in Scotland, for Scottish Natural Heritage (SNH 2001), has identified some key tourism transport issues. Although a major environmental impact from tourist travel worldwide arises from air travel, in Scotland the key impact is through use of the private car. The report categorises these impacts in five ways: air pollution; visual pollution; noise pollution; accidents and accident-risk fear; and congestion. It draws the conclusion that public transport has a potentially crucial role in reducing environmental impacts from leisure travel. Improved public transport is viewed as a way of attracting more of what they term 'deep green' visitors; but it is noted that this would require local authorities, transport operators and site managers to work in close partnership.

An earlier review of the environmental costs (disbenefits) of tourism in Scotland (STCG, 1992) focuses primarily on the destination where tourist activities take place. Although not particularly scientific, it provides a useful overview of the perceived problems caused by tourism. The main categories come under the headings: people pressure; traffic congestion; visual intrusion; untidiness; user conflicts. These clearly relate to visitor management issues, notably where the volume of visitors exceeds the carrying capacity of specific locations. More detailed analysis was carried out on five specific issues identified in the consultation process as being particularly troublesome: footpath damage; impact of caravans; impact of ski developments; intrusive activities such as jet-skiing, motor-sports and mountain-biking; wider environmental disturbance for example, loss and deterioration of wildlife habitats. The problems associated with tourism are recognised but the report stresses that for most people pressure difficulties are localised. The greatest concern is over the impact of tourism and day visitors on the countryside, particularly areas accessible to Scotland's population concentrations. It is concluded that where tourism is shown to have an influence on ecological change, these are confined to specific areas, are not severe and appear to be manageable.

More rigorous research reviews of the effects of tourism and recreation on the natural environment (Sidaway 2000; 1998; 1995; 1994) point to the lack of systematic evaluation of impacts and to the complexity and need to carefully classify impacts. Studies also stress that the effects of tourism and recreation on the natural heritage should be put into perspective: they are not usually the greatest threat to nature conservation. The report to the House of Commons on 'The Environmental Impact of Leisure Activities' (1995) came to this conclusion:

> We note that according to the balance of evidence we received, compared to other activities, leisure and tourism do not cause significant widespread ecological damage to the countryside. However there is no need for complacency. We believe that there are important issues to address, involving transport, rural culture, and leisure management, as well as local conflicts in specific areas. (House of Commons Environment Committee, 1995, xxvii).

There are however certain circumstances where the effects of recreation and tourism can be more serious, in particular when activities are coupled with the development of facilities and construction leads to loss of habitats in sensitive areas; when new technologies result in new potentially damaging activities such as jet-skis or 4x4 off-road driving; and where fragile habitats lack resilience due to low dynamic and long recovery cycles. Research into environmental impacts of recreation tends to be limited due to a tendency to focus on particular habitats and relatively few species and a lack of research that is pertinent to management needs.

All this indicates a need for closer links between researchers and practitioners and a closer examination of management practices. Attempts at detailed monitoring and evaluation of environmental impacts of tourism have been thwarted through a lack of expertise or resources to follow through recommendations. This was the case with the report on the Trossachs Tourism Management Programme environmental monitoring scheme that advocated comprehensive, detailed measurement of the physical impacts of recreation on the area (Dargie *et al*, 1994). A deficiency in hard information has led to an inability to have clear decision-making and effective management. This in turn has resulted in frequent, unnecessary polarisation of views between recreation and conservation lobbies. A pragmatic approach around this would be to identify critical locations, i.e. habitats and species, most vulnerable and liable to recreation demands and look to collective management involving researchers, managers and user groups. Sidaway feels the key issue is 'how do we manage recreation to ensure that wildlife interests of areas, that is important both to recreation and conservation, is maintained and enhanced' (2000:10).

Walking tourism: niche or mass market?

To consider walking as a single niche product or walkers as a homogeneous market niche is grossly misleading. Although data on the impact of and provision of facilities for walking continue to lump all walking together, there is increased recognition that a complex range of sub-segments exists: low recreational walking; hill walking and distance walking; climbing; organised walking holidays (Scotexchange.net, 2002). The 'Walking in Scotland' study in 1998 (System Three) came up with slightly different categories based on clusters of shared attitudes and benefits sought amongst walkers surveyed: casual interest/occasional walkers; family groups; committed, frequent walkers; ramblers; and mountaineers/hill walkers.

However, each of these categories tend to exclude the majority of walkers that tend to be tourists that list walking (less that 2 miles) as an activity undertaken during their visit or locals walking as part of their daily routine. Of activities undertaken by tourists to Scotland, 69% include walking, but this is less than 2 miles. Only 4% list hill walking or low level walks of more than 8 miles as a main activity undertaken (System Three 1988). Walking by Scottish residents equally indicates high participation rates but close examination shows that most walks are short (88% less than 5 miles), local (83% started from home) and not necessarily rural (53% of walks taken for pleasure were in towns and cities) - source: System Three (2000b).

The promotion of walking also raises issues from the supply perspective. These can be narrowed down to two related issues: access to the countryside and responsibility for provision and maintenance of facilities. Although recent legislation in the Scottish Parliament should address some problems, confusion has reigned in Scotland over the issue of the 'right to roam' with much of the population misguidedly believing there is no law of trespass in the country (Ralton, 2001). In fact, landowners and farmers have allowed access to their land for recreational purposes on the tacit understanding that those that pass through will respect the land and its needs. However access is granted on the understanding that something is expected in return (Parker and Ravenscroft 1999). This is reinforced by Scottish Natural Heritage who maintain that 'access should be based on mutual respect' (1994: 12). Although current frequent walkers in the countryside are generally aware of this need to respect and reciprocate the generosity of landowners, such understanding is often lacking amongst new or infrequent visitors. Indeed, fear of the unknown prevents many from participating. A related matter is the prioritisation of provision of walking facilities, such as footpaths. Should funding be diverted to areas with the greatest tourist demand or the greatest resident needs? In the past, long-distance paths and trails were accorded the highest priority (Kay, 1989). Even then, patterns of use and demand revealed that shorter walks were much more popular.

Opposition to recreational development of the countryside has always been strong. Conflicts of interest among environmentalist and conservation organisations, landowners and recreationalists, present potential difficulties in areas where paths are being developed and promoted. A further difficulty in the marketing of walking in Scotland is the question of responsibility. While local authorities are generally held responsible for provision, maintenance and promotion of public footpaths, they are under no legal obligation to carry out these tasks. The promotion of the 'walking tourism niche product' has implications for all infrastructure providers. The recent growth in voluntary organisations and initiatives is welcome as it bolsters the established providers such as the National Trust for Scotland and Scottish Natural Heritage. However if the growth of this niche is to be successfully managed to the satisfaction of all, much work remains in bringing together public and private landowners, and managers, the tourism industry and the full gamut of walkers.

Integrated management and promotion of niches: the role of public agencies

Planning and management techniques, carefully applied at the appropriate scale, mean that a balance can be achieved between tourism development and environmental conservation. If tourism is to last, it should be planned holistically: it should be ecologically bearable; economically viable; and ethically and socially equitable for local communities. Sustainable tourism should contribute to sustainable development and be integrated with all aspects of environment, respecting fragile areas and being careful that impacts do not exceed the capacity of those areas. However, achieving this, whilst integrating the policy of niche product development, presents organisational problems at national scale and practical implementation problems at local level.

In Scotland the economic importance of the natural environment in attracting visitors has been established, as has the physical impacts that occur through lack of management of these visitors. Therefore the maintenance and enhancement of this resource should lie near the heart of any strategy for the industry: this has been recognised and agreed in theory by tourism agencies and industry leaders. However there is still very little clarity on how niche marketing policies would achieve this at a practical level. Difficult questions are raised such as how to balance the interests of those in control of the environment, mostly private landowners, farmers and foresters, with those of the tourists and those who depend on them, such as hoteliers, retail outlets and tour operators. The organisation of coherent policies is hindered by fragmented and poorly defined niche markets, and the nature of tourism related businesses in Scotland, many being small scale and run by 'lifestyle entrepreneurs'.

In terms of public policy, some progress has been made in clarifying issues of access to the countryside and the establishment of national parks should eventually help plan and implement a better balance between conservation and development objectives. However the question of who pays for countryside maintenance has yet to be resolved. Promoting a niche product without reference to the owner or manager of the key attraction seems ludicrous. Since no way of charging for scenery has been devised (outside USA-style national parks) a combination of balancing land management regulations, visitor management and promotions and taxation/subsidisation are the only ways to proceed. As tourism depends on a mixture of private and public provision of attractions and facilities, private landowners, conservation organisations and local authorities question whether those who come and enjoy these features are contributing their proper share of the costs involved.

Recent access laws, agri-environmental measures and forestry practices have moved towards more visitor-friendly policies. The other side of environmental economics concerns damage to the environment through tourism activities. Although much can be done in raising awareness through education and interpretation to encourage responsible visitor behaviour, costs will inevitably be incurred. Footpath maintenance on private land, responsibility for clearing litter and restoring vegetation damaged by large numbers of visitors raises questions of finding methods of footing the bill through public sector involvement. Would the walking niche operators and the walkers themselves be prepared to foot the bill?

The influence of tourism on these problems is often exaggerated and a lack of clear, measurable indicators of change hinders rational remedial action. The connections between tourism and the environment are acknowledged by policy-makers but only in a general sense. The sources used in this discussion indicate a clear lack of accurate hard data on how this interaction works. There is insufficient measurement and monitoring of both the costs and benefits of tourism to the natural environment to allow managers on the ground to make rational decisions. Where there is a clearer relationship, as in the case of many wildlife tourism operations, the debate on management has focused on how to enforce controls. Alternatives, such as enforcing regulations through an official body, have been resisted by operators who advocate voluntary arrangements. However evidence suggests this does not provide adequate safeguards on protection of the wildlife resources. A compromise proposal is for the operators to develop self-regulatory agreements, linked to membership schemes with benefits and penalties. Organising and implementing this kind of arrangement has been problematic given the fragmented nature of the sector.

At the level of public policy making, there is also a lack of co-ordination and there are conflicting objectives of agencies concerned with tourism and environment related matters. Although sharing common sustainable development aims, SNH, SEPA, VisitScotland, SE, HIE, and the agricultural, forestry, waterways, rural policy agencies and, of course, local authorities, all, quite rightly, have different agendas and priorities. This is inevitably a constraint on the implementation of policies towards a tourism strategy advocating niche products that are sustainable. At individual project or site level this often results in a classic conflict between development of new activities and environmental conservation priorities. The co-ordination of public agency policies has not yet been clarified by the Scottish Parliament, where responsibility for tourism and environmental matters is spread across a range of departments. When they do come together round the table, such as TEF (see below), the partnership lacks funding and real policy making powers.

There are some positive signs of agreement that management of tourism and protection of the environment requires holistic approaches, involving both development and conservation interests. A variety of partnerships have been established at national (Scotland) and local levels. A great deal of work has been done in raising awareness of industry and integrating environmental variables into tourism quality grading schemes (Green Tourism Business Scheme).

Local sustainable tourism pilot projects (Tourism Management Programmes) set up by the Tourism and Environment Forum and its predecessor, the Tourism and Environment Task Force, have had varying degrees of success. Although these partnerships are still in their infancy and have demonstrated what can be achieved in balancing common goals there are signs that public support for them is dwindling. On the other hand, there is evidence of a shift in thinking in recent Area Tourist Board strategies:

> The challenge for the tourism industry in the Highlands will be to create tourism opportunities and eco-efficiencies through better use of our environmental resources, while effectively managing impacts on the environment brought about by tourism. (HOST 2000: 30).

However, there is scant mention in national tourism policy documents advocating the niche approach, such as 'A New Strategy for Scottish Tourism' (Scottish Executive, 2000), or the follow up Tourism Framework for Action: 2002 – 2005 (Scottish Executive, 2002).

Tourism development of niche products with local economic benefits requires improvements to the management of visitors and improved well-being and enjoyment of local people. They can in turn all result in enhancement to the quality of the natural surroundings on which a niche relies. But in order to achieve this effectively it is essential that accurate data is available to monitor and measure changing patterns of countryside usage: more day visitor surveys; in depth surveys; strategic network of people counters; dissemination of information to a wider audience.

Conclusions

The niche markets or niche products identified for Scottish tourism do not seem to fall within definitions in marketing theory. They are essentially product led with research into their potential markets following as an after-thought. The result is a muddled mixture of broad categories of 'forms of tourism' some with small niche markets within them, others appealing more to the mass market or an amalgam of visitor segments. Several categories depend on the natural environment including some of those identified as having high growth potential. Examination of these categories highlights a number of important issues including their economic value, environmental impacts, attractiveness to particular markets and management problems. The complexity of visitor motivations based on the natural environment and the inclusion of tourists, day visitors and local users makes identification of precise niche markets for environmental product based forms of tourism problematic: the focus on walking illustrates this point. Finally, the issue of connecting suppliers and managers of natural environmental based tourism with promoters suggests that much work is required in integrating niche promotions with visitor management and countryside protection if negative impacts and user conflicts are to be avoided. Although there are indications of partnership working, in particular at local level, recent national tourism policies that have underpinned the niche product approach have tended to ignore integrated, holistic policies that recognise all interested parties.

References

A & M Training & Development (1997) *Review of Wildlife Tourism in Scotland, Inverness*: Tourism and the Environment Task Force.

Arnold, H. (1997) *The Dolphin Space Programme: The development and assessment of an accreditation scheme for dolphin watching boats in the Moray Firth*. A report for the Scottish Wildlife Trust, Scottish Natural Heritage and the EU LIFE Programme.

Broom, G.F., Crabtree, J.R., Roberts, D. and Hill, G (1999) *Socio-Economic benefits from Natura 2000*. The Scottish Office Central Research Unit, Edinburgh.

Bryden, D. (1999) Sustainable Tourism and the Landscape Resource: A Sense of Place, in Usher, M.B.(ed) *Landscape Character: Perspectives on Management and Change*, London: Stationary Office, pp 66-77.

Crabtree,J.R. Appleton,Z. Thomson,K.J. Slee,R.W. Chalmers,N. and Copus,A.(1992) *The Economics of Countryside Access in Scotland*, SAC Economics Report No 37. Aberdeen: Scottish Agriculture College (SAC).

Crabtree, J. R., Leat P. M. K., Santarossa, J. and Thomson, K. J. (1994), The Economic Impact of Wildlife Sites in Scotland. *Journal of Rural Studies*, 10, 61-72.

Dalgic T and Leeuw M (1994) Niche Marketing Revisited: Concept, Applications and Some European Cases, *European Journal of Marketing*, 28, 4, 39 – 55.

Dargie, T., Aitken, R., Tantram, D. (1994) *'Trossachs Tourism Management Programme: Environmental Monitoring'*, Inverness: Highlands and Islands Enterprise.

Fraser Darling, F. and Boyd, J.M. (1964) *The Highlands and Islands*, London: Collins.

Highlands of Scotland Tourist Board (2000) *Highlands of Scotland Tourism strategy 2000 – 2005*, Inverness: Highlands of Scotland Tourist Board.

Highlands and Islands Enterprise (1996) *The Economic Impacts of Hillwalking, Mountaineering and Associated Activities in the Highlands and Islands of Scotland,* Inverness: Highlands and Islands Enterprise.

Holden A (2000) *Environment and Tourism,* London, Routledge.

House of Commons Environment Committee (1995) *The Environmental Impact of Leisure Activities, Volume I,* Report, together with the Proceedings of the Committee relating to the Report. London: HMSO.

Hunt, J. (2000) How do people enjoy the natural heritage?, paper presented at the Scottish Natural Heritage conference 'Enjoyment and understanding of the natural heritage: finding the new balance between rights and responsiblities' September 2000. Battleby: Scottish Natural Heritage.

Hunter, J. (1995) *On the other side of sorrow. Nature and People in the Scottish Highlands.* Edinburgh: Mainstream.

Hutchinson, P.G. (1997) *Town and Country Planning (Scotland) Act 1997 Report of the Helmsdale Wind farms Inquiry.* Edinburgh: HMSO.

Kay, G. (1989) Love affair with the countryside, in *Town and Country Planning,* vol. 58 (3), 78 – 81.

Kotler P (2000) *Marketing Management; The Millenium Edition*; Prentice Hall International, London.

Lister-Kaye, J. (1994) *Ill Fares the Land: A Sustainable Land Ethic for the Sporting Estates of the Highlands and Islands of Scotland,* Perth: Scottish Natural Heritage (SNH).

McGilvray, J. (1990) *The Impact of Sporting Shooting in Scotland,* Glasgow: Fraser of Allander Institute.

Mackay Consultants, (1989) *The Economic Importance of Salmon Fishing and Netting in Scotland,:* A report to STB and HIDB, Edinburgh: Scottish Tourist Board.

Mackay Consultants, (1997) *Jobs and the Natural Heritage in Scotland.* A report for Scottish Natural Heritage, Edinburgh.

MacLellan L R (2001) Tourism and the Natural Environment. *Scottish Environment Audits No. 5.* Scottish Environment LINK, Perth, Scotland.

Macpherson Research (1996) *Perceptions and Experiences of Access to the Scottish Countryside for Open Air Recreation of visitors from Mainland Europe.* A report for Scottish Natural Heritage. SNH: Battleby.

Masters D., Nautilus Consultants and Carter, J (1998) *Marine Wildlife Tourism: developing a quality approach in the Highlands and Islands.* A report for The Tourism and Environment Initiative and Scottish Natural Heritage, May 1998.

Mill R C & Morrison A M (2002), *The Tourism System (Fourth Edition)* Dubuque, Iowa: Kendall/Hunt.

Morrison, D. (1995) *Wildlife tourism in the Minch: Distribution, Impact and Development Opportunities.*Stornoway: Minch Project.

Parker, G. and Ravenscroft, N. (1999) Benevolence, nationalism and hegemony: fifty years of the National Parks and Access to the Countryside Act 1949, in *Leisure Studies,* vol. 18, 297 – 313.

PIEDA (1991) Review of Tourism and the Scottish Environment. Edinburgh: PIEDA.

Ralton, A. (2001) Access and Tourism, in *Tourism, The Journal of The Tourism Society,* Autumn, 2001.

Rayment, M. (1995) *Nature Conservation, Employment and Local Economies: A Literature Review*. Royal Society for the Protection of Birds, Bedfordshire.

Scotexchange.net (2002) Know Your Market, Activity Niche Markets; http://www.scotexchange.net/KnowYourMarket/Niche/walking.asp; 14/6/2002.

Scottish Executive (2000), *A New Strategy for Scottish Tourism*, The Stationery Office, Edinburgh.

Scottish Executive (2002), *Tourism Framework for Action: 2002 – 2005*, The Stationery Office, Edinburgh.

Scottish Natural Heritage (1994) *Enjoying the Outdoors – a Programme for Action,*Battleby: Scottish Natural Heritage.

Scottish Natural Heritage (2001) *Transport Tourism and the Environment in Scotland.* Battleby: Scottish Natural Heritage.

Scottish Sports Council (1998) *Sports Participation in Scotland (1987 – 1996)* Edinburgh: Scottish Sports Council.

Scottish Tourist Board (2000a) *Why British visit Scotland: UK Holiday Motivation Research 1996* in www.scotexchange.net/ Edinburgh: Scottish Tourist Board, Tourism Futures.

Scottish Tourist Board (2000b) Niche Product Identification, in www.scotexchange.net /KnowYourMarket/ Edinburgh: Scottish Tourist Board, Tourism Futures.

Scottish Tourist Board (2000c) Letter from STB Tourism Futures Department to the Scottish Tourism Research Unit regarding Niche Products. 24th May, 2000.

Scottish Tourism Co-ordinating Group (STCG) (1992) *Tourism and the Scottish Environment: A Sustainable Partnership*, Edinburgh: Scottish Tourist Board.

Sidaway, R. (1994) *Recreation and the Natural Heritage: a review of research and practice*. Edinburgh: Scottish Natural Heritage and Scottish Sports Council.

Sidaway, R. (1995) *Field Experience of Disturbance to Birds: a survey of research ornithologists' direct experiences of the effects of human disturbance*. Edinburgh: Scottish Natural Heritage.

Sidaway, R. (1998) Recreation pressures on the Countryside: real concerns or crises of the imagination, in Collins, M.F. and Cooper, I.S. (Eds.) *Leisure Management: Issues and Applications.* Wallingford: CAB International, 85-96.

Sidaway, R. (2000) The Effects of Recreation on the Natural Heritage, paper presented at the Scottish Natural Heritage conference 'Enjoyment and understanding of the natural heritage: finding the new balance between rights and responsiblities' September 2000. Battleby: Scottish Natural Heritage.

Slee B. (1998) Tourism and Rural Development in Scotland, in MacLellan, L.R. and Smith, R. *Tourism in Scotland*, Oxford, International Thomson Business Press, 93-111.

Slee B, Farr, H. and Snowdon, P. (1997) The Economic Impact of Alternative Types of Rural Tourism, *Journal of Agricultural Economics* 48 179-192.

Smout,C. (1993) *The Highlands and the Roots of Green Consciousness, 1750-1990,* Perth: Scottish Natural Heritage (SNH).

Surrey Research Group (1993) Scottish Tourism Multiplier Study. ESU Research Paper No. 31, Scottish Office Industry Department, Edinburgh.

System Three (1998) Study of walking in Scotland. Prepared for Highlands and Islands Enterprise, Scottish Tourist Board and Scottish Natural Heritage. Edinburgh: Scottish Tourist Board.

System Three (2000a) Tourism Attitudes Survey, 1999. Prepared for Scottish Tourist Board and Scottish Natural Heritage. Edinburgh: Scottish Tourist Board.

System Three (2000b) Scottish Residents' Recreational Attitudes: Survey of Walking. Prepared for Scottish Natural Heritage.

Chapter 17

Sustainable Visitor Management System
A discussion paper

Bill Taylor, David Masters, Peter Scott and Graham Barrow

Summary

The management of visitors to countryside and heritage sites has challenged site managers for decades. There is now renewed interest in a more systematic approach to visitor management, driven by new directions in countryside and access policy, increasing public expectations, and the broader 'sustainability' agenda.

This study revisits some of the key lessons that have been learnt over the last 30 years, and on the basis of this proposes a Sustainable Visitor Management System.

The resulting Sustainable Visitor Management System is a cyclical, iterative planning and management process. It is presented as a menu of procedures, processes and tools that can be used at a range of visitor sites according to their management

Introduction and Background

The Study Brief
Scottish Natural Heritage commissioned this study in response to needs identified by the Tourism and Environment Forum and various organisations that manage countryside sites in Scotland.

The brief identified a need to develop an approach to the management of countryside sites that was more dynamic, could inform site management and marketing, and was part of a regular cycle of reappraisal and adjustment. The brief noted 'It is critical such an approach is simple, widely applicable and recognised as a useful tool by site managers'.

Study Aims
The study aimed to provide guidance on a systematic approach to visitor planning and management at countryside sites, which has been

called the Sustainable Visitor Management System (SVMS). SVMS is presented as a system of procedures, processes and tools that can be used at a range of visitor sites and by a range of site managing organisations.

Key Assumptions
The findings of this study are based on certain key assumptions:

- Such a system must incorporate both planning and management.
- It must integrate with or take account of existing site planning and management procedures.
- It must be participatory.
- 'Countryside sites' include both small and large areas of coast and countryside and historic buildings and monuments in a landscape setting.
- 'Visitors' may be participating in both passive and active leisure activities, and may range from local residents to day visitors and UK and overseas tourists.

Methodology

Key Stages
Research and consultation

- UK reports and literature were reviewed.
- Research and consultation into visitor planning and management in Scotland was carried out.
- Research into systematic visitor planning and management in the National Parks of England and Wales was conducted.
- Requests were made for information on systematic visitor planning and management from agencies in England and Wales.
- Internet searches were made for international information and publications.
- Email discussions and / or meetings were made with recreation specialists in the USA, Australia and New Zealand.

Analysis and initial findings

- The results of the research and consultation were reviewed and an outline methodology developed.

Participatory workshops
- A workshop was held with the steering group agencies to review the initial research and analysis.
- A large, participatory workshop was held with invited site managers and site management staff from across Scotland to critique the outline the methodology.

Report preparation
- Draft and final reports were prepared.

Benefits of Sustainable Visitor Management

The study identified a number of key benefits of sustainable visitor management. The principle overall benefit is that an effective SVMS will help to secure, enhance and maintain both the quality of the environment and/or cultural heritage values of the resource and the visitor experience.

Benefits relevant to site managing organisations; to site managers and to the wider community and site users were identified. A clear understanding of these benefits will be important in the adoption of the methodology by site managing organisations.

Research Review

Background
Managing visitors to natural areas and to the countryside has been an issue since the establishment of National Parks in the USA in the late 19th Century. The growing numbers of visitors, particularly after the 1950's, led to the need for management, the reduction of the physical impacts of recreation, and concerns about interactions between different recreation users.

In the UK, concern for the impact of visitors in the countryside have been an issue since the 1960's and to some extent led to the Countryside Acts in the late '60's. At this time the concern was to measure the impacts of trampling and disturbance and to move towards some concept of reducing impacts through site management.

A review of literature from North America, the UK and Australia has identified five broad approaches to tackling these visitor and site management issues (see Appendix 2). The approaches can be classified broadly as follows:

Carrying capacity
Here the emphasis is placed on attempting to define a number of visitors which if exceeded will result in damage to the environment or to the recreational experience. Carrying capacity as a phrase is still powerful and has strong links to sustainability theory. It has social, economic and environmental components and makes little sense without clear management objectives, monitoring programmes and decision-making structures.

Limits of acceptable change
With its roots in the US Forest Service, the late 1980's saw attempts to introduce a different, but related approach (see Hendee *et al.*). Limits of Acceptable Change took the emphasis off visitor numbers - with its related implications of limiting use - towards measuring the state of the environment and agreeing management responses should predetermined thresholds be exceeded

Visitor impact management and monitoring
Jeff Marion at the US Geological Survey has attempted to introduce an approach which places even more emphasis on the monitoring of the impacts of visitors and the role of collective decision making. Farrell and Marion (2002), describe a system which combines elements of both LAC and carrying capacity. It recommends the formation of an expert panel, the use of zones, clear management objectives and the visiting in the field of the expert panel together with regular monitoring. The system is seen as being particularly applicable for use in protected areas.

Visitor experience and resource protection
Some experts have concluded that insufficient attention is paid to visitor satisfaction and their views of environmental quality. They conclude that any decisions concerning site management must be based on the views of users.

Recreation opportunity spectrum
Here the emphasis is placed on zoning the area and attributing different objectives and levels and types of recreational activity to the different zones. It has been the basis of many outdoor recreation management plans in both North America and the UK. Zoning remains a central plank of outdoor recreation management.

Current Extent of Systematic Visitor Planning and Management in the UK
The research identified very limited systematic visitor planning and management in the UK. In Scotland, a single example of LAC has been developed at Aonach Mor, with an adapted version in development at Cairngorm. The Brecon Beacons National Park has used LAC in its site management planning, focussing on ecological criteria rather than visitors. The Peak District National Park examined the possibility of an LAC approach but felt it was inappropriate to their needs. The Yorkshire Dales National Park has prepared an access strategy that combines zoning, quality-based indicators and standards, monitoring, management and stakeholder participation. This system is not dissimilar to that proposed below.

Lessons learnt
The key issues that must be addressed by any sustainable visitor management system can be summarised as follows:

- *The need for gaining acceptance of a systematic approach*
- *Setting clear objectives is central to the process*
- *Stakeholder participation and decision making structures are essential*
- *Suitable staff time and resources to follow any systematic planning and management approach*
- *Resources for regular data gathering*
- *Acceptable cost-effective methods for measuring "quality"*

The Scottish Context and Current Practice

Key issues evident from our review of site-based visitor management in Scotland are:

Some high quality visitor sites and management
Scotland has many visitor sites developed and managed to high standards that can compete with the standards of provision and management abroad. Similarly, many site managers and line managers are experienced and skilled in site and visitor management. Nevertheless, management organisations recognise that there remains scope to bring all sites and all staff up to the standards of the best.

Varied approaches to site management
Management approaches vary significantly between organisations and sites. Indeed, some sites will never justify substantial management intervention e.g. remote sites with very low levels of use and robust site characteristics. However, the extent or emphasis of management involvement has not always related to the requirements of sites. A review of past management involvement reveals examples of a conservation imperative where management organisations have developed management plans and practices that focus on natural or cultural heritage interests, without embracing opportunities for public appreciation or enjoyment of the site.

The range of current approaches includes the following: management according to the manager's values and experience; a market and income-generation imperative; crisis management and pseudo-/scientific approaches.

It is unnecessary to identify specific management organisations or sites to illustrate the above situations, but examples were evident during the consultants' research.

Issues of 'Ownership' of, and Commitment to, Site Management Plans and Prescriptions
Many visitor management plans and polices have been developed by HQ or other staff at a distance from day-to-day site management, or by consultants. In such circumstances, the management policies and prescriptions may not have been fully communicated to, or accepted by, site managers and rangers, etc.

Historically, site management has been the prerogative of the management organisations and their managers, with little external inputs from the local and wider communities and interest groups. It is still the case that few country parks and larger scale recreation sites/areas have arrangements for involving local and wider interest groups in their management.

Resource constraints
Visitor management planning, implementation and monitoring require staff and financial resources. Shortfalls in resources have often resulted in managers taking a 'fire fighting' approach to site management, rather than planning for future needs and seeking to pre-empt problems.

Shortfalls in Data and Awareness of Management and Monitoring Techniques and Good Practice
Site managers and others involved in managing visitor sites have identified constraints, which are inhibiting effective visitor site planning and management. The lack of information on visitor numbers and the need for advice on specific aspects of visitor management and monitoring are commonly mentioned.

Lack of Opportunities for Sharing Good Practice and Knowledge of Management Techniques

Drivers Towards More Sustainable Visitor Site Management
Representatives of conservation and visitor site management organisations have highlighted the appropriate timing of this study. In particular, they stressed its potential to contribute to their organisations' own programmes for reviewing and enhancing their visitor site planning and management procedures. Amongst the key drivers and influences for change are:

- *Sustainability, social inclusion and related societal agendas*
- *Responding to the new access legislation*
- *Recognition of the legitimacy and potential benefits of stakeholder interests*
- *Quality assurance*
- *Regulatory requirements*
- *Risk assessments and provision for the disabled*
- *Funding requirements*

Existing Constraints to Sustainable Visitor Management
Our review suggests there are a number of key constraints to implementing sustainable visitor management systems. These need to be understood and addressed by the SVMS, and are as follows:

- *No perceived problem*
- *Existing approaches perceived as adequate*
- *Work load / resource issues*
- *Costs of monitoring*
- *No management forum or stakeholder input*
- *Concerns about a structured appraisal*
- *Lack of proven application*
- *No common language for site planning and management*

Proposed Sustainable Visitor Management System

The key qualities of the proposed sustainable visitor management system are:

- It is a cyclical planning and management process
- It draws on existing models and experience, both in the UK and world-wide
- It is designed to integrate with wider site planning and management
- It is designed to be as simple as possible to apply to a wide range of circumstances

It is worth stating that this report is part of an experimental process, and that the following methodology will need to be rigorously tested to develop a fully operational and effective system.

Outline system

The system comprises a number of discrete but linked stages similar to the existing site planning and management cycle (**Figure 1**). The SVMS cycle can be initiated at any of these stages. The outline stages are as follows:

Defining the Boundaries of the Site

The site's boundaries are defined. For sites under single ownership this will be a simple task, but for sites in multiple ownership it may be more complex. The system is designed to operate at a wide range of scales, from a small site under single ownership (e.g. a local nature reserve) to a large area of countryside in multiple ownership (e.g. an extensive Highland glen like Glen Nevis).

Figure 1: The sustainable visitor management cycle

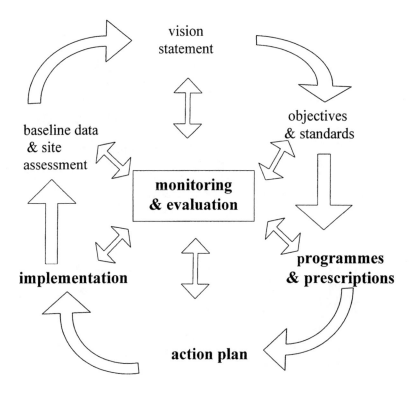

Baseline Information Survey and Assessment
Answers to some of the questions below will be contained in any existing management documentation or other databases and sources of information.

- What importance does the site have for natural and cultural heritage conservation?
- What importance does the site have for the local community?
- What importance does it have for other visitors?
- What importance does it have for research and education?
- Why do visitors come and what is / are their principle activities?
- What are the key visitor impacts and conflicts?
- What is the site's visitor context?
- Which stakeholders are concerned with visitor access?
- What is the current management practice?

Other questions may need original research, or might not be fully answered until the visitor and site monitoring is underway.

- What resources are available for visitor and visitor impact management?
- Are there opportunities for enhancing visitor use and enjoyment?
- What external pressures / influences need to be taken into account?

Any gaps that exist in the baseline survey and assessment should be identified and addressed later or at the first major review.

- What degree of management is needed?

The proposed SVMS uses a menu of planning and management tools, and only those relevant to a site should be used (i.e. a 'horses for courses' approach). As a guide we have developed three broad versions of the SVMS methodology:

Level 1: Low intensity management
Level 2: Moderate intensity management
Level 3: High intensity management

The majority of sites would require the 'low intensity management' approach. Some would need moderate intensity management. A few of the highest quality and / or most intensively used sites would need high intensity management. A decision would be made about which version the site needs. Answering questions such as below will suggest the degree of management likely to be required:

- To what extent does the site have a nature or cultural conservation value?
- To what extent does the site have a community or economic value?
- To what extent are existing visitor activities having an impact on the site's key qualities?
- To what extent are the site's key qualities vulnerable to increased visitor activities?
- How accessible is the site to a large population?

Vision Statement
A vision statement/s is prepared that articulates the broad goals (or 'aims') for visitor enjoyment of the site. It may look 20 or even 50 years ahead, should reflect the aspirations of relevant stakeholder organisations, and should not be unduly constrained by current funding and management arrangements.

Objectives and Standards
Key issues in setting visitor management objectives and standards are as follows:

Who should be involved?
It is important that the right people are involved in defining objectives and standards. A wide range of stakeholders may be concerned with the site and its potential visitor management objectives, some of whom may only be concerned with one or two very specific issues. Again, the principles of 'horses for courses' and open, transparent discussion should apply.

Stakeholder participation
The degree of stakeholder involvement should be commensurate with the scale of the site's visitor issues. At simple sites there may be very few relevant stakeholders, including its managing organisation (although different interests may exist within that organisation). At

complex sites there may be a wide range of stakeholders who should be involved in the site's management.

Not all stakeholders are the same: some will have a greater degree of concern than others, so a simple hierarchy may be needed of 'primary' and 'secondary' stakeholders.

It is important to communicate effectively with stakeholders to keep them informed throughout the process, and for them to be able to communicate with each other and the site manager in return. Email offers the simplest way to do this, although a web site or printed newsletter might also be considered. It is suggested that an effort is made to show early results in order to keep stakeholders enthused and involved.

Sometimes expert external advice and support might be needed to facilitate stakeholder involvement. There are also potentially important roles for stakeholders in applying the management prescriptions and monitoring visitors and their impacts.

Objectives

The visitor management objectives should set out what can be realistically achieved in a 5-10 year planning cycle (i.e. recognise the real constraints that exist). They should relate to all key elements of the visitors' activities and experience, and will be based on a collective judgement about what is achievable and desirable.

Some illustrative visitor management objectives are:

- The 'wild country experience' qualities of the site will be maintained and enhanced.
- Visitor levels and activities will be managed so that they do not risk causing any damage to the fabric of the historic monument.
- Conflict between walkers and cyclists will be minimised.

Some objectives may relate to the whole site whereas others may relate to specific zones. Simple sites may have very few objectives; complex ones will have more.

Standards

The visitor management standards articulate exactly how each objective is to be delivered, and provide specific, measurable goals to aim for (or limits not to be exceeded).

Each objective should have one or more standards set for it. Some would relate to site quality whilst others may relate to the quality of the visitor experience. Subsequent monitoring will enable the site manager and stakeholders to assess to what degree the standards are being met.

For example: Possible visitor management objective

The 'wild country experience' qualities of the site will be maintained and enhanced.

Potential visitor management standards to deliver this objective:
- There is a presumption against path surfacing, but any that is necessary (e.g. for reasons of cross-drainage) will use techniques and materials in keeping with the immediate environment.
- Path width will not exceed 0.5m in any remote zones.
- At least 90% of visitors visiting the remote zones will regard these zones as providing a satisfactory 'wild country experience' (as assessed in the annual visitor survey).

How prescriptive the standards proposed are will depend on the site, its visitors and its managing organisation. Where prescriptive standards are not appropriate, the visitor objectives must be detailed enough to guide management action.

Initial objectives and standards should be reviewed early on in the cycle (e.g. in year 2 or 3) to determine whether they are appropriate and achievable.

Management Prescriptions

A set of management prescriptions should be developed to deliver the visitor management objectives and standards. Initial prescriptions might not be comprehensive due to a lack of baseline or monitoring data. Over time, the prescriptions should become more focussed and reactive to the findings of the monitoring and evaluation.

Action plan
The management prescriptions are articulated in a costed, timetabled action plan: it indicates how they will be implemented and by whom. A new action plan should be prepared each year or as often as required.

Simpler sites may only need an action plan, amended as necessary, to take account of the results of the preceding monitoring and evaluation. Complex sites may also need a full visitor management and interpretation plan. This should set out objectives, policies and programmes for site management and visitor communication.

Implementation
Implementation is guided by the action plan. Possible visitor management actions are listed below:

- Increase or decrease marketing and promotion of the site
- Increase or decrease the size of the car park
- Open or close specific routes or areas
- Use signage, orientation and interpretation to influence visitors' behaviour
- Improve route surfacing
- Install or remove specific items of visitor provision (e.g. visitor centre, toilets, boardwalks)
- Adopt code/s of conduct or apply bye-law/s
- License or restrict specific activities
- Increase or decrease ranger presence
- Install or remove litter bins, increase or decrease frequency of litter collection, or implement a 'take your litter home' policy
- Engage conflict resolution mechanisms

Ideally the actions to be taken should be agreed by the stakeholder group. Some of these actions would show results within a single year. Others would take longer to implement and for their impact to show. Implementation could be delivered either by in-house staff, contractors or volunteers; or by a combination.

Monitoring
Monitoring is absolutely crucial to the successful application of the proposed SVMS. Monitoring techniques must be simple and effective, and be specifically linked to the visitor management objectives and standards. This must be inexpensive to implement and keep going and needs to be based on simple indicators and must trigger a management response.

Broadly speaking, two key elements are monitored: visitors' impacts (i.e. the state of the resource), and visitors' experience. Within this, four individual parameters may need to be monitored:

1. Levels of visitor use
2. Visitor activities
3. Visitor experience
4. Visitor impacts / the state of the resource

Of these, the visitor experience and visitor impacts / state of the resource are the more important parameters to monitor. Guidance on each of these is given below:

Levels of use
Every site should have some indication of its level of use. This can be easily monitored through: people counter/s; vehicle counter/s or spot count/s.

Visitor activities

The visitor experience
The visitor experience includes aspects such as accessibility, crowding, intrusions, queuing time, perceived safety, aesthetic qualities etc.

Formally monitoring the visitor experience is time-consuming and should only be attempted at sites with significant visitor management issues. For most sites the visitor experience can be assessed on the basis of information received on a voluntary basis from users through: stakeholder opinions; anecdotal reports; letters of praise or complaint or feedback sheets inserted in site leaflet.

Any structured monitoring of the visitor experience should be done through a visitor satisfaction survey, and would ideally relate satisfaction to expectations and motivation. Perceptions of overcrowding by visitors at peak times may be worthy of survey at very high intensity management sites. This could indicate trends over a period of years, but the data must be interpreted cautiously.

Visitor impacts / the state of the resource
Measuring and monitoring visitor impacts is the most technically challenging aspect of the monitoring. Broadly speaking, there are three kinds of visitor impact:

- Inter-user impacts
- Disturbance impacts
- Physical impacts

Inter-user impacts should be dealt with as part of the visitor experience monitoring outlined above.

Disturbance impacts have been debated by recreation ecologists and site managers for decades: there are so many variables that proving a causal link between visitor activities (e.g. dog walking) to disturbance effects (e.g. breeding birds are disturbed) to impacts (e.g. a reduction in bird population) is often very difficult without intensive research.

Physical impacts should be a primary focus of the visitor impact monitoring.

There are two broad approaches to physical impact monitoring[1]: observation and quantitative measuring.

Of these, we feel visual assessments have the best potential for a quick, pragmatic and structured approach to monitoring a range of impacts simultaneously. Visual assessments work as follows:

A scoring scale is chosen. One end of the scale is 'zero observable impact'; the other is 'very high degree of observable impact'. A 1-10 scale might be as follows:

- '1' is a site or zone where an experienced site manager can see no visual evidence of visitor impacts.
- '5' is a site or zone where either a range of minor impacts are observable (e.g. some litter, some erosion, some trampling of vegetation) or a single but more significant impact is observable (e.g. moderate degree of erosion).
- '10' is a site or a zone where major impact/s are observable (e.g. complete erosion of top soil, massive littering etc).

The site assessor/s travel around the site assessing the score for each zone, either annually or in summer and winter. Photographs could be taken if necessary as a back-up record. They begin by agreeing the score for two or three zones and then base the other scores on these. In this way an entire site can be monitored in the time it takes the

---

[1] See *Developing a Natural Resource Inventory and Monitoring Programme for Visitor Impacts on Recreation Sites: A Procedural Manual.* US National Parks Service Report NPS/NRVT/NRR-91/06. 1991

assessor/s to travel around it. The resulting data is simple to process and understand. To ensure consistent scoring, the assessors would need to be experienced site managers trained in the assessment process.

Public safety and public liability

Matters of public safety and public liability should also be monitored through regular site inspection, in line with the relevant legislation and legal requirements.

Evaluation

The monitoring data should be evaluated for individual zones and / or a whole site as follows:

- Visitor impact data will indicate whether or not the visitor impact objectives and standards are being met.

- Visitor experience data will indicate whether or not any visitor experience objectives and standards are being met.

- Levels of visitor use data will inform decisions about increasing or decreasing visitor numbers and their dispersal within a site.

- Visitor activity data may inform specific actions such as conflict resolution or changes in the way a site is promoted to visitors.

At its simplest, the evaluation will highlight four possible scenarios:

- A status quo situation that needs no action
- An improving situation that needs action
- A deteriorating situation that needs action
- An improving or deteriorating situation that does not require immediate action but should be watched in future

External influences (e.g. climate change, pollution, natural changes in population level etc) should be considered when assessing the relative importance of visitor impacts.

- When should evaluation happen?

Evaluation should take place when it is needed. For parameters where the impact and consequent rate of change is relatively constant, this can be on a regular (i.e. once yearly) basis. For other parameters, some form of trigger may be needed to initiate the evaluation. Evaluation must also feed back into the longer-term site planning and management cycle, for example during the site management plan review. The results of the evaluation will inform future management prescriptions. An additional key issue in the evaluation of monitoring data relates to who should be involved.

Once established, the cycle has three regularly repeating elements (see Figure 1):

- **Action** on the ground.
- **Monitoring** of site qualities, visitor impacts, the visitor experience and the results of past management.
- **Evaluation** of the monitoring data against the objectives and standards to identify what revisions are required to the management prescriptions and action plan.

It is important to keep the management statement / plan under periodic review to ensure its objectives and standards continue to be appropriate and to accommodate changing circumstances such as a new recreational impact on the site. It is recommended that site assessment, objectives and standards are reviewed every 3-5 years in line with any wider management plan cycle.

Wider ranging reviews of baseline information and vision statements could be undertaken on a longer-term cycle, perhaps every 10-15 years, when new individuals will almost certainly be involved in the site and its stakeholder bodies.

Initiating the Cycle and Keeping it Going

The proposed SVMS operates as an iterative cycle. In a theoretical world, it would begin as described above (i.e. with setting the site boundaries) and continue in a linear manner to the evaluation stage before starting again.

However, the real world is not so neat. For example, determining visitor objectives and standards will depend on good baseline information, which may not be available until some monitoring has been completed.

We suggest the first stage in initiating the system should be for the site manager/s to convene a meeting with the key stakeholders to discuss the need for, and benefits of, a systematic approach to sustainable visitor management. This should result in a series of action points that would initiate key early stages in parallel, including discussing the site boundaries, collecting baseline information, and developing vision statement/s.

There should usually be an emphasis on early monitoring to guide the objective setting. It is likely such monitoring will become more targeted and sophisticated as the cycle becomes established.

There are also further principles to follow in initiating and running the system:

- Don't rush the processes – SVMS is a long-term solution that should not be expected to work overnight.
- Don't expect to get it right first time: several cycles may be needed before the system as a whole, and its various feedback loops, work properly.
- Make sure that practical work begins early on to avoid SVMS being perceived as a 'talking shop'.
- Begin monitoring early on to provide important intelligence on the site and its visitors.

Possible Use of Management Triggers
This cycle will usually take place annually in line with the existing annual work programmes and budgetary and funding cycles. However, different visitor uses and impacts may take effect at different rates. Where these rates are significantly out of time with an annual work programme, some form of trigger mechanism may be needed to inform site management. In this scenario, the visitor management standards become 'limits of acceptable change'. Monitoring these parameters would trigger action when it is needed, not in time with an annual work programme. We suggest this more sophisticated version should be tested in a pilot exercise.

Project Management and Monitoring
Effective project management and monitoring will be needed. This would track, for example, actual expenditure on the various management actions, attendance at stakeholder meetings, publishing of minutes etc.

Organisational Structure and Commitment
To work, the proposed SVMS will need commitment at all levels in

the managing organisation.

There will be key differences in applying the system at sites under single- and multiple-ownership. Single ownership sites may need less attention to securing management consensus. Multiple-ownership sites will need a clear lead agency.

There is also the question of how best to apply the system at a suite of local or regional sites for which a single member of staff has responsibility, and which may share a number of key stakeholders.

Conclusion

The theoretical approach outlined above is the result of wide-ranging research, consultation and analysis. However, it will remain theoretical until an appropriate programme of pilot testing is undertaken. Piloting is the only way in which all aspects of the methodology can be tested in a range of practical circumstances.

Work has begun on this process (see Appendix 1), incorporating a wide range of sites and conditions. It is intended that this work will be developed over the next 18 months

Scotland is of a size where a national piloting programme such as this can be attempted that will finally provide answers to practical visitor planning and management issues site managers and their organisations have been struggling with for decades. The proposed SVMS could form the basis of a sustainability-based approach central to the objectives of the Tourism and Environment Forum, and for the future management of protected landscapes, heritage sites, nature reserves, and other countryside, cultural and coastal sites and areas.

Acknowledgements
The authors would like to acknowledge the support and assistance of the project steering group in undertaking this study. In particular, we would like to thank Bridget Dales and Jill Matthews (Scottish Natural Heritage), Paul Johnson (The National Trust for Scotland), Chris McGregor (Historic Scotland), Caroline Warburton (Tourism and Environment Forum) and Julie Snodgrass (Forest Enterprise) for their guidance and support.

SVMS Pilot Sites 2002/03

Glentress (FE)

Cross country bike routes where sustainability could be an issue. Well used by horses (and their riders!) and walkers. Lots of partnership funding coming in and new developments still planned. Franchised bike hire and cafe/toilets on site. Active forest: in terms of management of timber/replanting etc.

Falls of Clyde (SWT)

Popular gorge woodland site (includes woodland SAC) beside heavily visited World Heritage site. Significant infrastructure provision related to HLF project

St Abbs (NTS)

Coastal site: with SPA seabird colonies and coastal path. Long history of active visitor management planning

Flanders Moss (SNH)

SAC peatland: with SNH/SWT and private landowning interests. Significant habitat management works and proposed visitor infrastructure associated with LIFE project. Limited public access at present

Mar Lodge (NTS)

Large upland estate: with significant mountain and wildland assets, and some challenging activity base issues. Pinewood, upland and montane conservation interests.

Fife Coastal Path (Fife Council)

Complex coastal path with SAC/SPA interests, community involvement and tourism promotion issues

Ruby Bay, Elie (Fife Council)

Small beach with community involvement

Lochore Meadows CP (Fife Council)

Heavily used country park with water based activities

Appendix 2

Literature Review Sources: North America, UK and Australia

North America

Eagles P F J (1997) Prof. Dept of recreation and Leisure studies, University of Waterloo, Ontario, Canada International Ecotourism Management: Using Australia and Africa as case studies.

Farrell T and Marion J (in press, 2002). The Protected Area Visitor Impact Monitoring (PAVIM) Framework: A Simplified Process for Making Management Decisions. *Journal of Sustainable Tourism.*

Forman K C (1994) Environmental Studies Program, University of Nevada, USA. *Determining Recreational Visitor Carrying Capacity: The case of Black Canyon at Lake Mead National Recreation Area.*

Hendee JC, Stankey G H and Lucas R (undated) *Wilderness Management.* Ch 9 The Carrying Capacity Issue. USDA Forest Service.

Leung Y and Marrion J (2000) Recreation Impacts and Management in Wilderness: A State of Knowledge Review. *USDA Forest Service Proceedings* RMPS-P-15-Vol-5 2000.

Leung Y, Marion J and Farrell T (2001). The Role of Recreation Ecology in Sustainable Tourism and Ecotourism. Paper in *Tourism, Recreation and Sustainability* (Edited by S McCool and R N Moisey, CABI Publishing).

Leung Y, Marion J and Ferguson J (undated). Methods for Assessing and Monitoring Backcountry Trail Conditions: an Empirical Comparison.

Lundquist S S and Haas G E (1999). College of Natural Resources, Fort Collins, Colorado. Abstracts of papers. 1999 *Congress on Recreation and Resource Capacity,* Aspen, Colorado, USA

Manning R (1999) *Studies in Outdoor Recreation. Search and Research for Satisfaction.* Oregan State University Press

Marion J (1991). *Developing a Natural Resource Inventory and Monitoring Program for Visitor Impacts on Recreation Sites: A procedural manual.* US Dept. of the Interior - National Parks Service.

Marion J (1995). Environmental Auditing. Capabilities and Management Utility of Recreation Impact Monitoring Programs. *Environmental Management,* 19 (5).

Marion J (1996). Access and Management: Public Land Perplexities - Balancing Resource Protection and Recreation. National Outdoor Ethics Conference, St Loius, Missouri, April 1996.

Marion J (1998), Unit Leader USGS, Patuxent Wildlife Research Center, Virginia USA. *Recreation Ecology Research Findings: Implications for Wilderness and Park Managers.*

Marion J and Farrell T (1998). Managing Ecotourism Visitation in Protected Areas. Paper in *Ecotourism: a Guide for Planners and Managers* (Edited by K. Lindberg, M. Epler Wood and D. Engledrum, the Ecotourism Society, North Bennington, Vermont).

Marion J and Leung Y (2001). Trail Resource Impacts and an Examination of Alternative Assessment Techniques. *Journal of Park and Recreation Administration* Vol 19, no 3.

Marion J and Reid S E (2001). Development of the United States "Leave no Trace" Programme: A Historical Perspective. Paper in *Experience and Understanding of the Natural Heritage* (Edited by M Usher, Scottish Natural Heritage)

McCool S F (1996) Prof., School of Forestry, University of Montana, USA. Limits of Acceptable Change: A framework for managing national protected areas; Experiences from the United States. (paper delivered at workshop on impact management in marine parks, Kuala Lumpur, Malaysia, August 1996)

Shakley M (Editor) (2000) *Visitor Management: Case Studies from World Heritage Sites*. Butterworth-Heinemann.

Shenandoah National Park Backcountry and Wilderness Management Plan. (1998). Chapter 10 Research and Monitoring US National Park Service

UNDP. Sustainable Management of Water Resources and Aquatic Environment: the UNDP role to date and strategy framework

Williams P and Gill A (1991) Centre for Tourism Policy and Research, Simon Fraser University. Carrying Capacity Management in Tourism settings: A tourism growth management process. Prepared for Alberta Economic Development, Canada.

Yoo K (1995) University of Maine, The feasibility of visitor impact management in the Korean National Park system: an approach for technique transformation. Paper delivered to the 1995 Leisure Research Symposium, San Antonio, Texas.

United Kingdom

Bayfield N G and McGowan G M (1995). Monitoring and Managing impacts of ski development: a case study of the Aonoch Mor Resort 1989-1995. In *Landscape Ecology Theory and Application*. Proceedings of the 4th IALE Conference, Reading 1995.

Bayfield N G and Conroy J (2000). Environmental Audit of a Scottish Natural Heritage Area: The Cairngorms. In *Eco-Management and Auditing*, 7.

Bayfield N G (2001). Mountain Resources and Conservation. In *Habitat Conservation: Managing the Physical Environment*. (Edited by A Warren and J R French). Wiley and Sons.

Glasson J *et al* (1995) *Towards Visitor Impact management: Visitor Impacts, Carrying Capacity and management Responses in Europe's Historic Towns and Cities*. Avebury.

McGowan G M, Bayfield N G and Thurlow M (in press). Use of a Limits of Accceptable Change (LAC) Environmental Monitoring and Management Scheme at the Aonach Mor Ski resort, Scotland (1989-1999).

Moss R, Catt D C, Bayfield N G and French D D (1996). The Application of Decision Theory to Sustainable Management of an Upland Scottish Estate. *Journal of Applied Statistics, Vol 23*, Nos 2 and 3.

Scott P (1997) Calmer Waters: Guidelines for planning and managing watersports on inland waters in Scotland The Scottish Sports Council

Scottish Natural Heritage (1999) *Land and Communities: Openness in Ownership*, Scottish Natural Heritage

Sidaway R (1997) *Recreation Planning for the Care of Natural Resources.*

Scottish Natural Heritage

Australia

Australian Alps National Park (1998) *Managing Recreational Environments. Towards a Strategy for the Australian Alps National Park* (Rethink Consulting Pty).
Jacobs P and Mackay J (draft). Planning for Recreation and Tourism in the Australian Alps.
Queensland Parks and Wildlife Service (draft). Towards Best Practice Performance Measurement in Protected Area Management. Prepared for the ANZECC Working Group on National Parks and Protected Area Management, Benchmarking and Best Practice Program.

Chapter 18

Nature-based Tourism: A Paradoxical Niche?

Mhairi Harvey and Steven Gillespie

Introduction

What are niche markets and can their underlying philosophy be employed fruitfully in the promotion of nature-based tourism? Answering this question could be viewed as the culmination to the preceding chapters that have explored the relationship between tourism and nature in a variety of theoretical (and geographic) contexts. Nature, in its broadest sense, has been used as a backdrop for tourism activities ever since mass tourism was identified as a definable phenomenon. It has only recently, however, been viewed as a form of tourism in itself, a phenomenon borne from the desire by city dwellers to escape the challenges and constraints of urban living. The explosion of holidays in far-flung places, where nature is experienced in its most extreme form (treks to the Himalayas, expeditions to the Amazonian rainforest, safaris in the Serengeti), is testimony to a changing attitude towards nature and one that has been embraced by marketers worldwide. The promotion of such adventures may be relatively straightforward when provided with nature at its most magnificent and definable (big mountains, big trees and big cats), but presents a challenge when the nature is familiar, more genteel and 'home-grown'. This is a task for agencies such as VisitScotland who, recognising that there is a growing market for nature-based holidays, must somehow harness the essence of Scotland's nature and sell it to prospective visitors. The challenge becomes even greater at local levels.

It is at this spatial scale that the initial question will be explored, using Dumfries and Galloway in the south west of Scotland as an example. Dumfries and Galloway is a predominantly rural area with a number of market towns, of which Dumfries is the largest. From the M74 east of Dumfries (the main arterial link with the rest of Scotland and England) to Stranraer at its western most edge is a distance of some 100 miles. Whilst the region is close to potential English markets, it has proved very difficult to draw people off the M74,

tourists instead heading for the more high profile Highlands region to
the north or Lake District to the south. The Dumfries & Galloway
Area Tourism Strategy (D&GTB 2001: 6) describes the region as
thus:

> Overall Dumfries & Galloway's tourism 'offer' may be
> characterised as fragmented and small scale... Critically, the
> region has few 'must see' attractions – i.e. outstanding and
> well-known attractions of whatever type that will motivate
> people to visit...On the other hand, there is a wealth of small-
> scale attractions, mainly historical and cultural, for visitors to
> enjoy in the region.

The challenge for a niche market approach therefore is to de-fragment
the attractions to provide a dominant product, recognisable to the
tourist market. The question must be whether 'nature' can be utilised
in this way.

Successful promotion of nature-based activities should result in
increased visitor numbers in, predominantly, rural areas (that natural
places can be found in urban centres is recognised but beyond the
scope of this discussion). There is a danger that successful marketing,
by whatever strategy, may damage the very product upon which the
marketing is based. Nature-based tourism must be sustainable, a
concept which is often (rightly or wrongly) embodied in the term
ecotourism. A further question can therefore be asked. What is
ecotourism and can its underlying philosophy be employed fruitfully
in the promotion of nature-based tourism?

The term ecotourism has been adopted, some may say sabotaged,
by a tourist industry wishing to exploit nature in a manner that claims
to promote conservation of special landscapes and habitats and
preservation of indigenous cultures. The ubiquitous usage of the term
has led to it becoming meaningless to potential customers (Buckley,
2002). Ecotourism gained prominence as a mechanism by which
developing countries could obtain foreign exchange and as a
consequence the term often conjures an image of pristine
environments and primitive cultures. There may, therefore, be some
scepticism of its legitimacy in promoting tourism in a country such as
Scotland.

Despite this, the Dumfries and Galloway Area Tourism Strategy
(D&GTB 2001, p. 13) states:

> The region should position itself as a primary destination for environmentally friendly tourism or "ecotourism", as an integral element of the tourism strategy.

The view here is that ecotourism is a form of tourism that can be promoted as a niche, and it is the appropriateness of this approach that will be further discussed in the context of the question posed above.

Niche markets – defining the consumer

Marketing strategies, however envisaged, rely on being able to define consumer behaviour and supply goods accordingly. A variety of approaches can be taken, ranging from the wholesale promotion of goods to an undifferentiated market, to the selected promotion of unique product to a specified target market (niche). Those promoting a niche market must be able to define and target groups who will recognise and identify with the niche being offered. Not only that, if the concentrated marketing approach is to work, the marketer must be able to offer the identified segment something different, something that no one else can provide (Palmer, 2002).

Roberts and Hall (this volume) highlight an immediate problem with this approach to targeting the tourism market. A fundamental shift in the attitudes and expectations of the tourist has made market segmentation almost impossible. Within their context of rural tourism, they argue that this reflects a postmodern context where there is no such thing as a typical rural tourist. The postmodern tourist is neither structured, nor consistent in its choice of recreational activity, thereby rendering the market niche futile. Krippendorf (1987) further argues that tourism marketers must be more sensitive to modern tourists, who have a greater critical awareness of the tourism product being presented. Tourists demand a range of experiences to make their visit memorable: a feature of the new face of tourism worldwide as demonstrated by O'Brien (this volume) in his case study of Costa Rica. Within Scotland, walking has been identified as a niche market but MacLellan (this volume) argues there are many different 'types' of walker, none of whom who would readily place themselves within any particular tourist category. Indeed, Feifer (1985) argues that (post) modern tourists can be characterised by their active movement across different types of tourist experience.

In their strategy for 2001 – 2006, Dumfries and Galloway Tourist Board identify a number of trends likely to structure their future marketing:

- A greater number of older, travel experienced and affluent travellers
- People travelling singly or in couples
- Holidays with greater interest, self improvement and discovery, history and culture, and environment
- Consumers are aware of the options and opportunities available to them, they are more sophisticated and demanding, seeking quality experiences

These are the characteristics of the postmodern tourist: tourists able to make their own decisions about what (and where) to see and do. Despite this obvious recognition, a niche approach has been taken by the tourist board where:

> '…(t)here should be a very clear route to market – i.e. a cost-effective means of accessing well defined groups of consumers.

It should be noted at this stage that the Tourist Board's previous strategy aimed to raise awareness and improve selling of the *region* as a tourist destination, a geographic approach which has since been superseded by an activity approach.

Niche markets – defining the product

Identifying the niche consumer makes the formulation of niche markets in a nature based setting difficult, but problems also lie in identifying the product. What is nature and how can it be promoted?

It must be recognised that nature, like those visiting it, is not one-dimensional. Indeed nature is not a 'thing'. Rather it is a process, a palimpsest of generations of activities producing a transient image. Implicit in the recognition of nature in a Scottish setting is the cultural associations that have shaped the landscape, and it is perhaps this coexistence that will be appealing to the postmodern tourist. In Dumfries and Galloway much of the landscape is managed by the primary industries of agriculture and forestry. Areas of particular conservation interest are often managed under agreement with farmers. Indeed, in some instances, agriculture practises are vital to the preservation of landscapes that promote biodiversity: for example, many of the saltmarshes along the coast of the Solway Firth (designated as a Ramsar site and a National Nature Reserve) are grazed by sheep and cattle in order to maintain a sward diversity favoured by wintering wildfowl.

Rural tourism and nature-based tourism are often viewed as different things, with the former requiring a permanent human presence (Opperman, 1996) whilst the latter often precludes human intervention. In the context of Dumfries and Galloway, however, they are almost synonymous because it is the past and present activities of humans that provide the image of nature.

Roberts and Hall (this volume) provide a useful insight into the suitability, viability and indeed desirability of the term 'niche' as a philosophy for marketing rural tourism. Implicit in their questioning is an awareness of the multi-faceted nature of tourism in rural areas. Distinctions are drawn between "traditional rural tourism" (e.g. walking, bird-watching) and "prestige" or "contemporary tourism in rural areas" (e.g. munro-bagging, off-road driving, attending rural events). Neither aspect of rural tourism could be described accurately as niche because they could appeal to large number of tourists, rather than to a specialist few. It is further argued that the 'traditional' tourist was looking for some escape from the constraints of urban living, whilst contemporary tourists impose their urban values on their country pursuits: the adrenalin rush of off-roading or finding haute cuisine in the local pub. Distinctions are drawn between the recreational consumption of the countryside as a form of mass tourism, and true niche tourism that has connotations of small scale, low impact, distinctive and recognisable, socially divisive and is often priced at a premium. Rural tourism (active engagement with what rural areas have to offer) can therefore be distinguished from tourism in rural areas (using rural areas as a backdrop for recreational pursuits) but perhaps neither are best served by niche associations.

Nature-based tourism, as a facet of rural tourism, suggests that the visitor has a preoccupation with the physical elements of a place: landscape, flora, fauna; however, the attractiveness of this will be viewed against a cultural backdrop of those who live and work in these natural places. Promoting nature-based tourism as a niche outside of a geographic context may leave the visitor unclear as to what kind of place s/he is visiting. Such niche activities require the context of the whole experience to make them attractive.

Strategies in adopting niche marketing

The identification of niche markets may have its place in promoting nature based or rural based activities, if we accept a defining characteristic of its inception: that is, the identification and subsequent satisfaction of the needs of a few individuals, building to a uniquely practised product consumed by a specialist group. This bottom-up approach is not the basis of the approach adopted by VisitScotland, whose development of niche markets precludes geographic distinctiveness, focussing rather on activities which can be enjoyed anywhere in Scotland (and by extension anywhere else in temperate Europe). The Dumfries and Galloway Area Tourist Strategy (2001 – 2006) states:

> The focus of the marketing will be on the experience, more than the destination…an approach which is justified through lack of funds to establish significant market awareness of the Dumfries & Galloway brand.

VisitScotland have thus relegated nature to its historical role, that is, providing a backdrop to activities which occur within its setting: walking, mountain biking, wildlife watching.

This approach is not useful in a local context because there is no unique quality in the niche displayed. If nature based activities can occur anywhere, the difficulties for local tourist boards and businesses is to stress a given activity within a particular geographic context. Forbes (1998) describes the approach taken by Curry County in developing sustainable nature-based tourism. Promotional material, using the theme 'Oregon's Siskiyou Coast' emphasised the physical qualities of the area whilst also enforcing a regional identity. Modern tourists demand diversity and whilst they may be attracted to specific activities they require assurance of variety. Again referring to the Curry County example, Forbes (1998) notes that activities, such as mountain biking, kayak tours and lighthouse tours, were promoted as one or two-day events mixed within a week long package.

Dumfries and Galloway (by the Tourist Board's own admission) provides exactly what the postmodern tourist wants – diversity, small-scale attractions, high quality landscape, space, freedom and accessibility. Yet none of these qualities are represented in their tourism strategy because of the adoption of a niche approach. Such an approach may promote the activity, but not the area in which the activity takes place, which for regionally distinct tourist boards and activity providers may be a hindrance to successful product placement. Indeed, the identification of a niche may limit both the product (and the marketing of that product) and the consumer

(Roberts and Hall, this volume). A niche market or activity identifies one pursuit or experience and maps this to a recognisable consumer. The modern tourist does not want to be pigeon-holed into a category, nor do they necessarily want to be targeted with preconceived ideas of their interests. Nature-based tourism is not a single product which can be promoted, nor is it a single activity which can be marketed to a particular consumer segment.

Approaches to the promotion of nature-based tourism

Regardless of the approach taken by marketers, what is clear is that more people now 'consume' rural areas, meaning that careful management of these areas is required to protect or re-create the rural idyll sought out by the discerning tourist. A less structured approach to rural tourism, however defined, will mean challenges for those charged with managing rural areas. The postmodern tourist may well demand a range of experiences during the visiting period, but those demands may sit uncomfortably with the protection of natural, perhaps vulnerable areas, and sites of historical or cultural significance. Destruction of landscape and native cultural identities is usually laid at the door of mass tourism but such destruction can also be blamed on those seeking alternative forms of tourism, as the search for unspoilt areas drives people into vulnerable environments (Cater and Goodall, 1997). Such impacts must be recognised in the development of sustainable rural tourism. Both chapters by Dear and Taylor *et al* in this volume state the importance of protecting the foundation upon which tourism is based. Dear notes that 39% of all visitors to Scotland mentioned landscape, countryside and scenery as being important factors in their decision to visit Scotland, therefore emphasising the need to protect these characteristics from those, and for those, who wish to experience them.

O'Brien (this volume) provides a very useful definition of ecotourism which could be viewed as a strategy for ensuring that tourism in rural areas is developed in a sustainable manner:

> As a concept, ecotourism is primarily a sustainable version of nature tourism, including rural and cultural elements.

This promotes the idea that ecotourism is not a product in itself, as distinct from nature-based tourism or rural tourism but is an *approach* to these different forms. As a process, it has a variety of aims amongst which are that ecotourism generates financial support for protection and management of natural areas, there are economic benefits for residents living near natural areas, and support for conservation is promoted among these residents (Lindberg *et al.,* 1996). If we examine the characteristics of ecotourism outlined by O'Brien, we begin to recognise the value of this approach for rural tourism and in particular, nature based activities.

Rural tourism, especially that which is located on farms, reflects the objectives of ecotourism in that it is generally operated by small family-run businesses and therefore will have economic benefits for residents living in natural areas. Tourism activities in Dumfries and Galloway are mostly small in scale where businesses are family-run, a feature replicated in other parts of Europe (Fleischer and Felsenstein, 2000; Oppermann, 1996). The expansion of agricultural activities to embrace tourism is used as a diversification strategy for an industry that is often unprofitable: the experience of foot and mouth disease in Dumfries and Galloway, indeed across the country, outlined the vulnerability of the agricultural sector (see Lennon in this volume). There must, however be an appreciation that rural tourism, as with ecotourism, represents something more than just a form of tourism activity: it is an approach to living and a reflection of what rurality means (Nilson, 2002). Ecotourism is not just about the tourism product, it implicitly recognises that tourism must benefit local communities as well as tourists, a point emphasised by Hussin (this volume). These operators are not engaging in tourism as a replacement for their agricultural activities, rather tourism may allow these activities to continue by providing an economic cushion. Farmers as an indigenous group do not want their traditional values eroded in pursuit of tourist goals.

By protecting a way of life and ensuring the continuation of historical land management practises, the development of rural tourism achieves another goal of ecotourism by ensuring that the population takes an interest in conservation and that conservation objectives are supported by new income streams.

This is not to say that the term ecotourism should be used as a marketing strategy especially within the context of a niche market. It articulates a set of values by which the tourist provider and operator can work, thereby providing the modern tourist the product s/he is looking for. The role of ecotourism in the development of rural tourism is the subject of current research[1] in Dumfries and Galloway,

---

[1] This work is being conducted by S. Gillespie as part of his PhD: a project funded, in part, by Scottish Enterprise, Dumfries and Galloway, and supported by the Dumfries & Galloway Tourist Board and the Dumfries and Galloway Council.

the results of which should identify mechanisms by which the principles of ecotourism can be used as a framework for the promotion of rural tourism, rather than promoting ecotourism as a product.

Planning for visitor management is a crucial aspect of any tourism focussed activity regardless of its location. A growing awareness of the importance of environmental quality in rural areas, potential challenges presented by new access legislation and increasingly active recreational pursuits, means that a more proactive approach to visitor and site management is required (Taylor *et al,* this volume). The farming community is not the sole guardian of the Dumfries and Galloway landscape. Organisations such as Scottish Natural Heritage (SNH), RSPB, Wetlands and Wildfowl Trust and the Forest Enterprise, all have extensive sites actively promoted as centres for nature based activities. It is in these centres that a Sustainable Visitor Management System, promoted by SNH (see Taylor *et al*) will play its part in monitoring and ultimately protecting the natural heritage that people want to see. Implicit within the strategy is recognition that all stakeholders must be involved in the management and decision-making for the site, another key aim of ecotourism.

Of equal importance is to understand the needs of the visitors in terms of their expectations and ensure the quality of their experience reflects the quality of the site. Recognition of tourists' needs is a cyclical process reflecting the changing and sometimes inconsistent demands made by visitors to rural areas: these inconsistencies are described as a paradox by Hillery *et al.* (2001) whereby tourists to natural areas see tourism as a threat, yet they still want to visit these areas. Key then, is the need to ensure that carrying capacities of sites are established and respected. Carrying capacities may take the form of physical, ecological, economic and perceptual (Goldsmith, 1974): each taking precedence in different stages of development of a tourist site.

A recent project[2] attempted to establish a strategy to promote nature-based tourism sites in Dumfries and Galloway. The study began with the construction of an extensive database of all potential sites of nature-based interest in the area. Included in this list were sites that also contained cultural and historical interest. It was

---

[2] This project was undertaken by a group of Honours year undergraduates at the University of Glasgow, Crichton Campus. Advice for the project was given by the Southern Uplands Partnership: an organisation that addresses land use issues faced by those working and living in the Southern Uplands. The students were Lynn Brotherston, Elizabeth Garbutt, Lynsey Orr and Victoria Poynton.

recognised very early in the project that those participating in nature-based activities would not do so to the exclusion of other activities in the same area. The main aim of the project was to develop promotional material of nature-based sites in Dumfries and Galloway, in effect, to collate the numerous sites of interest, without labelling them as a niche product. The researchers decided not to aim this material at particular market segments because the sites being promoted would appeal to a wide audience. They did, however, include a children's education pack and 'site passport' in an attempt to include younger children into the visiting experience and decision-making process. Within the resulting promotional material there is a strong geographic focus. Information is structured around anchor sites with proven physical carrying capacities, the partial determination of which is the presence of a car park and facilities (e.g. shop, toilets). In addition, the anchor sites have a means of monitoring the ecological carrying capacity through the existence of a form of site management. In determining which sites should be used as anchor sites, the researchers asked managers to comment on visitor education opportunities, management strategies, voluntary participation in conservation and staffing: factors which are integral to objectives of ecotourism (see O'Brien, this volume).

Supporting the anchor sites (a number were chosen spanning the region) are a range of 'points of interest', sites which provide variety to the material but which are not directly promoted because of their reduced carrying capacities, either in terms of their physical or ecological characteristics. Sites identified from the initial database to be sensitive, vulnerable or inaccessible were specifically excluded from the promotional materials in an effort to protect them and ensure public safety. Although the anchor site is dominant in the material, the range of information provided means there should be a dispersal of activity with a commensurate dispersal of tourist impact. This project therefore, demonstrates an attempt to use the principles of ecotourism in the promotion of nature-based tourism, without the use of inappropriate labels or the use of niche targeting.

Conclusion

The promotion of niche tourism requires an identifiable product and an identifiable buyer. In this regard the promotion of activity-based niches is appropriate because both criteria are met. The use of this approach however is not appropriate when trying to promote nature-based tourism or rural tourism because neither the product nor the market can be defined. This is especially the case in promoting a place such as Dumfries and Galloway, where the tourism product is fragmented and small in scale but of high quality. In these circumstances, a geographic approach may be more appropriate, where the emphasis is placed on the diversity existing in a particular location.

Promotion of nature-based tourism sites, by whichever strategy, should ensure an increase in visitor numbers, which subsequently means that promotion must take account of the carrying capacities of the sites in question. Ecotourism can be used, not as a niche market, but as a set of guiding principles upon which promotion can occur. It should be regarded as an approach to recreation and tourism, rather than a form of tourism, thereby ensuring that the needs of the local community and the tourist are served without restricting either to unnecessary and unwanted stereotyping.

References

Buckley, R (2002) Tourism Ecolabels. *Annals of Tourism Research*, 29:1, 183 – 208.

Cater, E. and Goodall, B. (1997) Must tourism destroy its resource base? In *The Earthscan Reader in Sustainable Tourism.* France, L. (ed) London: Earthscan, 84 – 89.

Dear, S. (this volume) Sustainable tourism in Scotland.

Dumfries & Galloway Tourist Board (2001) *Dumfries & Galloway Area Tourism Strategy 2001 - 2006.*

Feifer, M. (1985) *Going Places.* London: McMillan.

Fleischer, A. and Felsenstein, D. (2000) Support for rural tourism: Does it make a difference? *Annals of Tourism Research,* 27:4, 1007 – 1024.

Forbes, B (1998) Curry Country sustainable nature-based tourism project. In *Sustainable Tourism: A Geographical Perspective.* Hall, C. M. and Lew, A. A. (eds) Harlow: Pearson Education Limited, 119 – 131.

Goldsmith, F. B. (1974) Ecological effects of visitors in the countryside. In *Conservation in Practice.* Warren, A and Goldsmith, F. B. (eds) London: Wiley, 217 – 231.

Hillery, M., Nancarrow, B., Griffin, G. and Syme, G. (2001) Tourist perception of environmental impact. *Annals of Tourism Research,* 28:4, 853 – 867.

Hussin, R. (this volume) Tourism and ecotourism development in Malaysia: An overview.

Krippendorf, J. (1987) Ecological approach to tourism marketing. *Tourism Management,* 8:1, 174 – 176.

Lindberg, K., Enriquez, J. and Sproule, K. (1996) Ecotourism Questioned: Case studies from Belize. *Annals of Tourism Research,* 23:3, 543 – 562.

MacLellan, R. (this volume) Niche tourism markets in Scottish tourism: an investigation of niche markets reliant on the natural environment.

Nilsson, P. A. (2002) Staying on farms: An ideological background. *Annals of Tourism Research,* 29:1, 7 – 24.

O'Brien, P. J. (this volume) Tourism and sustainable development: Green wash or natural allies? A case study of Costa Rica.

Opperman, M. (1996) Rural Tourism in Southern Germany. *Annals of Tourism research,* 23:1, 86 – 102.

Palmer, A. (2000) *Principles of Marketing.* Oxford: Oxford University Press.

Roberts, L. and Hall, D. (this volume) The Niche Pastiche. Or what rural tourism is *really* about.

Taylor, B., Masters, D., Scott, P., and Barrow, G. (this volume). Sustainable Visitor Management System: A discussion paper.

Valentina Bold is a senior lecturer and Head of Scottish Studies at the University of Glasgow's Crichton Campus in Dumfries. Her research interests include Scottish identity within the physical nation, and amongst the Scottish diaspora overseas, as well as Scottish poetry in the nineteenth century. Dr Bold's publications include the CD-rom *Northern Folk: Living Traditions of North East Scotland*, co-edited with Thomas McKean (Aberdeen: 1999) and an edited collection *Smeddum: A Lewis Grassic Gibbon Anthology* (Edinburgh: 2001). Her forthcoming monograph, *Nature's Making: James Hogg and the Autodidacts* is due for publication by Tuckwell Press in November 2003.

Sandy Dear is the Director of the Tourism and Environment Forum. Having spent a number of years working for tourism operators in Edinburgh and overseas he joined the Scottish Tourist Board's Development Division in 1995. As one of the first staff to join STB's new Inverness office he led STB's development and implementation of the ground breaking and highly successful Welcome Host training programme. Following a stint with STB's UK marketing department, he then led the Future Opportunities team in STB's newly created Tourism Futures Department. In 2000 he left STB to take over the running of the Tourism and Environment Forum that aims to promote sustainable tourism in Scotland.

Belle Doyle completed her PhD at the University of Sheffield in 1999. She now runs the South West Scotland Screen Commission that promotes the region of Dumfries & Galloway as a location for filming: for example *The Wicker Man*, BBC1's *Two Thousand Acres of Sky*, and *The Magdalene Sisters*. In addition, she programmes the art-house cinema, The Robert Burns Centre Film Theatre in Dumfries.

Steven A Gillespie is a graduate of the University of Northumbria (BSc Hons. Environmental Management) and the Graduate School of Environmental Studies at the University of Strathclyde (MSc Environmental Studies). Steven is currently reading for a doctorate in sustainable rural tourism at the University of Glasgow's Crichton Campus in Dumfries and is a member of the Crichton Tourism Research Centre. His PhD focuses on farm-based tourism as a sustainable rural tourism type, and the concept of ecotourism in Dumfries & Galloway, South-West Scotland.

Derek Hall is Professor of Regional Development and Head of the Tourism Research Group at the Scottish Agricultural College in Auchincruive, Scotland. He has a first degree in Geography and Anthropology and a PhD in Social Geography, both from the University of London. He has numerous publications on tourism and development in Central and South-Eastern Europe. His research interests include tourism and rural development, and EU accession issues in Central and Eastern Europe and the Central and Eastern Mediterranean.

Mhairi Harvey is Head of Environmental Studies at the University of Glasgow, Crichton Campus. Originally from Aberdeen in northeast Scotland, Mhairi graduated from St. Andrews University with a Joint Honours in Geography and Geology. Further study was undertaken at the University College of Wales,

Aberystwyth with the completion of an MSc in Environmental Impact Assessment. The dissertation associated with this course was concerned with the role of Strategic Environmental Assessment in the development of the Cairngorms in Scotland. This initial research has fuelled her interest in the relationship between sustainable development and tourism in areas valued for their natural heritage.

David Herbert is Professor of Geography and Senior Pro Vice Chancellor at University of Wales Swansea. He is author or editor of more than twenty books concerned mainly with urban studies. His interest in heritage tourism began in the 1980s with a set of projects commissioned by CADW (Welsh Historic Monuments). Relevant publications include *Heritage Sites: Strategies for Marketing and Development* (with R. C. Prentice and C. J. Thomas 1989), and *Heritage, Tourism and Society* (edited 1995). He has researched a number of literary places including the Jane Austen House at Chawton, Hampshire, and Dylan Thomas's Boathouse at Laugharne, Carmarthen. One current project is an analysis of the use of writers in place promotion policies for cities and regions.

Rosazman Hussin is a post-graduate student at the Department of Sociology and Anthropology, University of Glasgow. Currently he is studying ecotourism development and sustainable local community participation in the case of Sabah, Malaysia for his PhD programme. Since 1998 he has taught the Sociology and Anthropology of Tourism and Industrial Sociology at the University of Malaysia, Sabah. His major research interests are in the areas of ecotourism development, sustainable development, local community development and poverty issues.

John Lennon holds the Moffat Chair in Travel and Tourism Business Development. He has extensive experience within the tourism and hospitality industries and continues to teach and supervise the research of postgraduate students. He is also responsible for business development and consultancy with the Moffat Centre, based in Glasgow Caledonian University. His main areas of research include the management of visitor attractions, economic development in tourism, policy and infrastructure in developing countries and statistical analysis of tourism as part of the wider economy.

Rory MacLellan has degrees from the University of Aberdeen and Strathclyde and is currently Senior Lecturer in Tourism at the University of Strathclyde. His teaching and research interests include public sector support structures for tourism, rural tourism, sustainable tourism, and tourism and natural heritage. He has published on aspects of tourism and the Scottish natural environment including articles on wildlife holidays, sustainable tourism and has co-edited a book entitled *Tourism in Scotland*. He has carried out research on aspects of Scottish tourism for a number of agencies including Scottish Enterprise, Highlands and Islands Enterprise, Scottish Natural Heritage, the Scottish Parliament and Scottish Environment LINK. He is a part of the Scottish Tourism Research Unit and a member of the Tourism and Environment Forum.

Donald Macleod is Research Fellow in Heritage, the Environment and Tourism at the University of Glasgow and also the Director of the Crichton Tourism Research Centre. He has a doctorate in social anthropology from the University of Oxford and has done extensive research in the Canary Islands, Dominican Republic and Scotland on issues relating to tourism including development, cultural change, identity and environmentalism. He has published widely in journals and books and co-edited (with Jackie Waldren and Simone Abram) *Tourists and Tourism: Identifying with People and Places* (1997), and he has a monograph in press: *Tourism, Globalisation and Cultural Change: An Island Community Perspective.*

Phil O'Brien is a senior lecturer in the Department of Sociology and Anthropology in the University of Glasgow; he previously worked in the Institute of Latin American Studies. He has worked for many years on problems of development in Latin America and is author of various books and articles on Latin America, covering among others the Allende and Pinochet periods in Chile, the debt crisis in Latin America, problems of sustainable development in Latin America, and more recently he has been working on tourism and sustainable development in Latin America, particularly Costa Rica.

Mike Paterson was born in New Zealand and his interests lie in the cultural aspects of identity formation, and intercultural relations. His 2001 PhD dissertation for the University of Glasgow examined such issues in relation to Scotland's international promotion and marketing activity. He produces the international *Piping Today* magazine for the National Piping Centre, Glasgow, and is the creator and presenter of a course, *With Love: gifting your stories to grandparents* which encourages older people to pass on family lore to younger generations. He recently moved to Ontario, Canada, to further these and related activities.

Murray Pittock is Professor of Scottish and Romantic literature at the University of Manchester and head of the department of English and American Studies there. He was previously Professor in Literature at the University of Strathclyde and founding director of the Glasgow-Strathclyde School of Scottish Studies. His publications on nationality, identity and Jacobitism include *The Invention of Scotland* (1991), *Poetry and Jacobite Politics* (1994), *The Myth of the Jacobite Clans* (1995), *Inventing and Resisting Britain* (1997), *Jacobitism* (1998), *Celtic Identity and the British Image* (1999), *Scottish Nationality* (2001) and *A New History of Scotland* (2003). He was on the advisory committees for the Museum of British History (1996-7) and Glasgow as UK City of Architecture and Design (1998-9).

Lesley Roberts is Senior Lecturer in the Centre for Travel and Tourism in Newcastle Business School at Northumbria University where she lectures in subjects relating to tourism and its environment. She has worked on development programmes in Central and Eastern Europe and participated in international tourism programmes. Her research and consultancy focus on environments for, and processes of, tourism development, particularly in the rural context.

Jonathan Skinner is a social anthropologist lecturing in the School of Social and Health Sciences at the University of Abertay Dundee. His interests are in narrative and biography, performance, postmodernism and ethnographic representation. His most recent publications include *Scotland's Boundaries and Identities in the New Millenium* (co-edited with C. Di Domenico, A. Law and M. Smith, 2001).

Lesley Stevenson completed an MSc in Tourism at the University of Strathclyde in 2001. She is currently a doctoral candidate at the University of Glasgow Crichton Campus where she is a member of the Crichton Tourism Research Centre. Her doctoral research is focusing on the relationship between traditional music and tourism in Scotland.

Bill Taylor worked in conservation, land management and heritage interpretation for over 20 years: first in countryside recreation in central Scotland and Cornwall. He then worked in nature conservation on a large bog reserve at the UK's first National Nature Reserve in the mountains of NW Scotland. In 1992 he took over responsibility for a larger geographical area. From 1995 to 1998 he led a strategy for interpretation in the Highlands of Scotland, and then became responsible for assisting staff in developing major external projects. In early 2001 he was appointed as lead for tourism for Scottish Natural Heritage.